D1563546

THE COLD WAR AND THE 1984 OLYMPIC GAMES

THE COLD WAR AND THE 1984 OLYMPIC GAMES

A SOVIET-AMERICAN SURROGATE WAR

by

Philip D'Agati

THE COLD WAR AND THE 1984 OLYMPIC GAMES
Copyright © Philip D'Agati, 2013.

First published in 2013 by PALGRAVE MACMILLAN® in the
United States—a division of St. Martin's Press LLC, 175 Fifth
Avenue, New York, NY 10010.

Where this book is distributed in the UK, Europe and the rest of
the world, this is by Palgrave Macmillan, a division of Macmillan
Publishers Limited, registered in England, company number 785998,
of Houndmills, Basingstoke, Hampshire RG21 6XS.

Palgrave Macmillan is the global academic imprint of the above
companies and has companies and representatives throughout the
world.

Palgrave® and Macmillan® are registered trademarks in the United
States, the United Kingdom, Europe and other countries.

ISBN: 978-1-137-33061-1

Library of Congress Cataloging-in-Publication Data is available from
the Library of Congress.

A catalogue record of the book is available from the British Library.

Design by Scribe Inc.

First edition: May 2013

10 9 8 7 6 5 4 3 2 1

Transferred to Digital Printing in 2013

This book is dedicated to the Olympic athletes whose participation was sacrificed during the American-Soviet surrogate wars of the 1980 and 1984 boycotts:

The 1980 Olympians of
Albania, Antigua and Barbuda, Argentina, Bahamas, Bahrain, Bangladesh, Barbados, Belize, Bermuda, Bolivia, Canada, Cayman Islands, Central African Republic, Chad, Chile, Cote d'Ivoire, Egypt, El Salvador, Fiji, Gabon, The Gambia, Ghana, Haiti, Honduras, Hong Kong, Indonesia, Iran, Israel, Japan, Kenya, South Korea, Liberia, Liechtenstein, Malawi, Malaysia, Mauritius, Monaco, Morocco, Netherlands Antilles, Niger, Norway, Pakistan, Panama, Papua New Guinea, Paraguay, Philippines, Saudi Arabia, Singapore, Somalia, Sudan, Suriname, Swaziland, Thailand, Togo, Tunisia, Turkey, United Arab Emirates, United States, Uruguay, Virgin Islands, West Germany, and Zaire

The 1984 Olympians of
Afghanistan, Angola, Bulgaria, Cuba, Czechoslovakia, East Germany, Ethiopia, Hungary, Laos, Mongolia, North Korea, Poland, South Yemen, Soviet Union, and Vietnam

This book is also dedicated to the national Olympic committees whose commitment to Olympism has resulted in attendance at every Winter and Summer Olympiad: Australia, France, United Kingdom, Greece, and Switzerland

CONTENTS

TABLES

PREFACE

I was old enough to remember the Los Angeles Olympics and in particular the Reagan administration's random comments on what a huge mistake it was for us to boycott the 1980 Games. News stories appeared on a spectrum, suggesting the Soviet Union would appear, not appear, or just hold out until the last minute and show.

Nearly a decade after the 1984 Olympics ended, political studies posted everything from fear to bitterness to embarrassment as the reason for the Soviet Bloc boycott. Ultimately, the guesswork crystalized around the standard retaliation answer of tit for tat and was readily found in most over-the-counter studies on the Olympics.

The evolution of this study followed my evolution as an academic. Initially, I was a historian, and my interest in the Olympics was to understand their role in twentieth-century history. A few questions, especially the one that inspired this study, began shifting my interest from historical to political analysis. As such, this study began as a bridge between disciplines. The earliest manifestation of this book appeared as a short thesis as part of a degree in history that, as a few said, had too much theory and too little history. It was a valid criticism, as the thesis was written in the few months before work started on my doctorate in political science.

Political science changed my methodology, broadened my theoretical conceptions, and enlivened this study with a new question: What game was the Soviet Union actually playing? Tit for tat never seemed right to me, but placing it in a broader understanding of relevant theories and methodologies, it now just seemed like—to quote Vice President Biden—malarkey. A much needed break from my dissertation resulted in diving into this question using the tools I learned from my doctoral classes and resulted in a manuscript almost twice as long, grounded in a rational-structural argument on Soviet decision making.

Finishing the dissertation and my first book shelved the study once again, where it remained until the Republic of Georgia brought the topic back to life in August 2008. In the wake of the Russo-Georgian War, sometimes called the South Ossetian War, Georgian President Mikheil Saakashvili called for a boycott of the 2014 Sochi Olympics in response to Russia's invasion of his country. Comically, the story returned to public news just as this preface was being penned. Georgia had indicated its plan to attend the Sochi Winter Olympics.

Georgia's brief politicking with the Games, decidedly looking for international attention and an alternative avenue to challenge Russian interests in South Ossetia, Abkhazia, and Georgia, was reminiscent of Soviet politicking nearly thirty years earlier. As a result, this iteration of the study focused more heavily on a theoretical framework for utilizing sports politics as an alternative for traditional forms of conflict. This expanded the manuscript once more, required rethinking nearly every chapter, and resulted in the book you are currently reading.

ACKNOWLEDGMENTS

This book would not have been possible without the help of many people. First, I would like to start by thanking my academic mentors who guided me through the many iterations of this book: Gerald Herman and Harvey Green (in history) and Amilcar Antonio Barreto and William D. Kay (in political science). All four reviewed the manuscript in various stages spanning a ten-year period of transition from a work of history to a combination of historical and political analysis. To this day I will remain grateful for the generosity of time and mentorship that was provided when not required. It is a testament to the Department of History and the Department of Political Science at Northeastern University (NU).

Others provided their time and skills in the development of the final manuscript of this study. I would like to thank Holly Jordan for her invaluable help as my editor. She and Jared Simons, who assisted in editing sections of the book, did great work triaging my occasional mutilation of the English language. Also, I would like to thank Prof. Jeffrey Burds for his willingness to translate titles and sourcing from the original Russian. In regard to the production and publication of this study, I would like to thank Palgrave Macmillan and my two primary contacts, Matthew Kopel and Scarlet Neath, for their help and patience in the final stages of this project. Lastly, I would like to thank the staff at the following institutions for their cooperation, time, and assistance when needed:

United States Olympic Committee
Documentation Department, Olympic Museum
LA84 Foundation (formerly, Amateur Athletics Foundation of Los Angeles)
UCLA Special Collections Library (LAOOC archives)
University of Illinois Archives (Avery Brundage Collection)
Snell Library, Northeastern University

One of the challenges of writing this book was the complexity of the explanation of the Soviet boycott. Normally, simple and succinct, in other words the principle of Occam's Razor, is best when seeking causal relationships in many areas of inquiry. As a result, I took a very Holmesian approach to this study by seeking to eliminate all impossible and possible explanations until what remained was the only incontrovertible answer. In that regard, I sought the advice and opinions of a variety of friends and colleagues whose expertise included the full range of topics, subtopics, and tangents that may or may not have provided an alternative answer to the Soviet boycott. I wish to thank each of them here for their time and debating skills: Amilcar Barreto, Will Briede, Christopher Brummit, Oscar Camargo, Holly Jordan, Woody Kay, Dan McDuffie, Mark Mesiti, Jason Reilly, and Bret Sheeley.

I would also like to thank my larger circle of friends and family who provide stability, sanity, entertainment, encouragement, and many more things necessary to survive the process of my career and writing any book. Given the list of individuals, I have opted instead to thank them as groups instead of each by name. These include my family, including my parents, Anthony and Shirley, and my sister and brother-in-law, Deb and Tom; my inner circle of close friends, my colleagues at NU, my current and former students on the NU International Relations Council, and my music ministry at St. Augustine's in Andover; my broader circle of friends from Central Catholic, Merrimack College, and NU; and a small circle of forever undaunted friends who stretch across North America.

ABBREVIATIONS

BOA	British Olympic Association
FIBA	*Fédération Internationale de Basketball*
FIDE	*Fédération Internationale des Echecs* (Chess)
FIFA	*Fédération Internationale de Football Association*
FIG	*Fédération Internationale de Gymnastics*
FILA	*Fédération Internationale des Luttes Associées* (Wrestling)
GDR	German Democratic Republic
IAAF	International Amateur Athletics Foundation
IAF	International Archery Federation
IF	International Federation
IOC	International Olympic Committee
ISU	*Union Internationale de Patinage*
LAOOC	Los Angeles Olympic Organizing Committee
LSI	Lucerne Sport International
NOC	national Olympic committee
OAU	Organization of African Unity
RSI	Red Sport International
SANOC	South African National Olympic Committee
USOC	United States Olympic Committee
URSS	*Unión de Repúblicas Socialistas Soviéticas*
USSR	Union of Soviet Socialist Republics
USSR NOC	Union of Soviet Socialist Republics National Olympic Committee

OLYMPIADS BY TIME PERIOD

THE EARLY YEARS (ALL SUMMER GAMES)

1896 Athens, Greece
1900 Paris, France
1904 St. Louis, United States
1908 London, United Kingdom
1912 Stockholm, Sweden

THE INTERWAR YEARS

1920 Antwerp, Belgium (Summer)
1924 Chamonix, France (Winter)
1924 Paris, France (Summer)
1928 St. Moritz, Switzerland (Winter)
1928 Amsterdam, Netherlands (Summer)
1932 Lake Placid, United States (Winter)
1932 Los Angeles, United States (Summer)
1936 Garmisch-Partenkirchen, Germany (Winter)
1936 Berlin, Germany (Summer)

POSTWAR YEARS

1948 St. Moritz, Switzerland (Winter)
1948 London, United Kingdom (Summer)
1952 Oslo, Norway (Winter)
1952 Helsinki, Finland (Summer)
1956 Cortina D'Ampezzo, Italy (Winter)
1956 Melbourne, Australia (Summer)
1960 Squaw Valley, United States (Winter)
1960 Rome, Italy (Summer)
1964 Innsbruck, Austria (Winter)
1964 Tokyo, Japan (Summer)
1968 Grenoble, France (Winter)
1968 Mexico City, Mexico (Summer)

1972   Sapporo, Japan (Winter)
1972   Munich, West Germany (Summer)

BOYCOTT YEARS

1976   Innsbruck, Austria (Winter)
1976   Montreal, Canada (Summer)
1980   Lake Placid, New York (Winter)
1980   Moscow, Soviet Union (Summer)
1984   Sarajevo, Yugoslavia (Winter)
1984   Los Angeles, United States (Summer)
1988   Calgary, Canada (Winter)
1988   Seoul, South Korea (Summer)

Timeline of Events Relevant
to the 1984 Boycott

1967–78

October 14, 1964	Leonid Brezhnev becomes Premier of the Soviet Union
May 12–16, 1970	69th IOC Session, held in Amsterdam, Netherlands
	Montreal selected to host 1976 Summer Olympics
August 21–24, 1972	73rd IOC Session, held in Munich, West Germany
	Lord Killanin elected President of the IOC
October 16–25, 1974	75th IOC Session, held in Vienna, Austria
	Moscow selected to host 1980 Summer Olympics
July 17–August 1, 1976	Montreal Summer Olympics
May 12–21, 1978	80th IOC Session, held in Athens, Greece
	Los Angeles selected to host 1984 Summer Olympics

1980

January 4	President Jimmy Carter announces likelihood of a boycott of Moscow
February 13–24	Lake Placid Winter Olympics
July 19–August 3	Moscow Summer Olympics
July 10–August 6	83rd IOC Session, held in Moscow, Soviet Union
	Juan Antonio Samaranch elected President of the IOC

1981–83

September 1981	South African Springbok Rugby Team tours the United States
June 16, 1982	Yuri Andropov becomes Premier of the Soviet Union
August 1983	Soviet Union shoots down South Korean plan, killing 269 people.
November 1983	Soviet Union contacts East Germany about potential boycott
Late 1983–early 1984	Soviet hockey matches with the United States, in the United States

1984

February 8–19	Sarajevo Winter Olympics
February 9	Soviet Premier Yuri Andropov dies
February 13	Konstantin Chernenko becomes the Premier of the Soviet Union
March	LAOOC projects close to $200 million in profits for Los Angeles Games
April 24	Meeting of representatives of the IOC, LAOOC, and USSR NOC to discuss Soviet concerns over Los Angeles, held in Lausanne, Switzerland
April 30	Soviet Union decides to boycott Los Angeles
May 8	Soviet Union announces boycott of Los Angeles Olympics
May 8–10	Bulgaria decides to boycott Los Angeles Olympics
May 10	East Germany announces boycott of Los Angeles Olympics
May 13	Czechoslovakia announces boycott of Los Angeles Olympics
May 16	Hungary announces boycott of Los Angeles Olympics
May 24–25	Communist sports officials meet in Prague, Czechoslovakia, to discuss boycott
May 24	Cuba announces boycott of Los Angeles Olympics
May 24	Romania announces it will attend Los Angeles Olympics

June 7–8	LAOOC president Peter Ueberroth meets with Cuban president Fidel Castro in Havana, Cuba
June 16–17	Executive meetings of the Supreme Council on Sport in Africa decide not to boycott Los Angeles Olympics
June 27	Angola announces boycott of the Los Angeles Olympics
July 28–August 12	Los Angeles Summer Olympics

INTRODUCTION

OLYMPICS, SPORTS, AND BOYCOTTS
GAMES OF POLITICS

The modern Olympics returned from a 12-year hiatus from political and athletic competition following World War II. The process of revitalization occurred under the shadow of political turmoil between two opposing ideologies manifested as blocs of allied states. This conceptual contest between the United States and the Soviet Union posed a constant threat to the Olympic Movement, as both countries used the Olympics as a new field of battle to validate their respective political and economic systems. This conflict reached its zenith in the 1980 and 1984 Olympic boycotts. In spite of these challenges, the Olympics remained an attractive opportunity for athletes, cities, and nations to achieve greatness with the world as their audience. The contest of ideologies, far from being just a nuisance to the governing body of the Olympic Games, the International Olympic Committee (IOC), accentuated the entire Olympic Movement by attaching a deeper, more symbolic, and intrinsically more competitive spirit to its quadrennial events.

From 1948 to 1992, the IOC would evolve from Olympiad to Olympiad, expanding its global footprint while navigating problems posed by the heightened competitive atmosphere of the international environment. After World War II, the Olympics grew primarily due to the independence of several new states in the 1960s and 1970s. Many countries, regardless of age, political system, or economic development, viewed the Olympics as an opportunity to showcase the success of their newly founded political, economic, and cultural institutions. As the movement became more politicized, opportunities for political gain in the Olympics became more prevalent, and more and more states began to join.

In addition to new states, the Olympic Movement began to attract other groups, including nonstate actors; in the case of the latter, notable examples include the Mexico City (1968) protests and the orchestrators of the Munich (1972) massacre. Regardless of the goal of political actors, these examples all exist simply because the Olympics can be utilized as an effective platform for states, nonsovereign nations, and nonstate actors, giving them the same degree of international attention as the superpowers and their allies. In spite of the difficulties involved in the attempt, the Olympics offered an international venue that was arguably available for anyone that wished to try.

The real challenge became being able to attend the Olympics itself. Competitiveness, especially among European and American nations, fostered a surge of growth in advanced training methods, as well as other structural aspects of sports institutions, and created a situation that made it very difficult for smaller nations to find a global voice by either competing in or hosting the Olympic Games.[1] This created an increasing gap in performance between states whose athletes regularly won Olympic medals and states whose athletes rarely won. In time, this reality would restrict the number of states competing politically through sport to a small elite list. Concurrently, the opportunity of hosting the Olympics evolved to be a highly valuable but economically challenging prize.

With the increase in the number of participants, the number of sports competitions, and the need for larger and larger physical infrastructure, the economic benefits and challenges of hosting the Olympics multiplied. This progression had various effects on the Olympic bid process, but ultimately it restricted the number of states in the world fiscally and politically able to host the Games. While prestige was a direct result of hosting the Olympics, it was an option closed to most states participating in the Olympics.

By the 1970s, it became obvious that the political benefits of the Olympics were opportunities for an elite list of states whose wealth and development provided necessary means to exploit the Games. Within that elite list, the opportunities are still finite. Each of them has an opportunity every Olympic Games to maximize victory in sports. All other political opportunities, most notably bidding for the Games and hosting the Games, exhibit increasingly smaller circles of participation. For example, the IOC only accepted three cities to bid for the 2020 Summer Olympic Games.[2] Ultimately, only one will have the opportunity to host.

While it is clear that other states are limited in their political or economic opportunities at the Games, it is an oversimplification to state that both competition and the right to host are the only methods by which interested parties can capitalize on the Olympic stage. Other methods of politicizing the Games include the topic of attendance at the Games, which became a hallmark of the Olympiads of the 1970s and 1980s.

When hosting the Games or winning medals in sports competitions failed to achieve the political or economic goals of participants, the question of attendance introduced a new and troublesome political weapon in the Olympics. Boycotting the Olympics became an attractive alternative for states that had limited, if any, opportunity to either host the Games or win multiple medals. Boycott also offered states an opportunity to protest the domestic or international policies of other states in the Olympic Movement, either hosting or attending. The use of boycotts became so prevalent in international events that their implementation became an attractive option to all states in the Olympic Movement. There have been several examples of this, the first being the boycott threats against the 1936 Berlin Summer Games due to their plans to exclude Germany's Jewish athletes from competing.

Berlin's decision to disallow "non-Aryans" to compete on the German team was attacked by several states and athletes, who also declared their willingness to boycott the Games due to fascist German policy, particularly from France, Italy, and the United States. Individual athletes, such as African American athletes on the US track and field team, supported the United States Olympic Committee's (USOC) interest in boycotting the Games. The boycott was averted only due to the efforts of the British Olympic Association (BOA).

On March 7, 1936, *The Times of London* published a letter from the BOA stating that "it would be nothing short of a calamity if . . . this country [the UK] . . . were not fully represented at a gathering which will include athletes from almost every nation." The letter also stated, "[I]n sending a team to Berlin they are acting in the best interests of Sport."[3] The result of the letter, and the subsequent dialogue among several states, was that calls for a boycott abated and every state with a recognized national Olympic committee (NOC) attended the Berlin Games. The use of a potential boycott as a weapon failed to materialize and the tactic then would lay dormant for more than thirty years.

In the 1960s and 1970s, the South African apartheid challenge led to two boycott threats. In this instance, several African states used the boycott to protest the participation of states whose athletes competed with South Africa in any form of sports competition. The near universal policy of not competing with South Africa was a part of the overall isolation of South Africa as a protest against apartheid policies. Then the story of boycott would have another two chapters, this time involving the East-West Cold War dichotomy. In this scenario, the modern Olympics weathered two boycotts in the 1980s, one of which is the main feature of this study.

The purpose behind focusing on the Soviet boycott is to provide a viable explanation for several peculiarities about the facts of this event while challenging common academic and nonacademic explanations as to why it occurred. In the cases of the Berlin and apartheid examples, the boycott was exercised as a way to protest a policy that was not directly related to the Olympic Games. In the Soviet example, the Soviet Union claimed the boycott was used to protest specific failures of the Los Angeles Olympic Organizing Committee (LAOOC) and the United States, which culminated in an ineffective and inappropriate organization of the 1984 Games.

To complicate the story, the Soviet Union referred to their action as a "nonparticipation"[4] and stated it was different from a boycott simply because their decision protected rather than politicized the Games.[5] A primary purpose of this study is to explore this and other claims of the Soviet Union while identifying the true motivation behind their policy on Los Angeles. As this study will show, Soviet sports policy, with regard to the 1984 boycott, is far more complex than previously noted.

The complexities of the Soviet boycott easily surpass any prior example of boycotts against the Games. For the other boycotts, a simple "we will not participate because . . ." was deliberately stated by the authorities of the boycotting nation. Whether it was the Soviet invasion of Afghanistan, New Zealand's playing soccer with segregated South African teams, or Germany's anti-Semitic policies, all Olympic boycotts prior to the Soviet-initiated boycott had a clear political statement not aligned in any way with the Olympic Movement. The Soviet boycott is not as straightforward because its policy featured a complex series of complaints related to Olympic policy, Soviet security, and American organizational plans.

The lack of a simple nonparticipatory statement and the confused nature of the Soviet reasoning suggest a far more in-depth and complex set of goals than have yet been recognized by previous authors on the Olympics.[6] Due to the complexity of the Soviet explanation for the boycott, the unstable nature of their claims, and the partially successful diplomatic effort to alleviate the Soviet concerns, doubt is cast on the accuracy of their stated reasons for boycotting. The relative consistency of Soviet sports policy and strategy further challenges assumptions to date about the boycott. This fact does not, however, answer the question of retaliation.

As this study will show, Soviet interest in sports and their development of a significant sports policy lend credibility to any argument that there is a deeper and far more involved Soviet position at work in the boycott of 1984. Tying together this with standard Soviet sports policy goals and the dialogues between all pertinent actors, current explanations that the boycott was mere retaliation begin to look less and less convincing. A better understanding of Soviet goals and the Soviet Union's resulting decision to boycott is the main topic of this book. A more accurate explanation for the boycott rests on the development of Soviet sports policy and sports diplomacy and in the interaction of athletes and governmental systems, in a venue with a full spectrum of political and social beliefs present.

The Soviet Union masterfully manipulated sports competitions in what I will describe as *surrogate war* between itself and the West. Soviet sports history offers compelling evidence of the use of physical competition as a metaphor for the greatness of the Soviet state. The Kremlin endorsed international political competition as a means of demonstrating socialist supremacy without waging traditional war against the West. In short, the Soviet Union became well versed in the use of sports and competitions as surrogate wars.

The dichotomy between Soviet and Western Bloc politics in post–World War II international relations resulted in calculated efforts by both sides to maneuver their respective belief systems into the international limelight. The challenges between these two political-ideological camps occurred in many venues,[7] were carefully planned, and sought specific goals. In these instances, ideological, political, and state-level interests competed in a normally bloodless and nonlethal version of warfare.[8] The premise behind a surrogate war is that competitions are different from war by not featuring loss of infrastructure or life. Victory was granted to any state that could convince its fellow sovereign nations that its political and economic systems were the direct cause of their success.

Until now, historical and political analysis of Olympic boycotts denies the Soviet Union any degree of calculation in its foreign and domestic policies when determining how best to handle the Los Angeles Olympics. Instead, petty vengeance for the American boycott has stood as the universally accepted explanation. This study will offer an alternative explanation for the Soviet decision that will include a demonstration of actual goals of the Soviet state in its Olympic battle with the United States.

The American and Soviet boycotts both have their beginnings in the early post–World War II period. East and West interactions were strained during this time as former wartime allies began overtly challenging each other for international political clout. At the Olympics, this would mean a period of four decades of political maneuvering. Simultaneously, the situation was further complicated when many Asian and African nations gained independence from European colonial powers. The Cold War and the friction apparent in imperial-colonial relations complicated the processes of many international forums and multinational events. International sports competitions generally suffered the most during this period of sociopolitical unrest due to contentious international relations and foreign policy.

International sports competitions are of particular interest because athletic competition is often a substitute for actual warfare. In a time when traditional warfare was being shunned in the international community, the Olympics allowed the participating nations to compete against each other in an acceptable manner. The fact that most Olympic sports events involved direct physical competition between athletes of two or more states merely exacerbated the likelihood of this form of state competition. In terms of the Cold War, the Olympics presented a competitive atmosphere that allowed states from the two main ideological camps of the time to compete with each other. As concluded in this study, these competitions played an important role in the sports diplomacy of many nations, but particularly in the diplomacy of the Soviet Union.

The existence of this higher meaning of competitiveness in sports can be summed up quite eloquently by the lyrics of playwright Tim Rice, written for the Musical *Chess*, about the competition between Soviet and American chess champions. Molokov, a KGB assistant to the Russian player, states that "after all, winning or losing reflects on us all . . . The whole world's tuned in. We're all on display. We're not merely sportsmen."[9] While this is an exaggeration, it makes an important point. It offers an example of how competition in sport between the Soviet Union and the United States could be perceived to have a higher symbolic meaning. The 1980 "Miracle on Ice" victory of the US hockey team over the Soviet Union is a good example of how the media, spectators, and even political actors can easily be swept into the symbolism of sports victories over "enemy states."

Winning the game did not simply mean that one side was better at the sport than the other. Conclusions were drawn on more ideological grounds. It is crucial to understand this before the Soviet boycott of the 1984 Summer Olympics can be accepted in any context other than retaliation for the 1980 US boycott or because the Soviet Union was afraid of not performing well. Sports, from as early as 1952 and through 1992, were one of a few arenas for direct competition between the two superpowers, which had already rejected the use of actual warfare to settle the irreconcilable differences between them. Perhaps the most compelling evidence of this is Nikita Khrushchev's withdrawal of nuclear weapons from Cuba in 1962. The Korean and Vietnam conflicts also suggest that direct warfare between the United States and the Soviet Union had been abandoned by the two superpowers, but that is only superficially true. Korea and Vietnam were actually conflicts between "lesser" powers in divided countries that were struggling over the future government system for their nations. These wars were supported militarily and financially by stronger nations in the East-West conflict but did not feature direct confrontations between the superpowers on domestic or foreign soil.

The lack of a formal declaration of war in the latter of the two conflicts—the Vietnam "police action"—just adds to arguments about the waning popularity of official wars as a tool to settle differences. This is not intended to suggest that outright direct competition was an outdated artifact of history but instead to accentuate the fact that "warfare," defined for this argument as direct conflict between two or more states, could occur in many different ways. With the abatement of direct warfare along a more classical definition, something would likely appear as a substitute for conflict and conflict resolution. The result of this was that any international competition, especially sports, potentially became a new battleground.

Examples of sports being used in this manner exist between many nations. One of the most well-known episodes of sports politics occurred at the 1956 Summer Olympics in Melbourne, Australia. The Soviet Union had invaded Hungary earlier that year, an event that Hungary was in no position to protest militarily or politically. However, its athletes made the point clear during a water polo competition in which the match between the Soviet Union and Hungary was ended early due to the excessive violence and resulting amounts of blood in the water. Violent competitions between the Czechoslovakian and Soviet hockey teams highlighted several international competitions.

Another more political example, which did not actually involve competition, occurred at the Opening Ceremonies of the 2000 Sydney Summer Olympics. At these Games, the first display of a unified

Korea with a unified flag since the Korean War was introduced in the parade of nations.[10] The exuberant response of the audience brought the entire Opening Ceremonies to a halt as Korea made this prominent step toward peace.

While politics, particularly Cold War politics, played an important role in the events of the 1980s, this analysis will not attempt to use the Cold War to explain how the Los Angeles Olympics fell victim to the friction of differing ideologies; that should be self-evident. The goal herein will be to determine the actual motivation behind the Soviet boycott. In order to be successful, this study will need to accomplish two tasks. First, it must demonstrate that the Soviet Union has a history of using sports, particularly the Olympics, for foreign policy aims. More specifically, the Soviet Union used sports foreign policy and diplomacy in order to achieve certain goals. Second, this study must challenge statements made by the Soviet government in order to dismiss announced explanations of why Soviet athletes would not compete in favor of a complete delineation of the actual policy goals behind the decision. This second task requires us to dismiss the current opinions on why the Soviet Union boycotted the 1984 Summer Olympics.

The boycott will be studied in two contexts. First, the context of Soviet sports policy interests and the realities of the Los Angeles Games will demonstrate a series of likely purposes behind the Soviet boycott and will demonstrate that the likelihood of a cause beyond retaliation is sufficient to accept a more complicated explanation. Second, the context of an atypical conflict between the Soviet Union and the United States will also serve to provide an in-depth example of a surrogate war. As part of an effort to craft a new understanding of the boycott, we will need to dismiss several assumptions about it. These will be done throughout the many chapters of this book. However, before we can go much further, one question should be quickly handled: Was the Soviet boycott strictly due to the tension of the Cold War? The answer to this question is unequivocally no.

If the Soviet boycott was a direct symptom of the Cold War, then the Soviet Bloc would have boycotted the 1976 Summer Games in Montreal and an even larger number of nations would have boycotted the Seoul Summer Olympic Games in 1988 as well as the 1972 Summer Games in Munich, West Germany. The fact that the Democratic Republic of Germany (East Germany) and the Soviet Union attended the Munich Games in 1972 clearly shows that the Olympics could and did transcend the problems of the Cold War and that the Soviet Union was open to attendance in Western hosts.[11] Lastly, the boycott is clearly not a US-versus-USSR dynamic, or the Soviet Union would not have attended the Lake Placid Winter Olympics (1980). The Soviet appearance at the Lake Placid Winter Olympics casts doubt on any statement that Cold War sentiments made it impossible for Soviet athletes to compete in the United States. By noting the attendance of the Soviet Union and her allies in New York, we can quickly surmise that there must have been issues relevant specifically to the Los Angeles Games or events between 1980 and 1984 that ultimately caused the boycott in the summer of 1984. Simplistic and conventional explanations of the Soviet boycott are untenable, and the boycott can therefore no longer be seen as just a simple chapter in the history of the Cold War. This study offers a more dynamic and compelling story behind Soviet goals and actions in 1984—a story deeply grounded in long standing state policies with reference to international sports participation.

Other attempts to explain the boycott have suggested that the Soviet Union feared competition with the Americans. Peter Ueberroth, organizer of the 1984 Los Angeles Olympics, was convinced that the Soviet Union feared being defeated in the sports competitions at the Games and as such opted against attendance.[12] While this theory is more in line with Soviet sports policy than other current arguments, it is unlikely the answer when one considers the successful track record of Soviet athletes in the Games. Similarly unlikely is the claim of retaliation as the sole motivator.

Indicative of the usual analysis of 1984 boycott, Christopher Hill in his book *Olympic Politics: Athens to Atlanta 1896–1996* states, "[T]he simple explanation for the boycott is probably the right one—tit for tat."[13] This and similar explanations assume the Soviet Union's official policy on the boycott is rooted in nothing more than bitterness. Not only does this argument lack any proof of its accuracy; it is also inconsistent with sixty years of Soviet sports policy. Both the claims that the Soviets feared the competition and suggestions of strictly retaliation for the American boycott of Moscow are currently without significant merit. Analysis to come will first demonstrate the inaccuracy of these explanations and will then present compelling evidence in support of a new explanation for the boycott.

The Soviet Union has a rich sports history with a very active and consistent sports policy and sports diplomacy. The boycott was consistent with previous Soviet sports policy, none of which was based in retaliatory or strictly American-Soviet relations. Ultimately, events behind the selection and preparation of Los Angeles created a situation that prompted a Soviet boycott based on well-established Soviet sports policy. The highly capitalistic nature of the Los Angeles Games and very real differences in Soviet and American visions of the relationship between government foreign policy and sport also played roles in the decision of the Soviet Union to boycott the 1984 Los Angeles Summer Olympics.

When looked at in totality, the multiple facets of the boycotts will clearly be seen as a symptom of Soviet-American conflicts. A competition to host the Olympics, which began in the bid process for the 1976 Summer Olympics, culminated in a surrogate war between the United States and the Soviet Union over success in hosting the Olympics. This contest was exacerbated by hypercapitalist and nongovernmental tendencies in the Los Angeles Organization and failures in the 1976 and 1980 Olympic Games. Rolling all these factors together, we see a very clear and policy consistent motivation behind the Soviet "nonparticipation."

PLAN OF THE BOOK

Chapter 1 examines modern theories in international relations and defines the concept of a surrogate war. As this study's principle claim is that there was a logically constructed and historically consistent Soviet sports policy at work in 1984, it is ultimately necessary to explain a theoretical framework within which that policy exists. The chapter, therefore, outlines some key theoretical assumptions about interstate conflict, which emphasizes the basis of conflict with a concise understanding of war. Chapter 2 of this book sets the stage for the Soviet boycott by providing a concise history of relevant politics in the Olympics, emphasizing the roles politicization of the Olympics has taken. It should not be seen as an all-encompassing history of politics in the Olympics in place of a mere primer on how politics can and has been manifested in the Games.

Chapter 3 turns its attention to the specifics of Soviet sports history. The bulk of the work in Chapter 3 will address the growth of Soviet sports politics since its earliest formations, emphasizing key assumptions about the role of politics in the Soviet sports machine. Starting with Russian Olympic policy before the Russian Revolution, it discusses sports policy in general and then focuses on sports policy predominantly in the Olympic Movement. The bulk of the evidence that structures the historical consistency of Soviet sports policy will be presented in this chapter and the typical goals of Soviet sports policy will be established in order to understand the appropriate Soviet response to the situation revolving around the 1980 and

1984 Olympiads. Chapter 3 concludes in the early 1970s when Soviet Olympic sports diplomacy shifted its focus to the bidding process, the subject of Chapter 4.

The bidding process is a major factor in the Soviet boycott—far more than one would presume. As a result, Chapter 4 focuses on the actual process of bidding to host the Games. It explains the process and then turns its attention to the bids that are most important for this study: the bids to host the Olympiads of 1976, 1980, and 1984. In particular, it addresses the problems that complicated the bidding processes for those Olympiads and reports on the IOC's reasons for making the selections it did.

Chapter 5 offers a brief historical account of the events of 1980. Placing the events of 1984 in a stronger historical perspective, the chapter identifies key issues and events of the Lake Placid and Moscow Olympics. Because one of the standard explanations of the boycott has tended to suggest fear of failure, particularly in the wake of the US hockey team defeating the Soviet Union for the gold medal, the chapter turns to a recap of the sports competitions of 1980 and previous Olympiads, as far back as 1952. Ultimately, Chapter 5 will discuss the state of sports politics and US-Soviet relations after the 1980 boycott and the condition of the Soviet sports machine in an effort to dismiss wrong assumptions about the Soviet boycott.

Chapter 5 ends the historical perspective of the events leading up to 1984. With realities about Soviet sports policy articulated and unnecessary assumptions dismissed, the study refocuses onto disagreements between the Soviet Union, the LAOOC, and the IOC. Chapter 6 spells out the stated reasons for the Soviet boycott and addresses most of them. In addition, it provides background on the LAOOC and discusses its responses to Soviet concerns. Concerns presented by the Soviet Politburo and the Soviet National Olympic Committee (USSR NOC) are analyzed as the backbone of this analysis. All concerns of both bodies are discussed in this chapter except the security issue, which plays a key role in both the Soviet position and the analysis in this study.

Given the importance and complexity of the security question, it is given its own treatment in Chapter 7. This chapter also brings into the discussion the positions of Soviet allies and what it meant for the Soviet justification for boycott. The chapter rounds out the whole argument on the actual reasons for the Soviet boycott by looking at them from several perspectives, offering a clearer understanding of the role Soviet complaints played in the drama of the boycotts.

Chapter 8 concludes the book and explains the most likely reasons for the Soviet boycott, given the evidence presented and the contradictions among Soviet allies and Soviet officials. It gauges the merits of these assertions and calls back on the three key approaches to the methodology as a means of confirming the results. With the analysis concluded, the chapter theorizes the weight of "surrogate wars," accepting the topic of this book as a fitting example therein. It lends credibility to the analysis of events such as the boycotts of the 1980s as having a solid grounding in current trends in international relations theory and in modern interstate conflict.

DEFINITIONS

In order to accomplish the forthcoming eight chapters, we will first establish some common ground in language that otherwise can become quite complicated in Olympic analysis. Penultimate among issues of language is the Olympic concept of state and nation. First and foremost is the concept of state. The IOC does not limit itself by allowing into its members only fully recognized states. Therefore, when we discuss members we have to be careful not to use the wrong terminology.

For our purposes, *state* will refer to any entity in the Olympic community with the recognition of the United Nations as a sovereign state. In most cases, when we discuss entities within the Olympic Movement, we will use the term *nation*. *Nation* is usually defined as any group of people with a common set of traits unique enough to describe them as a unique grouping of people. In this study, however, the term *nation* will be used indicate an entity with political, economic, geographic, and cultural traits that is recognizable as such in the international community. The IOC often uses the term *nation* and, as a result, so shall we. To offer a brief example, current nations with recognition in the Olympic Movement but without international recognition as sovereign—therefore not holding voting rights in the United Nations—include Chinese Taipei (Taiwan), Palestine, Puerto Rico, and Guam. Several IOC decisions on the matter have revolved around their definition of nation.

After World War II, Germany was not allowed to compete as two separate states until 1972. According to the IOC, the German nation was represented by the unified German team consisting of athletes from the states of East Germany and West Germany. The two Chinas issue fell under this categorization as well. Furthermore, this is also why US citizens can compete for Olympic teams of other countries, because they, and the nation they are competing for, recognize that Italian Americans, Samoan Americans, Latvian Americans, and so on, while citizens of the United States, are also culturally and historically tied to the nations of Italy, Samoa, Latvia, and elsewhere.

In addition to the terminology needed to reference IOC member nations, this study will regularly use the terms *sports policy* and *sports diplomacy*. Most states or nations that conduct a sports policy do so on a domestic and an international front. Domestic sports policies include issues such as the building of sports stadiums, the incorporation of new sports leagues, sports programs, health education systems, and so on. International sports policy refers to the formal position of a state or nation with regard to its participation in international sports programs and competitions. A state needs neither domestic nor foreign sports policies to have the other, although it is rare for an international sports policy to be formulated without a prior domestic policy already in existence.

For the most part, this study will refer to an international sports policy in which a nation must have responses to the following:[14]

1. Why or why not should they participate in the international sports community?
2. How should they participate in the international sports community?
3. Which sports federations should they join and organize teams for competition?
4. Which invitations for participation in a sports event should they accept, and which should they refuse (boycott)?
5. Should they choose to host international sports events, and which events should they host?
6. What role will an international sports policy play in the overall foreign policy objectives of the state?

Most nations that conduct an international sports policy have answered all these questions at one point, and many of them have revised their answers on a number of occasions. In this study, time will be spent establishing the standard sports policy of the Soviet Union in order to demonstrate how it would go about responding to its concerns with the Los Angeles Games as well as to indicate likely explanations for the boycott. When we bring the issue of boycott and other such disagreements on sports policy between nations, we shift from simply discussing sports policy to also discussing sports diplomacy.

CHAPTER 1

THE SURROGATE WAR, THE BOYCOTT,
AND THE SEARCH FOR A HIDDEN STORY

A CALL FOR A DEEPER UNDERSTANDING

The assumption that began this study was simple enough: the Soviet Union, a state with very complex and interrelated domestic and foreign policies, would most likely have a goal behind its decision to boycott the Olympics. Given the nuanced decisions behind most of Soviet policies, it is not unreasonable to assume that the Soviet decision to boycott the 1984 Los Angeles Olympics was not simply retaliatory. Hans Morgenthau illustrated that diplomacy is neither haphazard nor uncalculated.[1] His study of international relations is actually an excellent presentation of precisely how deliberate and carefully designed foreign relations are between states. Of even greater significance is Thomas Schelling's study of conflict, in which he delineates the concept of bargaining between two or more states.[2]

One of Schelling's most important contributions is that international relations are not always a zero-sum game; international relations do not exist at an extreme in which one state gains completely and another state loses completely. Instead, he explains, it is a non-zero-sum game in which bargaining plays a crucial role in determining degrees of success and failure of each participant. Moving forward with Schelling, it becomes increasingly hard to assume that the Soviet Union would opt for automatic noninvolvement instead of entering into a bargaining game with the Los Angeles Olympic Organizing Committee (LAOOC) and the International Olympic Committee (IOC) as an attempt to arrive at a conclusion with a better outcome for the Soviet Union than boycotting.

The simple fact that, as will be demonstrated in Chapters 6 and 7, the Soviet Union did have both demands and diplomatic encounters with the LAOOC and the IOC during the months before the Los Angeles Summer Games suggests there is more to this story. Therefore, with the simple application of Schelling's theory, we are able to immediately dismiss statements that the simplest answer—"tit for tat," as Christopher Hill put it when describing the boycott[3]—is automatically the correct one. This does not, however, dismiss the explanation of vengeance as the final answer. Morgenthau and Schelling's theoretical notions would suggest that the Soviet Union would have considered many options for their sports policy in the 1980s, with the possibility of boycott likely being one among many.

To fully understand the purpose behind the Soviet boycott, we have to first understand what goal(s) Soviet officials had in their participation or nonparticipation in Los Angeles. As we will see, the boycott may actually have been the method of achieving a goal rather than the goal itself, thus making the current explanation of vengeance inaccurate. The American boycott, followed by an American Olympics, provided a "competition" between the superpowers. The decision to boycott must have been a result of a careful decision process, resulting from the conclusion that they would gain more by not attending the Games. Soviet officials must have seen the nonparticipation as preserving the state's sports authority instead of as mere retaliation, with retaliation being only a side effect of the actual decision and not the decision itself. The added benefit of retaliation with a Soviet nonparticipation was most likely an incentive to ultimately decide not to go. The question in this study is not whether retaliation played a role—it would be naïve to assume it did not—but to place retaliation in its proper context as a part of the decision process: the greater process of which the retaliation was a part of—what I will define as a longstanding surrogate war against the United States.

This study relies on a belief that international sports can serve as a form of surrogate war. As such, concepts and theories on war are pertinent to this study. In particular, Bruce Bueno de Mesquita's study on the causes of war offers a particularly interesting justification for challenging current explanations for the Soviet boycott.[4] In his account for war, termed the *expected utility of war*, Bueno de Mesquita explains that war only occurs when the benefits from going to war outweigh the potential cost of the war. Additionally, he states that decision makers are rational maximizers: they will act in a manner that provides a positive outcome while simultaneously being willing or unwilling to take risks in their actions.[5]

The expected utility of war is perhaps the best explanation for Soviet sports policy. As Chapter 3 will reveal, the Soviet Union had a history of attending only those sports competitions in which they could guarantee victory. In war terminology, they would only go to war if they "expected" that the outcome would be in their favor. As Chapter 4 will indicate, hosting the Olympics represents its own form of competition, which would also fall within the scope of Bueno de Mesquita's arguments.

In addition to Bueno de Mesquita, we need to note there is a possibility of multiple levels of competition within a single event. These layers, *nested games* as George Tsebelis referred to them,[6] are used to explain how suboptimal choices, made by an actor, might actually be rational if placed in the context of a larger goal—meaning that they appear suboptimal because the focus of the research is on the wrong question. These suboptimal choices—nested games—become particularly relevant when analyzing complex foreign policy goals in surrogate wars.

Nested games are a reminder that actual observed outcome is not necessarily the main goal of an action. For our analysis, this would mean that the Soviet goal was not to boycott; rather, it was to achieve some other goal, which boycotting would help to attain. Current explanations assume that the boycott was the direct result of a desire to punish or embarrass the United States for its decision to boycott the Moscow Olympics. However, it is also possible that the boycott served a more important goal of the Soviet Union and that retaliation was not the primary objective. Current theories on international relations and the history of Soviet involvement in sports all suggest that the Soviet Union's involvement in the Olympics represents a calculated strategy to attain specific goals of the state. Where previous studies saw the boycott as a means to its own ends, this argument sees it as merely the process to attain the actual objectives of a well-crafted Soviet sports policy that was far more sophisticated than "You didn't come to ours, so we aren't coming to yours."

THE PATH TO A NEW UNDERSTANDING

The two interrelated goals of this study are to establish the actual Soviet objectives that led to the boycott and to replace current understandings of the boycott with a theory based in a more rigorous understanding of Soviet sports enterprises. This study will focus on the choices that Soviet actors made in their sports diplomacy. Recognizing that these choices are made through the institutions and regulations of the Olympic Movement, the rational choice framework will be constrained by structuralist factors. To that end, the study is informed by the arguments of Morgenthau,[7] Schelling,[8] Kenneth Waltz,[9] and others on the deliberate and calculated nature of the decision process of international relations while accepting statements, by Ira Katznelson and others,[10] that structural realities influence outcomes of decisions. Lastly, the process of establishing Soviet interests and objectives in participating in the Olympics will be established through historical perspectives on Soviet sports policy decision making.

Additionally, it must be noted that the theoretical framework of this study will be deeply influenced by historical analysis. It will be demonstrated that Soviet sports policies are consistently designed around meeting the same set of specific goals—namely, to seek the promotion of the Soviet political, social, economic, and cultural system as superior to all others with particular emphasis on a comparison with Western and capitalist political systems. Granted that every individual example of Soviet sports diplomacy had its own unique situation and therefore its own specific goals, the underlying purpose behind Soviet involvement in international sports, and therefore the broad goals for that involvement, remained consistent.

By recognizing that international sports competitions represented a recurring opportunity for Soviet objectives, we find that there is a roughly sixty-year period of history from which consistent strategies of Soviet sports policy can be established. By placing this study into a historical perspective, we are able to establish a pattern of Soviet decision making and judge the 1984 decision to boycott accordingly.

SURROGATE WARS: FIELDS OF COMPETITION FOR STATES

On a more theoretical level, this study serves to systematize the concept of a surrogate war through a close look at the 1984 boycott. This concept may have many similarities to a traditional war, but its unique nature has attributes that distinguish it from traditional war. To start, I define *surrogate war* as a conflict between two or more states that features a direct competition between representatives of those states but does not feature as an expected outcome property damage or severe personal injury, including loss of life. The expected nonlethal nature of surrogate wars is a key point of differentiation from traditional wars and proxy wars. These differences made surrogate wars, particularly during the Cold War, an increasingly popular option in twentieth-century politics.

The definition of *surrogate war* differs from a similar concept, *proxy war*, in a few key ways. William Safire defined *proxy war* as "great-power hostility expressed through client states."[11] By logical extension, proxy wars can include the use of nonstate actors in this capacity as well. The key difference between surrogate and proxy wars is the type of engagement. While proxy wars are the same engagement concept as traditional warfare, just waged by different actors, surrogate wars are more commonly waged by the primary state's nonmilitary capabilities, in various forms or manifestations of competition.[12] The focus of our analysis will be not only types of surrogate wars but also the capabilities that are used to wage them.

The interaction of all states, when in conflict, is conducted as a facet of war. Each state's participation in war is conducted by a means consistent with that state's capabilities and the perceived likelihood of victory from its preferred method of participation. For some states, this results in a traditional concept of war. In other cases, a traditional war becomes untenable and states instead must seek alternative venues for conflict. One attractive alternative is a surrogate war, in which states settle disputes in a manner that, while structurally distinct from more traditional concepts of war, is no less valid and no less theoretically bounded.

First, it must be noted that potential surrogate wars are not limited to any specific "type" of engagement. Far from encompassing a set list of types of conflicts, surrogate wars indicate a concept of conflict, which can manifest itself in many different ways. Carl von Clausewitz's definition of war states that war is politics by other means.[13] If we accept this context and suggest surrogate wars are "wars by other means," then surrogate wars too are politics by other means. A surrogate war becomes another option in the arsenal of state conflict, allowing states to define and meet objectives that are otherwise outside their capacity.

While the usage of surrogate wars can be seen as nothing more than war with nonlethal tactics, that would be overly simplistic. A surrogate war allows for direct contest between states in circumstances in which traditional concepts of war are either not practical or not possible. In some cases, this is the logical result of the cost of war in certain circumstances. The lack of significant direct conflict between the United States and the Soviet Union during the Cold War and the use instead of "competitions" in sports, technology, economics, and industry offers initial evidence of this.

While conflict between "enemies" is what most would assume plays out in surrogate wars, this is not a required feature of the relations of participants in a surrogate war. Arguably, another use of surrogate wars is in a rivalry between allied states as a means to abate rivalry rooted in nationalism and to diffuse interstate conflict among them. In such a scenario, surrogate war allows for confrontation and competition between these states without weakening or fragmenting alliances and their benefits.[14]

Surrogate wars, therefore, fall within the current theoretical understandings of war, but with a few additional conditions. These conditions include four elements: degree, competition, luck, and outcome. First, surrogate wars, even more so than situations of brinkmanship, allow for a conflict between two states that does not result in excessive costs and the risks of traditional war. The formula of expected utility, while still valid, often has different outcomes for surrogate wars simply because the cost involved can be much less. This is not to suggest that the terms, conditions, and outcomes of surrogate wars are trivial. Instead, it suggests that surrogate wars offer solutions to interstate challenges that are not contestable on a traditional battlefield.

Degree

Surrogate wars vary in degree of cost and planning, much like the spectrum of concepts from brinkmanship to total war. Arguably, we can analyze surrogate wars in a similar fashion, by identifying the amount of resources a state is willing to commit to them. This is only superficially useful though. Ranging from spontaneous to multiyear planning endeavors, the degrees of complexity of surrogate war are *ipso facto* conditions for the likely structures and outcomes of those events.

An element of degree is the context of battle versus war. Surrogate wars can manifest themselves as a singular event, separate from other forms of conflict between two states, or they may be embedded into a broader conflict with many "battles." During traditional wars, states often claim victory in a variety of potential venues, like trumpeting the control of the skies in World War II as a moment of pride and rallying for England. Within a war, states seek many avenues to accept victory for many purposes. Surrogate wars can manifest individually, as a series of contests, or even as an event within a traditional war. It should be noted that celebrations of "victory" in a traditional setting of war, as a means to maintain morale or for some other purpose, are merely interpretations of the circumstances of war and not surrogate wars.

Competition

The degree of sophistication of the structural element of a surrogate war, in other words the concept of competition, needs careful consideration. To be valid, a surrogate war must be a *deliberate* contest between representatives of two or more states, through which a structured means of determining a victor is present.[15] While the terms of victory may be somewhat up for debate between participants, the effectiveness of a contest as a surrogate war is lessened if determination of victory is cloudy or open to contestation between the represented states. Competitions that are structured around a set of governing rules tend to be more effective than those that are more haphazardly drawn.[16] As a result, sporting events are a common and effective type of surrogate war.

As I define them, surrogate wars do not require physical competition. The objective can be attained through physical prowess, mental capability, ingenuity, or some other capability of the individual(s) involved. Any ability of a citizen that the state can claim to have been partially or fully responsible for developing or that can be attributed to the overall capability of members of a specific national identity is a necessary condition for a surrogate war. Acceptable examples would be any sport where physical prowess determines victory. Competition is not, however, a factor solely of physical ability. The Space Race,[17] arms race, or even chess represent surrogate wars of intellect, engineering, and state capability. Competition therefore requires success to be contingent on the abilities of the competitors that would be a legacy of state policy.

Strict rules for competition are required in surrogate wars because the concept of surrender does not readily exist in most examples of surrogate war. In a war, the moment of victory for one side is the surrender or destruction of the other.[18] In surrogate wars, surrender can be an outcome, but so can a structured stopping point, such as a length of time or a set point-total earned. Competitions, ultimately, must possess mutually accepted terms of victory to bolster the legitimacy of declared outcomes. Victory must be a definable reality; otherwise, nothing is clearly gained, as the "losing" side can argue it did not really lose.

Luck

Ambiguity can also be a result of the role of luck in surrogate wars. In war, many factors determine victory, including luck. Because the point of a surrogate war is to rank states in terms of their success, victory must be determinable and the result of factors arguably within the control or influence of the state. Luck, therefore, cannot be a necessary precondition of the competition. In traditional war, surrender is the admission of loss; therefore luck is inconsequential for determining who won. Either way, one side said the other side won. When the competition exists within a frame of limitations, then outcomes are *post facto* debatable. The degree of luck or uncertainty involved in the competition will exacerbate postcompetition arguments over which side is the actual winner and will diminish the value of the victory in competition.

Therefore, haphazard or luck-based competitions do not provide effective examples of surrogate wars. This is of course not to suggest that luck must be discarded. Indeed, many generals have attested a victory to the presence of God, Lady Luck, or another mystical explanation. Even so, luck is often manifested as favorable conditions within which we must still perform. Luck is not totally dismissed. If the competition is determined with an outcome of surrender, then luck is a condition both sides must seek to overcome. However, as the conditions for victory become more arbitrary, luck becomes a more potential justification for failure. For a surrogate war to be effective, all competitors together must be in control of the outcome, with luck playing a minimal role, if at all. To illustrate this point, consider two games: roulette and chess.

While gamblers may claim to possess a hidden skill in determining what number will come up in roulette, and while there are different methods of betting that have a higher likelihood of paying off, the results of roulette are still a system of random chance the result of which is that any number has an equal chance of coming up. The methods by which one plays can be carefully strategized, but that process has no influence on the outcome of the spin. In chess, however, the rules of the game place both players on an equal plane in terms of options for the game. The player with the strongest strategy attains victory. Luck is perceived to still be present in the game, as the player that makes a horrible mistake thanks God that their opponent "didn't see it." However, the outcome of that scenario is due to failure on the part of both players: the first who made the mistake, and the second who failed to capitalize on it.

In the roulette and chess examples, we find a useful explanation for the dismissal of luck. Should two states compete in roulette, neither can claim the surrogate war's outcome represented any real ability of one state over the other. The winning state, unless it cheated to "rig" the outcome, did not use any actual capabilities to create its victory. In chess, however, the Soviet Union and the United States saw a repeated contest between American and Soviet chess masters, both sides of which claimed supremacy over the other as an American or a Soviet bested the other with strategy. Victory was based on which state system produced the smartest and most effective chess players. Claims of luck in this endeavor were either modesty on behalf of the winner or a justification on behalf of the loser. In summation, the more luck plays a role in the outcome of competition, the less important skill becomes. Once skill is dismissed as the precondition of victory, the outcome of the surrogate war loses meaning.

Outcome

The importance of the minimization of luck and of having systematized rules set for determining victory are both linked to the problem of outcome. Warfare has, if you can call it a benefit, the luxury of not ending until either both sides accept a draw of some kind or one side of the war admits defeat. While a draw allows both sides to claim they performed better, it is meaningless, as the accepted outcome of the conflict was a state of no victory. A claim of victory is arrived at in one of three ways. First, victory is achieved through limited action. The state has a predetermined objective and victory is attained when the objective is met. Second, victory occurs through surrender—when one side of the war admits defeat. Third, victory is realized when warfare exacts a toll on one side to the point of which no military or governing structure is present for its continuation or for their surrender. In well-planned surrogate wars, victory is a mutually accepted condition that either side attains while following mutually accepted rules. In unplanned, spontaneous surrogate wars, victory is often a case of which side accomplishes something first or when one side surrenders. The most complicated surrogate wars are those competitions in which the conflict begins before an agreed-on condition of victory.

To place the concepts of competition and outcome into a clearer context, consider the infamous water polo match between Hungary and the Soviet Union that took place at the 1956 Melbourne Summer Olympics. The 1956 Games took place shortly after the Soviet Union invaded Hungary to quell an anticommunist uprising. The Hungarian team actually left for the Games at the very start of the revolution. The Hungarian Revolution, which would fail to attain even a single military success, conducted an impromptu surrogate war providing the Hungarians a "battle" they had a better chance at winning.

The Hungarian water polo team decided to challenge Soviet political authority through a symbolic victory in sports. As Hungary had little hope of matching Russian military capacity in Budapest, water polo provided a field in which capacity was level and victory was based on the merits of Russian and Hungarian athletes. The match, which turned bloody, ended when referees called the match a few minutes early to avoid further injury in the pool and to quell angered Hungarian fans over a Russian cheap shot. Hungary triumphed with a symbolic victory over the Russians, leading to a gold medal that would later turn into an even greater symbol at the award ceremony: the Bronze-medal-winning Soviet team silently stood watch as the Hungarian flag was raised to the playing of the national anthem—the tradition for the state taking the gold medal.

In summation, within the current understanding of international conflict, we find a necessary expansion of the concept of conflict to include war, sports, diplomacy, and other "competitions" within the same in theoretical terms, differing only in the rules, tools, and processes by which it is contested. The scope of political analysis in terms of states in conflict must be broadened to include any venue in which a state vests a higher meaning, in terms of international politics, than it inherently possesses. Avenues of interstate inquiry have been only limitedly considered, cloaking the actual policy goals of some states in international decisions. Given the political and strategic nature this study applies to Soviet sports policy, it becomes evident that the Los Angeles boycott may fit into the definition of surrogate war, if the decision can be seen as a means of victory in a Cold War contest.

BOYCOTTS AND STRATEGY

To start this analysis, we should first define the term *boycott* in general and how it will be used in a political context. The term *boycott* is defined as "withdrawal from social or commercial interaction or cooperation with a group, nation, person, etc., intended as a protest or punishment."[19] Integral to the concept of boycott is the coercive tendency of the action, which often seeks to influence another actor to change course on some specific action as a means of avoiding stated "protest or punishment." For our purposes, the word *coercion* is a key element of the definition. Coercion is the utilization of force in order to elicit a specific behavior or action. While it is often expressed in terms of literal infliction of force, in other words physical harm or pain, it can also be more psychological and emotional. In that sense, blackmail, peer pressure, and other sociocultural expressions of coercion are viable examples. Consideration of boycotts on a psychological or emotional level is more attuned to this study than more traditional notions of the use of force. Such an outcome would require rallying enough states behind a boycott so that the Games are wholly undermined, relocated, or cancelled. The IOC is not likely to move the Games, cancel the Games, or take any other action that would truly and clearly harm the host. Therefore, it is illogical to argue that the boycotts presented significant infrastructural or economic harm. As such, the boycotts result more in a blow to the ego of the host state than any long-term harm. Boycotts have limited the host from successfully claiming that its Olympiad was largest, most inclusive, most competitive—in other words the best—Olympics ever, but these claims are ancillary to the majority of goals of the host state. These claims are also not endorsed by the Olympic committee, so they carry little authority.

The coercive nature of the boycott presents a single conundrum to the host: give in on policy demands of the boycotting state(s) or live with an Olympics short a few states and athletes. In some instances, this included athletes whose performance would increase the profile of specific sports competitions. In short, the boycotts—as with most surrogate wars—featured a less violent and arguably less costly means of exercising politics than more violent forms of coercion and war.

As this study will indicate, boycotting was a political strategy and weapon that occurred multiple times through the history of the modern Olympics. As a means of alternative political conflict, boycotts had the potential of being a venue for surrogate war in which states could use their participation or nonparticipation as means of fostering state policy on matters irrelevant to the Olympics or sports competitions in general. The debate of the inviolability of sport versus political protest would play itself out several times in Olympic history. While boycott is a simple enough concept, it is inaccurate to state that they were all structurally the same. In fact, this analysis identifies two distinct types of boycotts that can be recognized from the five examples.

The two types of examples differ on the basis of the cause of the boycott and in how the boycotting state justifies it. In the first category, the boycott is motivated by a desire to change the domestic or foreign policy of an offending state by the use of a punitive measure if the state does not back away from the policy the threatening states are upset over. The boycotts in this category include the boycott threatened against Berlin in 1936, the African boycott in response to South Africa, and the American boycott of the 1980 Moscow Games. The aforementioned attempted boycott against the 1936 Games was in response to Nazi policies toward Jewish athletes. The two boycotts threatened by the African Bloc were in response to the participation of states that had violated international agreements isolating South Africa due to apartheid. Lastly, the 1980 American boycott was chiefly caused by the inability of the American government to deter Soviet aggression against Afghanistan, thereby changing their foreign policy decisions.

The examples in this first category have little to no actual pertinence to the Olympic Movement. The boycott was nothing more than using the Olympics as a venue to protest state actions that were either irrelevant or only partially relevant to the Olympics. They illustrate a boycott that attempted to focus the attention of the global community on a current issue in the domestic or foreign policy of a nation. This is a reasonable description of the failed boycott of the 1936 Nazi Olympics, the African boycott of the 1976 Olympics, and the American boycott of the 1980 Olympics. Comparing this description to the Soviet boycott is not as simple and requires some consideration of language on the part of the Soviet Union.

The assumed goals of the Soviet Union are no different from the other examples given, when one considers the announced motivation of the Soviet boycott. Chapters 6 and 7 will detail Soviet concerns over the Los Angeles Olympics and their eventual announcement of the boycott. For now, it is sufficient to note that the Soviet Union's announcement claimed there were numerous failures in Los Angeles's plan to provide a safe and successful Summer Games. This suggests that previous definitions and political analysis should sufficiently describe the actions of the Soviet Union. However, in their statements on the situation, Soviet representatives never used the term *boycott* formally. Instead, they called their response a *nonparticipation*. The change in syntax was likely a means of avoiding use of a label they demonized four years earlier,[20] but it's worth noting how this terminology may affect our analysis of the Soviet Union's goals in utilizing it.

As participation simply implies one's willingness to take part or be involved with something, a nonparticipation is a choice to not share in something or take part. This is a reasonable definition of what the Soviet Union and the United States did, but the definition lacks specificity, as there is no limit or expectation as to the motive behind the decision. The term *boycott* implies political motivation in response to the actions of another state, but it does not indicate any specific types of motivation. Therefore, all previous examples of *boycott* can comfortably use this term instead of *nonparticipation*, which is necessarily lacking focus. Part of the difficulty in comparing the 1984 Soviet "nonparticipation" to prior boycotts is the clumsiness of terminology. Forthcoming chapters will demonstrate that every potential explanation for the Soviet nonparticipation has political inferences. Regardless of what state policy termed its action, the Soviet decision was a boycott. The term unfortunately has several connotations that make it less favorable, but we should not allow these factors to influence our understanding and analysis of the event. Therefore, regardless of the validity of state claims, the noble or ignoble motivation behind such claims, and other factors surrounding the decision process, a state's political decision to refuse to participate in a specific event is a boycott. With this definition of boycott in mind, the Soviet Union's protesting of American and LAOOC handling of the Olympics was a boycott, not a nonparticipation.

While the Soviet Union actively claimed its nonparticipation was motivated by pure commitment to the ideals of the Olympic Movement, many Soviet statements were outright attacks on the United States and its corruption or manipulation of the Olympic Charter. The IOC maintains sole authority to act on interpretations of the charter. While other organizations and governments may comment on the charter and how states implement the ideals enshrined within it, it is not within their power to act on these opinions. As it will be shown, the IOC accepted the details and validity of Los Angeles's plans to host the Games. This rendered Soviet claims that Los Angeles was operating outside of Olympic ideals invalid and suggests Soviet concerns were more political and less altruistic than they claimed. Had the IOC agreed with the Soviet Union, then the claim of nonparticipation may have been valid.

Acting in defense of the charter is the only logical means of a nonparticipation, as the Soviet Union was describing it. If the Olympic Movement was being harmed by Los Angeles's plans, then the nonparticipation is a deliberate choice to not support the Games that were, as the Soviet Union was implying, harmful to the Olympic Movement. With the IOC dismissing this as invalid, all that remains are self-interested motivations that provided some benefit—most likely political—for the Soviet Union. This creates a logical divide between nonparticipation and boycott that is rooted in the motivation of the state.

In summation, *boycott* implies a political opinion or position that drives the decision to not participate. Neither the Soviet Union nor the United States were willing to outright admit to politicizing the

Olympics. While both were eager to accuse the other of doing so, they both adamantly insisted that their decisions were not politically motivated. For the United States, this was a far more complicated argument to make because their decision to not participate was entirely unrelated to Moscow's Olympic Games. It was easier, but yet ultimately unsuccessful, for the Soviet Union to claim they were not politicizing because their stated reasons for the boycott were related to the facts of the Los Angeles Olympics; as this study will demonstrate, the actual reasons for the boycott were far more political and far less pertinent to LAOOC organizational efforts than they claimed.

Whatever may cause a boycott, we must not forget that states manifest power through strategy. Thomas Schelling defined strategy as the exploitation of potential force.[21] By focusing on the strategy of conflict, Schelling reminds us that we are dealing with a bargaining situation.[22] For the study of a boycott, this assertion becomes even more pertinent. Having already theorized that boycott is a type of state conflict, and having established that all boycotts are a form of political protest over the actions of another state, then we see the benefit of Schelling's understanding of bargaining. Boycotts can therefore be seen as a means of increasing the cost of a state's action.

The process of bargaining in a boycott scenario involves making nonparticipation appear to be a damaging enough result of an unwanted policy of another state. A part of the bargaining game is one of perceived threat. The United States had to perceive the Soviet threat of boycott as real and not a bluff. Because of this, the process of boycott is always a form of tacit bargaining. Tacit bargaining, or a negotiation in which communication is either incomplete or outright impossible,[23] is a commonality in limited warfare and other forms of conflict that involve diplomatic encounters. As this is not solely a study on bargaining, I will limit myself to two brief observations on bargaining in a boycott situation.

First, a negotiation on boycotting always involves a competing interest between two or more states in which neither state is aware of what extent the other is willing to risk boycott to attain a specific state objective. Both states must weigh the value of the boycott and compare it to the overall cost of that boycott occurring. As the boycott will mean different things to each state, the potential success, failure, and outcomes of diplomacy are hidden from some actors in the negotiation; thus, a boycott negotiation will always include some aspects of tacit bargaining.

Second, both sides must be looking to avert the boycott. This needs be true for a political boycott to have any relevance. There is not a boycott if the threatening state would not attend had the justification for the boycott not occurred. Also, the state against which the boycott is conducted must perceive the boycott to be damaging. Should it see the boycott as without cost or purpose, the state threatening the boycott would see no benefit in the attempt and therefore gain nothing.

The main point of understanding a strategy for conflict and bargaining, coupled with a utilization of current trends in theories of the causes of war, is to aptly demonstrate how the elements of political theory are pertinent for both the study of boycott and the study of international sports policy. By grounding this study in mainstream international relations theory, and by restricting ourselves to an analysis of actor choices and the structures through which these decisions are made, this study will be able to effectively establish the motivation of the Soviet boycott.

Regardless of how effective or ineffective one may assume that sports diplomacy is, the simple fact is that several states and nations practice it. The sheer number of states that practice it implies that a properly managed sports diplomacy is likely more effective than not. Both the Soviet Union and the United States conducted very active and complicated sports diplomacies and encouraged their allies to do the same. It is worth noting that more than just states and nations conduct both international sports policy and sports diplomacy.

The International Olympic Committee has within it examples of both states and nations that conduct sports policy and sports diplomacy. In addition to this, other international organizations whose main purpose is not sports related manage sports policy and conduct sports diplomacy. For example, whenever a nation violated the isolation of South Africa sports teams, the Organization of African Unity (now the African Union) got involved in the situation and aggressively pushed for sports boycotts of the offending party. The outcome was that the OAU made the decision to compete with South African teams too costly to risk. Businesses often conduct sports policy and sports diplomacy by seeking ways to endorse athletic teams, athletic events, and so on in the hopes of gaining a better reputation, some advertising, or some other policy goal. A very recent trend in business involvement in sports policy involves efforts on the part of major media outlets attempting to influence the selection of locations for competition so as to allow for the best possible opportunity to broadcast the event to the largest population.

In some of the most complicated controversies within international sports, states, nations, international organizations, businesses, religious and nongovernmental organizations, and even individuals have attempted to influence the outcome of the situation. The full scope of sports diplomacy as a tool of international conflict has been evident in the history of the modern Olympics, for more than a century. Sport diplomacy can become as complicated as any other manifestation of diplomacy and, as such, requires careful analysis with as much attention to theory, methodology, and detail as other forms of international conflict and cooperation.

THE SEARCH FOR AN EXPLANATION

The rest of this book will involve answering the following key question from multiple perspectives: what actual interests and goals motivated the Soviet boycott of the Los Angeles Olympics and to what extent was retaliation a part of that logic? As the Soviet-stated justification for the boycott, and the actual underlying causes of it, are multifaceted and complicated, this study will need to address the question through those various areas. The process of this methodology will be to seek evidence of the Soviet objectives through several avenues. The hope behind the effort of this methodology is that a broader mode of analysis will produce more meaningful results. Beyond the goals of this methodology, this approach solves an otherwise critical problem. A primary cause of this methodology is routed in the fact that the Soviet Union's objectives are not apparent given the available evidence.

The easiest answer to the main question of this book would be to simply read the internal correspondences of the individuals who made this decision. This of course assumes that they would be an accurate reflection of their thought processes. A relatively uncooperative modern Russian Government, particularly the Russian Olympic Committee and the Russian Embassy to the United States, dismissed this as an option, so this study needed to use a more elaborate research design. A deductive method of analysis, which would work with three distinct assumptions and avenues of research, took shape to provide a valid process of analysis.

The first assumption rested in the already present body of analysis on Soviet sports policy. By identifying consistency in the inherent rationality of the decision process of the Soviet Union's sports policy, we can accept that this decision would follow the same rules as all previous Soviet sports decisions. Recognizing that international sports are always conducted through a system, the effects of the system on these decision outcomes remains a reality. However, fluctuations within that system, unless quite large, are relatively unimportant to this study.

As this study focuses more deeply on Soviet decision processes than on IOC or international sports structures, the fact that the structures exist and constrain decision processes is more pertinent than how these structures changed during the past sixty years of Soviet sports policy. This assumption is strengthened in the next chapter, where it becomes apparent that Soviet sports policy has maintained consistency over that period of time, suggesting that changes in the structures, should they have occurred, are clearly not a significant influence on those decisions. Studying political phenomena within a system that is constant enough to not significantly influence outcomes only more sharply focuses analysis on the goals of actors within that structure, which represents our second assumption.

Second, the general goals of the Soviet Union's participation in international sports will be considered constants unless there is evidence of a change of direction in Soviet policy. Soviet decision making on international sports phenomena remained consistent from its earliest manifestations up to the boycott era in the Olympics. Unless there is evidence that their sports policy goals changed during the actual events studied in this book, the fundamental elements of that policy will be expected to have significant influence on Soviet decision makers addressing the issue of the Los Angeles Olympics. In this sense, the historical framework of this analysis will provide ample evidence that the decision processes of the Soviet Union maintained stable throughout all segments of this analysis.

As this study focuses on the interests and objectives of the Soviet Union as found within the statements of the Soviet Union, the accuracy and authenticity of such statements must be maintained throughout all aspects and directions of this study. The overarching requirement placed on usable material was that they are an accurate depiction of the Soviet point of view. Anything that appeared to be interpreted or otherwise altered by anyone with an agenda other than the Soviet Union's or that of a clear and earnest attempt to get the Soviets to attend was simply dismissed. Sources articulating the Soviet point of view needed to be either directly from the Soviet Union or from individuals within the International Olympic Committee or the Los Angeles Olympic Organizing Committee as they attempted to alleviate Soviet concerns.

Requiring a reasonable expectation of authenticity in Soviet diplomacy on the boycott also requires strict consideration of any sources on the Soviet position that were interpreted, controlled, released, or summarized by the American political system and/or the American news media of the mid-1980s. While these sources are not outright dismissed, they are considered cautiously in order to find uncontestable proof of the accuracy or bias of those sources to the Soviet position. This includes American allies, particularly the United Kingdom, Canada, and France, all of which produced several reports and statements on the Soviet position as it developed. This left only three avenues of research, all of which proved to be productive and remained within both the theoretical framework of this study and the litmus tests for accuracy.

As a result of strict methodological requirements for the selection of evidence, there are limited, but ultimately fruitful, avenues of research. First, and clearly the most limited of them, involves studying the positions of Soviet allies. As will be demonstrated later, several claims of the Soviet Union involved issues that affected more than just the Soviet Union and its athletes. If they were real concerns, they would also be evident in the positions of other nations. As a result, the positions of several other nations were analyzed to judge whether Soviet claims were the actual reason for boycott or if these claims were a smokescreen for other clandestine reasons. Fortunately, the positions taken by Bulgaria, East Germany, Romania, and Cuba offer significant facts that can be used to understand and judge the Soviet viewpoint. This, however, posed some of the same problems of access that made retrieving Soviet documents impossible. Previous research into the Romanian and Bulgarian positions was available and written in what appears to be language lacking the Cold War political rhetoric that has plagued many accounts of Soviet Olympic history. Bulgaria also published its own explanation for its boycott, something the Soviet Union never actually did. Sources on other nations, particularly Cuba, Czechoslovakia, and East Germany, rounded out the pool of evidence.

A second avenue of research was the correspondence between the IOC and the LAOOC. The LAOOC, which was run by a businessman instead of a part of the American political establishment, had divorced itself from the American government and was acting as an independent entity not directly linked to or under the control of the White House or even the California government. This, in the end, was probably an advantage in organizing certain aspects of the Games, but a critical roadblock in Soviet-USOC negotiations. The LAOOC wanted to avoid political turmoil and had several meetings and many correspondences that tried to legitimately address the concerns of the Soviet National Olympic Committee (USSR NOC).

LAOOC President Peter Ueberroth had made it clear on several occasions that he wanted to avert the boycott and work with Soviet representatives in order to guarantee their state's attendance. Whether the LAOOC agreed with Soviet claims or not, the issues raised by the Soviet representatives had to be dealt with by the LAOOC, Ueberroth, and his vice presidents. The Soviet Union also had to deal with a Los Angeles businessman and not a government official. Not only did this not legitimize the LAOOC in the view of the Soviets, but it would be a serious problem for the LAOOC to gain Soviet trust during negotiations. This unique relationship complicated matters for the LAOOC but allowed for another source of inquiry.

The result of the relations between the USSR NOC and the LAOOC was a series of correspondences and meetings between these two organizations and the IOC. The correspondences provide previously unexamined statements of intention to boycott by the Soviets and responses from the LAOOC and the IOC. They demonstrate a concerted and earnest effort on the part of all three parties to resolve the dispute. The documents put forward delineate Soviet, USSR NOC, LAOOC, and IOC goals. The goals for all but the IOC are fairly obvious and do not need further comment here. The IOC's goals, however, are important to briefly note.

The IOC's goal during this period was garnering the attendance of the Soviet Union and her allies and demonstrating the IOC's willingness to act as mediator to resolve similar problems so that the issue of boycott would not reoccur in 1988. In order to meet this goal, the IOC managed a complex series of correspondences between the USSR NOC, the LAOOC, and the United States Olympic Committee, while also playing an active role in negotiations with all parties involved. These correspondences provided a collection of original documents that can be analyzed to discern Soviet intentions and, due to a clear disagreement between the Kremlin and the USSR NOC on boycotting, more accurate conclusions can be drawn than originally thought.

The most useful documents uncovered from this approach would be the correspondences of the LAOOC and the IOC with each other, the Soviet National Olympic Committee, and the Soviet and American governments. Therefore the goal of the research was to find and assess the work that the LAOOC and the IOC did, not for their successes, their weaknesses, and their eventual failure, but to determine the actual Soviet position. This could then be studied, and through careful research into the LAOOC responses and the position other Soviet Bloc nations took, one could begin to understand which concerns of the Soviet Union eventually became the ultimate causes of the boycott.

Third, it is necessary to gain an understanding as to how the Soviet Union has used the Olympics to further their own political aims.

This will help to understand the placement of the Olympic Movement in Soviet diplomacy. The nature of messages the Soviet Union believed their decisions involving the Olympics sent will be gleaned from personal statements of the Soviet government and of Soviet IOC representatives made when dealing with other Olympic issues. The arrival of the Soviet Union into the Olympic family, and the concerns they had in initially joining, contain information that can explain shreds of the political/athletic situation in the 1980s. This history and the documents and statements that are an integral part of it formulate the basis of the third aspect of the research methodology. Fortunately the topic of the inclusion of the Socialist states in the Olympic Movement has been well analyzed by historians of sports, sports diplomacy, and the Olympics.

The Soviet viewpoint is well documented in those histories with letters and correspondences of the Soviet sports authorities, the Soviet National Olympic Committee, and the IOC. A comparative method of past Soviet decisions to the questions elaborated in this study will in the end help to discover the most plausible explanation for the Soviet decision to boycott. Due to the role the Soviets played in the history of the Olympics and the overall role politics has played in the movement, a political history of the Olympics is required to understand how the Soviets viewed the Olympic system. This history is not so much a total story of the movement from its beginning to the present but is instead an overview of the methods in which nations or groups have used the Olympic Movement to their own advantage. This will help to explain how the Olympic Movement tantalized the Soviet hierarchy and how that nation's history in the Olympics led to their decision to boycott the 1984 Los Angeles Games.

CHAPTER 2

A PRIMER ON POLITICS
IN THE OLYMPICS

THE AGE OF INNOCENCE

From 1896 to 1925, the International Olympic Committee (IOC) founder and second president, Baron Pierre de Coubertin, and his close-knit group of sports-loving friends controlled the decision processes of the early modern Olympics. They determined the locations of each Olympiad, the list of competitive sports, and the nations that would receive invitations to attend. The site selection process, now a complex bidding system performed by cities and states that wish to host the Games, was then nothing more than the result of the whims of the IOC's leaders. With the benefits of hosting the Olympics steadily increasing for the past one hundred years, the process is now more systematic and highly competitive. The changes in the bidding process, particularly the creation of a competition for the host selection process, played a key factor in the setup of the adversarial Olympic atmosphere between Canada (site of the 1976 Summer Games), the United States, and the Soviet Union, and assumed a key role in the Soviet decision to boycott.

As early as 1920, the use of the Olympics to make political statements was becoming more prevalent in the movement. This was mainly due to the fact that the IOC did not discourage the process and, in fact, even participated in the politicization of the Games. Political decisions—namely, on the bidding process and invitations to the Games—grew out of a direct result of World War I. As we shall see, IOC political games took on many goals, particularly as either rewards for the winners of war or a careful balancing act between opposing sides of the current political situation. During the interwar period, for example, the need for ideological "balance" in the political messages affecting IOC decisions became the overwhelming factor from 1920 to 1938.

The first, and by far the most obvious, of these political statements came as punitive responses to the states defeated in World War I. The overall success of the 1908 London Games and the 1912 Stockholm Games helped the Olympic Movement to survive World War I by demarcating the Games as a worthy endeavor and fostering enough interest that they would survive the cancellation of the 1916 Games. With the Games in abeyance for eight years, most would expect them to fail; after all, they were not yet even twenty years old when World War I began. Yet, due to aforementioned successes, the IOC was able to find a host for the 1920 Games almost immediately after the war ended.

War and Peace and War

The restart of the Modern Olympics took place in Antwerp, Belgium. The IOC did not make any attempt to hide this decision as overtly political and in fact said the Olympics would be a fitting tribute to show that the devastation during the German occupation of Belgium, from roughly 1914 to 1918, was in the past and that Belgium had begun reconstruction of its major cities.[1] In other words, the decision was a symbolic one to show that the German occupation did not result in long-term damage to the nation of Belgium. This justification for decisions would be repeated many times in the next three decades.

On another political level, the aforementioned successes of the Olympics allowed it to remain, in 1919, an attractive opportunity for reconstruction of devastated cities as well as providing newly recognized European nations a chance to gain some respect and visibility on the international level. Belgium had a lot to gain from the IOC's symbolic decision to place the Games in Antwerp. The Games offered a chance for a faster reconstruction, at least of Antwerp. The Games also breathed life into Belgian society, its pride, and other socialeconomic factors that were damaged by the German occupation. These benefits extended to future hosts and, in a more limited fashion, to those nations attending the Games.

The new opportunities of the Olympics were particularly important to several once-suppressed nationalities that achieved independence when the war ended. It was of little surprise when the newly independent states of Poland, Czechoslovakia, and Hungary immediately formed national Olympic committees and applied for IOC recognition.

All newly independent states that applied for membership were granted it except Hungary—the only state to apply that fought with the Central Powers, specifically as one part of the Austro-Hungarian Empire.[2] Germany's position in the Olympics raised another complicated facet of this form of political manipulation of the Games. Germany had been a member of the Olympic Movement since its inception, competing in the Athens Games of 1896 and every Olympiad held from 1896 to 1912. It had gained enough respect and IOC support that Berlin was selected to host the 1916 Games, the Olympiad later cancelled due to the outbreak of the war. When the Games were restarted in 1920, two questions were immediately raised. First, should Germany be allowed to attend? After all, it had been a founding member of the Olympic Movement. Second, and probably more complicated, if Germany, and Hungary incidentally, were allowed back into the movement, how do you handle a Belgian government that, many in the IOC assumed, would not be receptive to that suggestion?

The Belgians were obviously not very amenable toward the Germans just two years after the armistice. The IOC was also hesitant to take a position, mainly because inviting Germany meant that German athletes would be interacting with Belgian athletes and fans, most of whom suffered under German occupation or in the war. The very heart of the problem was that some members of the Olympic community were unwilling to simply deny the Germans entrance because of the war. The Olympics, in theory and spirit, were supposed to transcend such political disagreements. On the other side of the issue sat both Belgian and other officials that were uncomfortable with German attendance so soon after the war.

IOC Chancellor Otto Mayer reflected the opinion and decision of the IOC with regard to Belgian discomfort when he said, "The problem of German participation was discussed. Solemnly to proclaim any kind of ostracism in the wake of the conflict which had just drenched Europe in blood would have been a violation of the Olympic constitution as it then was. The solution was quite simple. There was, for each Olympiad an Organizing Committee which . . . sent out invitations."[3] Historian Allen Guttman summarized the IOC position in 1994: "[T]he Belgian Organizers were not instructed by the IOC to exclude representatives of the defeated powers, they were simply encouraged not to invite them."[4] In short, the IOC avoided both questions by leaving it up to the Belgian organizers to send invitations to states at their discretion.

Without much surprise, the Belgians (and four years later the French) "lost" the necessary invitations, thus forcing the Germans to miss the 1920 and 1924 Summer Games. They also missed the inaugural Winter Games, held in 1924, because the French government was just as unwilling to allow Germany attendance in Charmonix (Winter 1924) as in Paris (Summer 1924). Germany would not appear in Olympic competition until St. Moritz, Switzerland, hosted the Winter Games of 1928, followed by the Summer Games of that same year in Amsterdam, Netherlands. The selection process of host cities became highly political and was an important factor in the 1976, 1980, and 1984 Summer Olympics.

It should be noted that IOC decisions, particularly in host city selection, were not unchallenged. Even though the IOC members were blatantly honest that political purposes influenced the selection of Antwerp to host the 1920 Games, there were still objections to the decision. Regardless of Germany's violation of Belgium's prewar neutrality, many in the League of Nations thought it would have been more appropriate to select a nation that remained neutral throughout the war. It was a reasonable request from the League of Nations, since placing the Games in a neutral state would have made German and Austrian attendance easier and would have also been a step in the direction toward reconciliation and peace. While the IOC would ultimately not change its decision, future host selection decisions suggest the criticism did not go completely unheeded.[5]

The selection process for the 1924 Summer Games was already under way in 1920, and Baron Pierre de Coubertin was clearly in support of placing the thirtieth anniversary of the Games in Paris. League of Nations outcries and IOC member criticism of having two consecutive Games in major cities of the victors of World War I were so rampant that de Coubertin had to work hard to guarantee that Paris would host for the second time. He announced his retirement in order to gain sympathy for Paris, but the voices of the opposition were not silenced or ignored. The decision process for the Winter and Summer Olympics of 1928 would answer requests for a neutral host.

Amsterdam, the capital of the Netherlands, was selected to host in 1928 mainly because the Dutch had been neutral during the war. This decision process was reflected in the Winter Olympics, too. The original plan was to have a state selected to host both the Winter and the Summer Games for a specific Olympiad. Therefore, with Paris hosting the 1924 Summer Games, France was given the option to place the Winter Games in one of their Alpine cities, of which they chose the southeastern resort of Charmonix. The practice was temporarily abandoned for 1928 because of the environmental inability of the Netherlands to host a Winter Olympics.[6] Just as Amsterdam was awarded the Summer Games due to Dutch neutrality in the war, the Winter Games were awarded to St. Moritz, located in the then neutral state of Switzerland. Thereafter, the sites of competition oscillated between Great War victor and loser cities until they were suspended again because of World War II. The Games in 1932 went back to a victor state, as the United States played host to Summer and Winter Games at Los Angeles and Lake Placid, respectively. Germany, one of the defeated states, hosted both seasons of Olympics in 1936, with Berlin hosting the Summer Games and Garmisch-Partenkirchen hosting the Winter Games. The 1940 Games, cancelled due to the outbreak of World War II, were awarded to Japan,[7] which had been allied with France and England and involved itself in the Great War by attacking German interests in Asia. After this, it would appear that the alliance balancing system was coming to an end, since London was selected to host the 1944 Summer Games, and Cortina D'Ampezzo, Italy, the 1944 Winter Games.

While postwar tensions remained a feature of this period, the interwar era was a time of compromise and growth for the Olympics. Though politics did play a regular role in the roughly twenty-year period, it was predominantly domestic politics that swirled around sport instead of international relations. The issues of this short era in sports were centered on questions of amateurism, the degree to which women should compete, and the use of performance-enhancing drugs. Beyond attendance and who hosted, international political issues remained relatively quiet. In fact, the majority of the IOC's problems were symptoms of the process of expansion in similar ways that growth affects any organization. This radically changed when Berlin hosted the Olympics.

When the Nazis gained power in Germany, the scope of the 1936 Winter and Summer Olympics changed drastically. The Germans understood the true power that hosting the Olympics possessed, and Adolf Hitler was more than capable of exploiting that opportunity. Hitler used the Olympics to showcase the progress the German nation had made under Nazi control. Possessing a crippled infrastructure and economy, the Weimar Republic collapsed under the terms of the Treaty of Versailles. The Nazi Party had taken control of the state, and under its system, Germany began to prosper. As with all other aspects of German society and policy, its participation in the Olympics quickly and obviously changed from 1920 to 1936.

For eight years, Germany was ostracized from the Olympic Movement. Once Germany had been readmitted, the Germans quickly regained respect as an active and vital member of the Olympic family.

Less than four years after their return to the Olympics, the Germans were awarded the right to host the 1936 Games, thus ending a period of isolationist IOC policies that restricted the Germans, and others, from participating fully or partially in the Olympic Movement. The shadow of discrimination that hung over the Olympic Movement was not fully gone. It reemerged, due to Nazi policy, two years after the Americans hosted the Summer Games in Los Angeles.

The Olympics had left behind, or so the IOC thought or hoped, any form of discrimination against participation, whether that was of a whole nation or of a segment of a nation. Women, although not represented in as many events as men, gained ground in the Olympic Movement as policies that ostracized their participation faded. By the time of the Berlin Games, 328 women competed, as opposed to 64 at the Antwerp Games in 1920.[8] That was a 400 percent increase, compared to a barely 50 percent increase in the number of men competing.[9] At this time, there were no formal policies of discrimination against people by means of race, ethnicity, or religion. Discrimination did occur in some aspects but was waning. By 1936, all forms of restrictions on participation had more or less become an artifact of history. While some restrictions on the participation of nations or individuals of nations persisted, none of this was official IOC policy, and the IOC made a habit of working with hosts and participants to broaden the definitions of inclusion in all areas, except for the question of amateurism.

Discrimination, whether on the basis of race or religious background, did occur informally all through the early history of the Games. Its existence was tolerated more as a means of avoiding argument within the movement than anything else. However, protests over discrimination became visible in the years just prior to the now infamous Nazi Olympics. The end of the silence was caused by three colliding circumstances: the blatant German policy excluding athletes on the basis of racial or religious identity and the shifts from silent objector to vocal objector both on the part of IOC representatives and officials and on the part of governments both within and outside the Olympic Movement.

Berlin wanted to formally reject all black and Jewish athletes from competition. This met with furious opposition in the IOC and in several member nations, particularly the United States. As a result, the first real threats of boycotts against the Olympics began in 1935 with the Berlin Games only one year away. President of the Amateur Athletic Union of the United States Avery Brundage worked diligently to avoid a boycott of the Games. Surprisingly, to his credit, every state or nation with a recognized national Olympic committee sent a team to the 1936 Games. The boycott was averted for several reasons. First, the IOC president was able to keep the United States from being too vocal about its opposition to the Nazi-hosted Games. Second, the only real alternative to the Games, which was suggested by the Soviet Union, was Barcelona, Spain. This recommendation was unproductive at best for two reasons: The Soviet Union was not a member of the Olympic Movement and had no rights to make such a suggestion, and Spain was practically falling apart because of the already under way Spanish Civil War. Therefore, not only was the Soviet suggestion not taken very seriously due to their noninvolvement in the Olympics, but Spain was not a very good option due to war. In short, for all the heated debates against Berlin as host, there simply were no other viable options.

Third, the British Olympic Committee made several efforts to keep the United Kingdom and her allies from boycotting. According to a March 7, 1936, letter from the British Olympic Association, not only would it be a calamity for the United Kingdom to not attend, but it was also in the best interest of sport to keep such political situations from adversely affecting the Olympics.[10] The British position was convincing enough to keep others, especially France and Italy, from boycotting. In addition to those convinced to not boycott, several nations chose not to politicize the Games, so they were automatically going to attend regardless of actions by the aforementioned individuals and governments. Finally, Hitler himself did work to block a boycott.

Hitler realized that the true political power of the Olympics rested in attendance, not through the lack thereof. The point of the Games was to display Nazi glory, innovation, architecture, and so on, in addition to the superiority of the Aryan race. Displaying them is worthless if the stadium seats are empty. Besides, the greatest goal, that of proving the intellectual and physical superiority of the German people, was best served in competition with what he felt were "inferior" races. In short, Hitler capitulated on all the Nazis' hardline views on participation in order to garner the attendance of the world and provide a stage where Aryan athletes could demonstrate their superiority against non-Aryan athletes. The magnitude of Hitler's capitulation included openly allowing German Jews to represent the Reich in competition.

The "Nazi Olympics," as the Berlin Games are now immortalized, may have been problematic in the years leading up to the Games, but in the end, and notwithstanding the achievements of Jesse Owens being snubbed by Hitler, the Germans put on an impressive sports festival that showcased Nazi precision, authority, and the arrival of a revitalized German state in Europe. Three years after the Berlin Games, the world returned to a period of warfare. The Winter and Summer Games of 1940 and 1944 were both cancelled due to World War II. However, just as with World War I, the Games lay dormant, waiting for their resurgence when peace was eventually restored. In 1945, with the end of the war rapidly approaching, surviving IOC members started discussing how to get the Games back on their feet in time for the Olympiad of 1948.

The Start of Cold War Games

Once the restart was officially under way, the Olympic Movement encountered the same problems in the late 1940s as it had done in the early 1920s, made worse in some ways because several IOC members died during the War, including then IOC President Henri de Baillet-Latour. Indeed, entire national Olympic committees were dead or dispersed, making it even harder to get a sense of what was left of the Olympic Movement. Refocusing on politics, the IOC found itself in a situation similar (and arguably worse) to 1919.

The two main questions from 1919, that of who should host and who should attend, were back, but this time, the IOC had precedents to aid in the decision process. The problems were exacerbated by the fact that the Games had grown much larger than they were in 1920, which made addressing concerns of all the members far more difficult. By the time of the 1952 Olympiad, countries from six continents were competing, both in the athletic competitions and in the host city selection process. The IOC was left with several problems that required them to make difficult decisions, while member (and some nonmember) nations vocalized their opinions on each question.

In the midst of all this, the world was once again divided into camps of victors and vanquished, and the IOC made no secret of the fact that it was going to attempt some sort of balance, much like it had done in the politics of the 1920s. In addition to all this, the advent of the Cold War created another set of ideological camps, resulting in requests for inclusion from several socialist states, not the least of which was the Soviet Union.

In 1948, London was awarded the first postwar Games, echoing the selection of Antwerp 28 years earlier. Switzerland's resort of St. Moritz took the Winter Games for a second time, offering a neutral host for the Winter Games. Much like 28 years prior, the German occupation zones were simply not sent invitations by the British or even the Swiss. The Soviet Union raised a similar, but far more complicated problem. The Soviet moves to control its Eastern European neighbors, turning them into satellites, raised many questions in the early Cold War atmosphere. Since the Soviets did not have a national Olympic committee before the war, the IOC found it easiest to ignore the Russians by simply stating that the requirement of having an established NOC was not met. Incidentally, this excuse worked well with "unwelcomed" states and other groups that wanted, but were denied, recognition as part of the Olympic Movement.

In short, the Germans, the Russians, several Eastern European states, China, and Japan were all ostracized, which would slowly change as the IOC addressed the requests and concerns of all parties involved with the membership of these states. The delay was justifiable, given the state of the IOC in the late 1940s. After the war, a new Executive Council of the IOC was needed, and half the national Olympic committees needed to be reformed. As such, it took great efforts on the part of organizers and the IOC both to get the 1948 Games off the ground and to decide on the hosts of the 1952 Games in mid-1947 in order to give them sufficient time to prepare. Membership issues were delayed as a result, though they were never fully ignored.

London, as was noted earlier, was selected because of the symbolism of it being the capital of allied Europe and also as a consolation for the cancellation of the 1944 London Summer Olympics. St. Moritz was selected for three reasons. First, it was neutral in the war, thus balancing the decision to place the Summer Games in London. Second, only St. Moritz and Lake Placid, New York, had held the Winter Olympics previously and had not been bombed, occupied, or otherwise harmed. The necessary equipment and venues were already in place for an Olympics that was scheduled to start less than three years after the war ended. Third, St. Moritz was chosen over Lake Placid because of a combination of the first reason and also because the financial hardship of getting the European teams to the United States just three years after the war ended was far larger of a problem than getting the Americans, the Canadians, and a few others to Switzerland.

The politicking continued for the 1952 and 1956 Olympics, although in a more limited capacity. Since the bidding process was becoming more competitive and, at the same time, the International Olympic Committee was growing in size, the decisions of the body became less malleable for any reason, including political biases.

Decisions that were once made by an elite inner circle were now open to debate with a much larger field of individuals offering opinions openly to the members of the IOC. However, even though the system was less politicized, one can still see a clear attempt at guaranteeing some form of balance of hosts along political lines. While it is a true statement that this "balancing act" was fading away and became less and less apparent, it took a full twenty years for that political game to end. By 1960, comparisons on this level become untenable.

In 1952, the Olympics went to two Scandinavian cities, both of which were occupied during the war. The first, Oslo, Norway, was given the Winter Games. The Germans had occupied them during one of the bloodiest campaigns of the war. The second, that of the 1952 Summer Games, went to Helsinki, Finland, which was occupied and annexed by the Soviet Union. In 1956, the International Olympic Committee surprised the world by sending the Summer Games to the southern hemisphere, placing them in Melbourne, Australia. With the Summer Games in a former allied state, the Winter Games naturally went to a former axis state. Cortina D'Ampezzo, located in the northern Alpine region of Italy, played host to the Winter Games. Arguably, one can claim that the pattern continues in 1960. The Summer Games of 1960 went to Rome, the capital of a former axis state that switched sides in the war, while the Winter Olympics went to Squaw Valley, a resort town in central California.

By 1960, an era in the Olympic Movement was quickly ending and another was about to begin. Until this point, the history of the Olympics shows how the Olympics were used to further the political messages of many groups. Often it was the voice of those victorious in war, or, alternatively, it was the voice of a changing nation trying to demonstrate its new situation to the world. After World War II, the Olympics had grown enough in scope to be useful for more overtly political ends. It was this critical shift in the political weight of the Olympics that led to the change in the political atmosphere of the Olympics. Before 1956, the Olympics and politics combined where the Olympic Movement and the people within it chose to politicize decisions or to make political statements. The only real exception was the 1936 Olympics that were disturbingly visionary in their manipulation of the Games.

By 1948 and up through 1960, the Olympics began to shift from being a solely a political actor to also being a tool for political opportunists inside of and outside of the Olympic Movement. This transition period, if any real "end" can be labeled, shifted into the new relationship of politics and the Olympics in 1958, when states began using the Olympics as a platform, a tool, sometimes a weapon, and always as an opportunity to make a statement.

The Olympics were now seen as a potential force for social change in many parts of the world, and political activists immediately started making use of this force. In 1958, South African Sports Association founder Dennis Brutus began the protests against South African participation. Though South Africa had no official rules on the matter of segregation in athletics, the reality was that athletes were separated on the basis of racial difference.[11] The unofficial status of this segregation became overt state policy when the South African government formally adopted apartheid in 1948.

During the early 1960s, the apartheid system in South Africa came under renewed and expanded criticism, provoking the IOC to call for a ban of the South African National Olympic Committee (SANOC). The situation was so volatile that the IOC had to move its 1963 session from Nairobi, Kenya, to Baden-Baden, West Germany, because of fears that Kenya would not admit representatives from SANOC.[12] The IOC did not, in the end, fully ban SANOC, because it was believed that the Olympic community could come up with an equitable solution that both South Africa and other African states could mutually accept. During this period of negotiation, South Africa did not compete. Instead, it spent much of its time working diligently with the IOC in an attempt to find a compromise to the situation.

To solve the SANOC crisis, the IOC sought a pledge of non–racial discrimination in South African sports on an international level. As it would turn out, the IOC would fail in this endeavor but would get enough concessions to consider readmitting South Africa to competition. The South African Government and SANOC's offers to the international sports community seemed more of a placation than anything else to many African states. As a result, more than thirty states threatened a boycott of the Mexico City Games for that year if SANOC was not immediately expelled and South African athletes were denied the right to compete.

This crisis for the Mexico City Games represents the second significant effort at a boycott of the Olympics. The challenge began when Algeria and Ethiopia threatened to boycott the Mexico City Games if a racially segregated South African team was allowed to compete in the Summer Olympics.[13] African protests prevailed as the IOC and Mexico City agreed to not invite South Africa to quell a growing voice of opposition to apartheid.

Due to the large and vocal group of states protesting, the threat of a boycott proved to be a successful means to protest the policy

Germany and the German Democratic Republic had separate national Olympic committees and separate teams. The IOC, whose preference is to have nations instead of states in competition, was not particularly happy with the decision of the Bonn and Berlin governments, but they took consolation in the fact that no one else had accomplished what the IOC achieved. With the future of Germany uncertain, the Olympics succeeded in unification, something that would not happen again for forty years. Simultaneously, the IOC was also deliberating the China question. This question, however, did not result in a quick success story.

The China question would eventually become one of the IOC's many successes, as it is one of only a few political-representative bodies that count both Chinese entities as members. The situation began in the wake of the Chinese Revolution, which resulted in a communist government in Beijing and the relocation of the nationalist government to the island of Formosa (Taiwan). The problem for the IOC, specifically, arose because the IOC has had a longstanding rule disallowing a state to have more than one national Olympic committee. Success, albeit temporarily, with the German question added weight to this IOC policy. Once the Chinese revolution ended, both the nationalist Chinese and the communist government organized national Olympic committees to represent China. Since the Chinese had an Olympic committee prior to the revolution, it was a valid claim that some entity was the heir to the IOC's prewar recognition of a Chinese Olympic Committee. Both entities claimed to be the rightful representatives of China and to ownership of China's history in the Olympic Movement. The situation quickly split IOC members on the issue along ideological lines.

The Soviet representatives and their allies backed the People's Republic of China, while the US representatives and their allies backed Taiwan. Unlike the previous situation in Germany, the two sides of the China issue were unwilling to work together. Because the separation of the two German states was imposed on Germany by outside forces, the source of the friction between them was not initiated by either of the two German states. Therefore, it was easier to get them to work together with only a little friction between them. The Chinese situation was the exact opposite, growing out of a revolutionary movement that divided one Chinese state into two politically different Chinese states.

The separation of the two Chinas was a result of a violent revolution that left both sides hating each other. Furthermore, the ideological basis for the revolution translated into incompatible governing systems for the two Chinas that further inhibited any chance of a unified Chinese team. Finally, powerful political positions, such as China's permanent United Nations Security Council seat, exacerbated the competition for the title of *China* and all privileges that went with it. The result was that the IOC needed to recognize only one China but still find a way to have both entities involved in the Games, or it would fail at being a truly global organization.

Avery Brundage, IOC president from 1952 to 1972, announced the IOC's formal position in 1959, which forced the Taiwanese NOC to resubmit its application with a different name. They had originally submitted themselves as the Republic of China, which the IOC determined was unacceptable. In this statement, the IOC confirmed that it would accept the People's Republic of China as the heir to the Chinese Olympic Committee. The decisions infuriated everyone involved.[15] The Soviets and the Americans were both angered by the decision because they wanted only one Chinese team recognized. Taiwan resented the fact that they could not be recognized as the Republic of China, and the People's Republic of China resented the fact that Brundage's decision allowed Taiwan to have a national Olympic committee independent of Beijing.

Brundage's decision was a geographic one. In short, he stated that the IOC would recognize two spheres of the Chinese nation. One sphere would be mainland China, governed from Beijing, and the other would be the pacific island of Taiwan, governed from Taipei. Brundage, who believed strongly that the Olympics dealt with geographic regions and not governments, stood behind this belief with his decision to keep both Chinas as members but to also ask the government on Taiwan to change the name of its Olympic committee. The People's Republic of China would maintain the title of, and national Olympic committee for, *China*, while the Nationalists, in Taiwan, would have to submit papers for recognition of the island as a separate part of the Olympic Movement under a name different from its claim as the Republic of China. A long series of boycotts by either the Nationalists or the Chinese would follow for decades.

The Chinese boycotts are not generally discussed as part of a history of Olympic boycotts. This is mainly due to the fact that it was either the People's Republic of China or Taiwan that was boycotting. There is currently no evidence that any state other than the two Chinas boycotted an Olympic Games due to the host's policy on the Chinese situation. Furthermore, there is no evidence that any member of the Olympic committee threatened to boycott over the Chinese situation other than the two Chinese Olympic committees. Several states, including the United States, did vocally object to some decisions of the host, but the problem never heated up to open threats of boycott. By the late 1970s, signs that the end of the Chinese question, at least as far as the Olympics were concerned, seemed eminent.

In 1984, the IOC successfully arranged the presence of two Chinese teams: The People's Republic of China and Chinese Taipei.[16] Under the agreement, Taiwan would be formally recognized but would not use the symbols of China. Instead, it would march with the Olympic flag and anthem. Eventually, Chinese Taipei would have its own Chinese Olympic flag (like the aforementioned unified German flag) and be a member of the IOC and attend all Olympiads from 1984 onward. The People's Republic of China, after its first appearance in competition at the Los Angeles Games in 1984, also continued to compete at every winter and summer competition.

China and Germany offer examples of how the Olympic Movement has been used as a tool to press for foreign policy changes of one or several states. South Africa can be utilized to provide an example where the Olympic Movement was used to promote domestic policy changes. In the case of South Africa, the Games were used as a constant voice demanding that racist policies of South Africa, official and unofficial, be struck down. In the case of the two Chinas, the IOC demonstrated how it could transcend Cold War politics and act as a unifying force in the international sphere.

We saw a situation similar to the two China story, but ultimately temporary, over the two Korea question at the 2000 Summer Olympics in Sydney, Australia. The China situation was first approached from the perspective of having one Chinese Olympic team. Ultimately, the IOC capitulated on this goal but continued to press for the participation of Chinese athletes from both China and Taiwan. The first instance of both teams appearing together, ironically, was at the Los Angeles Olympics. The IOC sought a similar outcome for the issue of North and South Korea. Most attempts to unify Korea, in any political or social sphere, outright failed. The Olympics, however, have seen an expression of cooperation from both sides.

The Sydney Games played host to the first uncontestable depiction of a future Korean unification with the presence of a Unified Korean team at the opening ceremonies, marching in with a unified-Korea flag, an action that would be repeated four years later in Athens, Greece amid very contentious relations between South Korea, North Korea, and the United States. Efforts continue to develop an integrated Korean Olympic team and Olympic committee.

In these three examples, the Olympic Movement used its own rules and regulations to guide its thinking process and decisions. In all these cases, other states also attempted to use these same rules to force the IOC to arrive at their own policy goals. While maintaining the rules of the Olympic charter is preferable for the sake of the movement, states and individuals seeking to use the Olympic stage for their own interests have often ignored these principles.

Many political actors have hijacked the Olympics in attempts to garner political objectives through misanthropic displays or actions. For example, Black September terrorists seeking Palestinian Liberation through the murder of Israeli athletes at the 1972 Munich Olympics stands as the most chilling example of how the Olympic Games offer a stage that is used outside the bounds of Olympic rules. Another example occurred at the 1968 Mexico City Olympics, where two African American athletes gave a "black power salute" and disrespected the flags and anthem of the three winning athletes during their medal ceremony. The actions were a protest over domestic racial policies in the United States and Australia.

The Black September Munich attack and Black Pride examples, plus the boycotts mentioned thus far, all share two commonalities. First, they were all deliberate and inappropriate attempts to make use of the Olympics to further political objectives not directly relevant to the Olympic Games themselves.[17] Second, in all examples, the IOC had very few options to stop the political protest while also staying out of the elements of the political dispute not relevant to the Games. Actually, in some cases, attempting to circumvent IOC policies and even the IOC itself has made using the Olympics for political purposes easier and more effective. The Soviet Union was aware of this and also realized that taking advantage of such things would lead to a greater amount of influence in international sports with each passing year.

Here, a distinction must be made on using the Olympics as a political tool. The process can be done in two ways. First, the Olympics, for good or for bad, can be used in a variety of methods to affect a policy peacefully and vocally. This often involves using the opportunity of the Olympics to demonstrate opinions of a state to the international community. This is what a boycott usually entails. In most cases, these methods entail demonstrations or statements on the part of participants or hosts. Typically, these statements are crafted to either explain or strengthen a foreign policy objective. The vast majority of these do not willfully attempt to subvert, attack, or destroy the Olympic Movement. However, there is one other method, which should be discussed here, that I call *hostage tactics*.

Hostage tactics describes a scenario where the Olympics are seized for malicious or subversive goals of an actor (nation, individual, or group) in which the sanctity of the Olympics is neither revered nor protected by the actor. In these situations, of which there are thankfully very few examples, the Olympics are still seen as an opportunity to further an agenda regardless of the harm it may cause the Olympics or the Olympic Movement. Hostage tactics are generally against the spirit of the Olympics and, when conducted by a nation, are typically against the spirit of diplomacy as well.[18]

Protests, violence, and political grandstanding, all of which have threatened the Olympic Movement, are examples of this form of political maneuvering in the Games. They all share in common the use of an Olympic opportunity to hijack the attention of the audience and then promote any political goal of interest to the purveyor of the message. Before continuing, allow me to clarify that this tactic is mentioned as it is a political utilization of the Olympics and not because it is directly relevant to the Soviet boycott.

As you will see in Chapters 3, 5, and 6, the Soviet Union politicized the Games only when they saw a tactical advantage for their own policy aims within a situation affecting the Olympic Movement. Accusations, threats of boycott, and general complaining on the part of the Soviet Union all had at the heart of the issue a connection back to their stated views of the ideals of the Olympic Movement. Whether you wish to accept their positions or not, the Soviet Union saw itself as working within the structure of the movement in order to improve it. This explains the use of the term *nonparticipation* by the Soviet Union.

The Soviet's term *nonparticipation* was an attempt to make the decision to not attend appear less political. As Chapter 1 noted, the term *boycott* is an objective concept that merely indicates a political influence in the decision to not participate. Therefore, the terminology is semantic but still illustrates the Soviet interest in working through Olympic structures instead of against them. In fairness, there are copious examples of the Soviet Union abusing these rules to attain their own goals in the Olympics, but these situations were usually done more subtly than as hostage tactics. At times when the Soviet Union politicized the Olympics for less auspicious reasons, the politicization took place at IOC meetings or through letters and publications between Olympic Games. The Soviet Union rarely grandstanded during the ceremonies, which is necessary for the action to be considered a hostage tactic.

Remaining for discussion is actual participation in the events of the Olympics. Participation involves one of two methods. The first,

and by far the more common and most obvious, is winning medals in competitions, which often lead to domestic and international
rivalries. When other avenues of competition between two nations
are not a viable or preferable option, sports can become politicized
as an alternative means of conflict. The infamous rivalries between
Soviet and Eastern European hockey teams or the bloody water polo
match between Hungary and the Soviet Union at the 1956 Games
offer examples in which political aggression was turned into aggressive
sportsmanship.

THE HOSTING GAME

The second participatory method involves the process of hosting.
Regardless of whether we are talking about the Summer or the Winter Olympics, hosting brings with it huge opportunities. Utilizing the
chance to host the Olympics was briefly examined in the example of
the 1936 Berlin Games. Berlin is the natural place to start that analysis, as it was in the Berlin Games that the political opportunities presented by playing host to the Olympics were fully realized. Prior to
Berlin, however, it was a different story.

The early days of the Olympics were met with a marked resistance
to host the Games by many nations. The financial, political, and
logistical problems were simply too much for some to shoulder, and
there was no clear evidence that the host benefited in any way from
its efforts. In fact, France did not initially want the second Olympiad
and "demonstrated a lack of enthusiasm," though Paris eventually did
host the 1900 Summer Games.[19] More recent Olympiads have seen
many states vying to host the Games as opposed to the early days of
the Olympic Movement. In 2001, five countries fought doggedly to
gain the IOC's approval to host the summer Games of 2008. In 2004,
five cities (London, Madrid, Moscow, New York, and Paris) spent bil-
lions of dollars to win the right to host the 2012 Summer Olympics.

In the shift from the early 1900s, with no one asking to host, to
the early 2000s, with states fighting each other for the opportunity,
the role the bid process has played in Olympic politics has steadily
increased. Initially, the IOC outright asked countries to host, as they
did with France for the 1900 Olympics. As state interest in hosting
increased, IOC political power also increased. The downside for the
IOC is that their selection process met with regular accusations of
political preference. By the 1970s, the IOC encountered significant
resistance to the fact that no Soviet Bloc state had hosted the Olympics. A previously untold story of the Soviet boycott exists in the bids

for the 1976, 1980, and 1984 Summer Olympics. Los Angeles bid for all three and Moscow bid for the first two. As a result, the competition to host the Olympics played an important role in the story of the boycott years.

Antwerp, Paris, Los Angeles, and Berlin all realized the benefits of hosting the Olympics, but they had not openly bid for the Games without assistance and persistence on the part of IOC members. As early as the late 1940s, cities began to recognize the benefits of host- ing the Olympics and subsequently sought the opportunity to host the Olympics without the need for IOC encouragement. Among the benefits, none stood out more apparently than the chance to simply display political and cultural successes on a global stage.

The Olympics offered any location the opportunity to showcase itself to the world. In the case of Japan, Tokyo's opening ceremonies of the 1964 summer Olympics marked "it's reentry into the world as a full participant in the international community."[20] The opening ceremonies of the Atlanta Summer Games gave Atlanta, Georgia, and arguably the entire southern United States, an opportunity to demon- strate uniquely Southern cultural identity and traditions.

Such benefits offered not only the chance of demonstration but also the opportunity of promoting international opportunities for economic and political growth. In 1981, Seoul, South Korea, was awarded the 1988 Summer Olympics, yet the two Koreas had dif- ficult international relations. The peninsula had been split into a northern communist state and a southern republic after World War II. It remained divided after the Korean War, and many nations rec- ognized only one Korean state—whichever was in line with their own political ideology. As a result, South Korea did not have relations with the Soviet Union, Romania, Bulgaria, East Germany, and many other socialist/communist states, while North Korea was not recognized by many Western-oriented states.

In spite of this, in 1988, the Seoul Olympics were the first boy- cott-free Summer Games in 12 years. Even the Chinese, the military supporters of North Korea, and the Soviet Union, the leader of the Eastern Bloc during the Cold War, attended the Olympics in the capi- tal of Republic of Korea. The Olympics opened new avenues of trade and economic growth for South Korea simply by creating a bridge to nations that had previously been out of their political and ideological sphere. They realized, as did the Germans in 1936, that the Olympics brought more than just international approval; they brought eco- nomic revitalization.

These benefits combined to make hosting the Olympics not just a viable option but also a potentially beneficial one. They became a source of competition between potential hosts. In short, the benefits alone led to the politicization of the host selection process and therefore the Olympics themselves. These facts combined to lead to the boycott years because of the political messages that now existed behind hosting, attending, and so on.

African protests over the Mexico City and Montreal Games were founded by an unwillingness to involve themselves in any event that tolerated South African apartheid policies either by allowing teams that were segregated to participate or by allowing other states that competed with segregated South African teams (i.e., New Zealand) to compete at the events. Calls for a boycott of the 1936 Games were justified by an unwillingness of several states to associate themselves with fascist policies. The United States, in Vice President Walter Mondale's speech to the United States Olympic Committee House of Delegates on April 2, 1980, and in numerous other White House statements, stated that the US government "made it clear that the Olympic boycott is a genuine element of America's response to the invasion of Afghanistan."[21] The concern of the White House and others in the US government was that America's appearance at the Moscow Games would be read as tacit approval of Soviet foreign policy.[22] These kinds of political statements attached to hosting, boycotting, and so on severely complicated sports politics in general and particularly added difficulties to any attempt to find an equitable solution to the boycotts.

So far, we have discussed primarily the international benefits of hosting the Olympics. Due to its impact on several cities and therefore Olympiads and bid processes, we should briefly mention one important domestic impact. Beginning in Berlin, in 1936, governments and private citizens have used hosting the Games as a stimulus for urban revitalization. In 1936, the Germans undertook an entire remodeling of the capital. Berlin officials constructed an Olympic Village that served as a residence for the athletes. This new sector of Berlin later became housing for government officials, demonstrating how the Olympics could be used as an opportunity to revitalize and reconstruct a city.[23]

Sydney, Australia, built an entire new section of the city in an outlying and previously undeveloped area, which, when the Games ended, became a vibrant part of Sydney with infrastructure and transportation systems already in place and in operation. Another example, however, involves a failed attempt to host. Osaka, Japan, is one of many

Japanese cities that has been rapidly running out of land for expansion. The Osaka bid included in it a daring plan to build up the seabed in Osaka's harbor to actually construct a new island for a major international airport and other facilities. If Osaka had won the bid, the city would have gained new land for development as well as a new airport and a transportation system to link it and other islands completely into the infrastructure of Osaka. The failed New York City 2012 Summer Olympics bid involved making use of a north-south water transportation system and revitalizing shorefront property in New York City. In short, the Olympics offers a city a chance to revitalize or create whole new areas of a city as a part of a major project that would have its own funding, revenues, and planning. These types of projects would likely never get done if they were not being handled as part of a much larger planning operation that would have economic and political benefits for the city far beyond the specific projects themselves.

In conclusion, the inroads of politics into the Olympics overly complicated many issues. It is with both these benefits and complications in mind that dozens of cities have fought—sometimes viciously—to win the opportunity to be selected as an Olympic host. It was also with this backdrop that the Olympics were forced to face a series of politically driven ideological confrontations and challenges. The result of these confrontations was the politicization of the Olympics to levels that actually began to threaten the Olympic Movement as opposed to being minor nuisances or unnecessary and unwelcome political maneuvers that coexisted (sometimes peacefully) with the Olympic Movement. As we shall see in the next several chapters, this politicization created an atmosphere that led to the Olympic boycotts by the United States and the Soviet Union, which came close to crippling the Olympic Movement.

CHAPTER 3

SOVIET SPORTS HISTORY AND THE OLYMPIC MOVEMENT

THE EARLY YEARS: A PRE-SOVIET RUSSIA AND A YOUNG SOVIET STATE

The rich and competitive spirit of Soviet culture helped to drive many of the policies of the Soviet Union, including those involving their participation in international sports. The Soviet practice of utilizing international sporting events for political purposes helped to shape the history of sports in the Soviet Union, especially after World War II. Although it relates only peripherally to the main points of this book, it should be noted that the Russians were competing in the Olympics prior to World War I and the founding of the Soviet Union. They had made sporadic appearances in the Olympics from the early planning stages of revitalizing the Games through the Russian Revolution.

In what remains a strange series of events concerning their participation, Imperial Russia was one of the founding members at the first Olympic planning meeting, held in Paris in 1894; however, it failed to compete in any Olympiad until the London Games of 1908.[1] This is most likely due to its involvement and its defeat in the Russo-Japanese war, which ended in 1905 and precipitated the abortive 1905 Revolution. Even when the Russians were able to compete, their performances were not very successful. Prior to 1952, the only times Russian athletes brought home medals were at the 1908 London Games and the 1912 Stockholm Games.[2] They won one gold and two silver medals in London, and two silver and three bronze medals in Stockholm. In the medal count, this ranked the Russians twelfth out of 23 attending nations in London and sixteenth out of 28 attending nations in Stockholm.[3] The Stockholm Olympics were last Olympics to see Russian competitors until after World War II.

SOVIET ABSENCE FROM THE INTERWAR YEARS

The Soviets' absence from the Olympics during the interwar period was due to four key reasons. The first of these actually had nothing to do with the Soviet Union, but instead with the International Olympic Committee (IOC). The Soviet Union and other communist nations were not eagerly encouraged to join the Olympic Movement, because IOC president Henri de Baillet-Latour was not convinced that the communist nations would be able to become part of the Olympics due to ideological differences between communism and Olympism. He even went so far as to suggest that the Soviets would not make a very good (or necessary) contribution to the Olympic Movement.[4] In the interwar period, the IOC chose not to pursue Soviet membership, and the Soviet Union made no attempts to convince the IOC to let it join. The IOC's attitude would be very different after World War II, when Soviet influence over Eastern Europe made the Soviet Union a necessary member of the IOC, especially if the Olympics had any hope of universal membership among European states.

Political and ideological differences between the Soviet Union and the IOC ultimately meant the two were incompatible in the 1920s. This incompatibility, the second reason for Soviet absence in the 1920s and 1930s, was due to the Soviet view of the Olympic Movement. V. P. Kozmina stated that the Soviet absence from the Olympic Movement was due to the notion that the Games were created to "deflect workers from the class struggle and train them for new imperialist wars."[5] This may sound simply like ideological rhetoric, but there is a policy-oriented dimension to this statement by the Soviets on sports policy. The lack of a Soviet presence in the Olympics may have indicated the Soviet Union's unwillingness to cooperate with an organization that was to some degree incompatible with socialist ideology. There is evidence for this, as the Soviet Union did not completely withdraw from international sport competitions during the interwar period. In most histories on Soviet sport of the 1920s and 1930s, the focus is mainly on a series of exploits in soccer competitions.

Soccer was probably the best choice of competitive sport with western nations for the Soviets for a couple of reasons. First, soccer's international federation, the *Fédération Internationale de Football Association* (FIFA), had not outlawed competitions between its members and nations that were not members. Second, soccer was one of a few sports that continued competitions on an international level during World War I. These competitions took place mainly in neutral states—namely, Sweden and Switzerland—further justifying the prior statement that there was unwillingness on the part of the Soviet Union to compete under western jurisdiction. Another key reason for the selection of soccer is that it was both the most popular sport in the Soviet Union and a sport in which Soviet athletes excelled. The fact that Soviet sports policy demonstrated a general trend toward noncompetition with "imperialist" sports organizations bolsters the argument that they were less willing to compete under Olympic auspices. As a result of this standoffish policy, the Soviet Union was isolated from competition against many. International federations generally blocked their members from competing with athletes from states that were not members of the federation. This means that the list of sports the Soviets were excluded from on the international level was extensive.

The Soviet ability to compete successfully, the third reason for Soviet absence from the Olympics in the interwar period, was a key factor in the selection of soccer as its sport for international diplomacy. Success was a paramount concern of the hierarchy of the Soviet government when they considered any international competition, and generally the Soviet Union did not partake in any events where they did not expect to emerge victorious. Soviet sports diplomacy was never just about international relations; it always included a display of the success of the Socialist system through victory in international sports encounters. Nikolai Romanov, chairman of the Committee on Physical Culture and Sport in the Soviet Union from 1945 to 1948 and 1953 to 1962,[6] offered a keen insight on the placement of sport in Soviet policy, stating, "Once we decided to take part in foreign competitions, we were forced to guarantee victory . . . That actually happened. To gain permission to go to international tournaments I had to send a special note to Stalin guaranteeing victory."[7]

Soviet soccer competitions on an international level had several benefits that provided a great vehicle for promoting relations between the Soviets and both nations sympathetic to the Soviet Union and those near the Soviet borders. First, as James Riordan pointed out, it allowed the opportunity to normalize relations between the Soviet Union and other Eastern European nations after World War I. For the most part, the Soviet Union was as ostracized in the international community as Germany was. Formal recognition of the Soviet Union did not begin until 1924, first by Britain (which withdrew it a year later and would continue to sporadically change its mind on the issue) and then by the United States, which formally recognized the Soviet Union in 1933.

Soviet sports diplomacy was a useful method of encouraging this process. The Soviet Union began its ascendance into the international community by first approaching neutral and sympathetic nations and opening foreign relations with those nations through sport. Sweden, a nonaligned nation in the interwar period, and Hungary, a nation also trying to improve its image in the international community after its defeat and subsequent partition after World War I, serve as excellent examples. As will be discussed later, socialist sports organizations in the Soviet Union and in several European states would help facilitate Soviet outreach toward Belgium, Czechoslovakia, and Finland. This slow process of acceptance in the international community is an integral part of the fourth factor that caused the absence of the Soviets from the Olympics during the interwar period: isolation from the West.

Without recognition, the Soviet Union did not have any nation to help bridge the gap between themselves and the Western leaders of the IOC. Furthermore, the hosting nations could not provide that bridge because of the same isolationist issues. Belgium, France, Netherlands, and the United States, all of which hosted Olympic Games from 1920 to 1932, had no contacts with the Soviet Union during their duties as host of the Olympics. Consequently, the Soviet Union could not use host countries as a means of facilitating their incorporation into the Olympic Games. Only after Soviet sports diplomacy had opened political and economic ties with Finland, Sweden, Czechoslovakia, Hungary, and other nations did the Soviet Union start acting as a significant contributor to international sports. However, by the time that happened, Soviet-German relations would keep the Soviet Union out of the Berlin Games of 1936.

The fourth reason for Soviet absence from the Olympic Movement incorporates both the lack of any strong international relations with hosts or key competitors and the circumstances surrounding Soviet, German, and Spanish relations in the 1930s. The majority of Olympic nations did not recognize the Soviet Union until 1933, but it would still not join the movement until after World War II. The 1936 Summer Olympics were in Berlin, which posed several challenges to the Olympic Movement and Soviet participation. The call for boycotts against Berlin notwithstanding, Soviet foreign policy on fascist governments placed the Soviet Union and Germany at odds with each other. Exacerbating the situation was Moscow's position that the 1936 Games should be relocated to Barcelona, Spain. The irony of this request is that Berlin defeated Barcelona in its bid to host the Games.

The IOC met in Barcelona in April 1931 to decide where to stage the 1936 Summer Olympics. Political instability in Spain coupled with outbreaks of violence made attendance in Barcelona too unsafe for most IOC members, so many submitted votes in absentia. In the end, Berlin received 43 votes, Barcelona received 18, and 8 members abstained.[8] Political instability in Spain culminated in 1936 in a civil war between the democratically elected popular front and a national fascist movement under General Francisco Franco y Bahamonde. The Soviet Union backed the populist government while Germany and the Italy backed the fascist dictatorship. All three nations would become deeply involved in the Spanish Civil War.

As Soviet and German differences on Spanish and German domestic policy pulled the two nations apart, the Germans, now under Nazi control, worked diligently to entice the nations of the world to attend the Berlin Games. The Soviet Union made this very difficult for Germany by pressing Olympic member nations to withdraw support from the German-organized Games. This pressure culminated in the call for relocation of the Games to an antifascist state that, conveniently, had already been considered by the IOC as a potential host.

Soviet diplomacy does show that the Soviet Union was ready, by 1936, to enter the international sports movement at the Berlin Games. The Soviet Union saw political benefits in the Olympic Movement, and consequently, they began taking a more vocal role in Olympic matters. In response to fascist policies in Germany, the Soviet Union advocated the revocation of the Olympics from Berlin. In the past, the Soviet Union had simply ignored the Olympics as a "bourgeois" event. But in this situation, the Soviet Union, as part of its efforts to organize an antifascist front, attempted to take a leadership role in the concerns over the Berlin Games by working with Spanish and Catalan authorities to organize an alternate Olympics in Barcelona.[9] The Barcelona Olympics, to have taken place roughly one month earlier than the Berlin Games, were cancelled due to the outbreak of the Spanish Civil War.

In these examples, sports diplomacy had very clear political benefits; in addition, there were economic benefits as well, including the opportunity to foster growth in the Soviet economy.[10] In some cases, Soviet sport decisions were made purely for diplomatic reasons. A series of soccer matches with Finland in the early part of 1923 opened a dialogue between both states and fostered new levels of cooperation. This led to a July 1923 agreement that normalized shipping in the Gulf of Finland.[11] In fact, a great deal of Soviet sports diplomacy in the 1920s and 1930s involved improving relations with nations that either were within a reasonable land or sea trade distance of Moscow, Leningrad, Novgorod, or Rostov or were nations with a strong socialist movement. The former, such as Finland, Sweden, Estonia, Czechoslovakia, and Hungary, were nations that previously had some form of relations with Russia and with whom the Russians wanted relations reinstated or normalized. The latter, such as Germany, Belgium, Norway, Spain, and Turkey, were nations in which the Soviets were hoping to foster greater sympathy toward their revolutionary ideas.

Thus, the Soviet decisions on sports competitions from the 1920s through the end of World War II focused primarily on two goals: to promote its own system of beliefs and to strengthen relations with European nations on an economic and diplomatic level. The promotion of Soviet ideology constituted a dismissal of western ideology and an affirmation of Soviet socialist ideals. This also strengthened and coalesced the relationships and efforts of other socialist/communist countries and movements throughout all Europe. With regards to inter-Europe relations, all sports encounters of Russian athletes during the interwar period satisfied both of these conditions. The Olympics, however, simply could not provide the Soviet Union such an atmosphere in the 1920s and 1930s. This was mainly due to the nature of politics in the Olympic Movement in those two decades as well as the list of invited and uninvited states due in part to politics and the aftermath of World War I.

Given the Soviet Union, for a variety of reasons, was not participating in the Olympics and several other international sports competitions, it opted to establish its own sporting leagues that sought to benefit its ideological biases. The early 1920s witnessed the formation of two new international sports organizations, existing solely to control the realm of socialist sport: the Lucerne Sport International (LSI) and the Red Sport International (RSI). The LSI was a central European organization, consisting primarily of Austria, Switzerland, part of Germany, and Belgium. The RSI was a Soviet-led organization that consisted mainly of Eastern European nations, such as Czechoslovakia, Bulgaria, and that part of Germany not in the LSI. The two organizations did not go very far to foster growth and competition between each other. Eventually, in 1927, the LSI forbade contact with the RSI.[12] Attempts to create non-Western international festivals—for example, the Workers Olympiads, the Spartakiad, and soccer tours of their respective members—met with some success, but they eventually fell apart due to constant calls for boycotts by either the LSI or the RSI. The RSI ceased to exist just prior to World War II,[13] since socialist sport was waning during the spread of fascism. Part of this demise was the disappearance of Austria and Czechoslovakia from the list of sovereign states and the arrival of more conservative dictatorships in states such as Bulgaria and Germany. Soviet ostracism of Germany and many other nations during the 1936 Olympics only added to the division of the international sports world. Member nations elected to take part in more widespread international competition offered by the international federations, and the IOC would strike their own devastating blows to socialist sport movements. The failures of the socialist sports organizations left the IOC as the only surviving option when the Soviet Union started to normalize its relations after World War II and sought a return to international sports competition that the now defunct RSI and LSI could no longer offer.

POST–WORLD WAR II POLITICKING AND THE MISSING SOVIETS

The IOC was neutralized during World War II. Its president was trapped in occupied Belgium, several members were drafted into the Soviet, German, and British armies, and others died during occupations across Europe, Africa, and Asia. After World War II, the IOC started to put the surviving pieces of its organization back together. This was no easy task, since the war had left the IOC with several problems, most notably a lack of leadership. President Baillet-Latour had died in Belgium during the war, and many other IOC members had perished during the war years. Still others were representatives of nations that were no longer independent after World War II had ended. Despite these problems, the IOC began the process of reconstruction.

The surviving members began the process of reinstituting the Olympics and quickly announced London as the host of the 1948 summer Olympics and St. Moritz, Switzerland, as the host of the 1948 winter Olympics. Several IOC members argued that the Olympics should be postponed to 1952, but IOC President Sigfrid Edstrom and Vice President Avery Brundage saw crucial symbolic meaning in restarting the Olympics after the end of the war. By having the Games occur on the first possible Olympiad after peace was declared, it established the hiatus as a temporary cessation of the Games and not an end to the movement. It also demonstrated the resiliency of the movement in the face of significant political upheaval. Furthermore, Edstrom and Brundage also understood the role an international sports festival could play in the process of reasserting peace. London, even though severely damaged during the war, agreed to host the Games. With the return of the Olympics, sports diplomacy roared back to life, though not immediately involving the Soviet Union. The London Games had many problems to deal with: damaged and inadequate facilities, scarcity of supplies and food, and other logistical problems that one would expect in a city that only four years prior was being regularly bombed. These widespread problems, along with the IOC's need to replace old members and reappoint its leadership, forced the IOC to ignore issues of courting the Soviet Union to join the list of participating nations. At the same time, the Soviet Union did not show any immediate interest in joining the movement.

In the immediate postwar years, Soviet sports were in disarray. According to Norman Schneidman, "Soviet athletes were not yet ready to enter the international sport scene as full fledged members of the international sports community."[14] The reason, he adds, is that Soviet athletes would not be able "to perform at a level required by both the party and the state."[15] The Soviet response to this situation came from the Party Central Committee through a resolution it passed in December 1948, which stated that Soviet physical culture "should include provision for the development of a mass physical culture movement in the country and for the rise in the level of sport mastery of Soviet Athletes. The fulfillment of these objectives should secure the victory of Soviet athletes in the world championships in the most important sports in the near future."[16] With these words, the Central Committee openly attacked the state of Soviet physical culture and sport.

Once the 1948 Winter and Summer Games were over, the process of addressing the postwar political climate's impact on the Olympic Movement began. The desire for sporting competitions between the two postwar political camps of the Cold War would be the main factor that brought the IOC and the Soviet Union together. For the most part, this can be credited to the steady increase in the formal organization of international sport that was in place after World War II. International federations now governed almost all major sports competitions.[17] These international federations were the governing bodies that made decisions on the rules of a given sport and also regulated the participation of nations in those sports. They would govern the competition, confirm building sites, approve tournaments, and confirm officials. Changes that would, in any way, alter the sport were processed through them. Sports federations, including the International Amateur

Athletics Foundation (IAAF), which governs all track and field events, began creating strict rules for membership and competition. The Soviet Union found itself unable to compete on an international stage due to its lack of recognition by the IAAF. It was a fairly common practice for international federations to restrict competitions to only accept athletes from member states. The Soviet Union would not have been allowed to compete in the 1948 Summer or Winter Olympics because it was not recognized by many of the sports federations that governed Olympic sports, and it also lacked a recognized national Olympic committee. Swim meets, soccer matches, track and field competitions, even chess tournaments were closed to Soviet athletes because the Soviet Union had not become a member of the sports federations that govern the rules of the various sporting events. Now that the control of international sports was becoming more centralized, an increasing number of international federations had rules forbidding member states from allowing their athletes to compete with the athletes of nonmember states, thus excluding the Soviet Union from nearly any internationally federated sport.

This organizational structure of international sports competitions and common rules of international federations helped frame all sports diplomacy from 1945 onward. It is because of this backdrop that the Soviet Union and other states would eventually capitulate on international requirements for their involvement. Before continuing this discussion, let us look at the stage on which Soviet sports diplomacy turns from isolationist to participatory. To do so, we must first look at the situation in Europe at the start of the Cold War.

One interesting and important exception to Soviet ostracization was a series of soccer matches between the Soviet Union and the United Kingdom in 1945. Immediately following World War II, Soviet sports began its usual multinational interactions again. For instance, a Soviet tour of England in November 1945 saw a Moscow soccer team face several British teams in England and Scotland. The reason for this deviation from the typical selections for Soviet competitions, besides the obvious effect of cementing relations among World War II allies in the postwar period, was that of pride. The British had established the modern rules of soccer as well as its first associations and organized competition, and because of this, they held a special symbolic place in the sport. That being said, the Soviets recognized that victories and draws in the series in Britain demonstrated the Soviets' ability to compete effectively on a world stage. This was one of the many instances where Soviet sports diplomacy showed a very methodical and repetitive decision process. The aforementioned soccer matches between Sweden and the Soviet Union were staged in part for the same reason. Both the matches with Sweden and with Britain were an attempt to "reestablish contacts with top-class international competition so as to be able to assess the level of Soviet play and improve on it."[18] In other words, these competitions were a chance to assess Soviet progress in sports development prior to appearing in larger and more visible competitions.

THE EMERGENCE OF THE RUSSIAN (SPORTS) BEAR

The Cold War was at first a stalemate in Europe. The West and the East had carved up Europe after World War II and left a map full of countries that were satellites of either the Soviet Union or the West. Without open warfare, which was highly unlikely since neither side was willing to go through another major war, one of the obvious forms of competition open to these two camps was that of sport. Sports diplomacy from the 1950s through 1980s was in many cases an opportunity for bloodless war.[19] Schneidman remarks, "Soviet authorities [did] not miss an opportunity to point out the success of athletes from socialist states in international competition."[20] In fact, Soviet officials went even further and drew "conclusions which would lead one to believe in the superiority of the social system existing in most Eastern European countries."[21] Soviet statements on results of sports competitions often used such language as "defeated the Americans," as opposed to noting Soviet victories over the entire field of competitors. For the Eastern Bloc to take advantage of this method of diplomacy, the Soviet Union and her allies had to start the process of joining international federations. The IOC was the culminating point of that process for many states, since membership in the IOC required involvement in the international federations whose sports were a part of the Olympic Games. For both the Soviet Union and the international federations, this was not a simple process.

The process of uniting the international federations and the Soviet Union was a painful one for both sides. After the war, diplomatic relations between the Soviet Union and the non–Soviet sphere nations were either severely limited or nonexistent. To make matters worse, no one really knew how to deal with the Soviets or with Stalin, and problems started occurring immediately. Soviet athletes appeared unannounced at IAAF and IWF competitions, usually wanting to compete without invitations. In some cases, they were allowed to participate, but more often Soviet athletes found themselves increasingly left out of competitions due to the lack of formal Soviet recognition. In response to this isolation, the Soviets began sporadically joining international federations throughout the period from 1946 to 1951. Among them were FIFA, *Fédération Internationale de Basketball* (FIBA), *Fédération Internationale de Gymnastics* (FIG), *Union Internationale de Patinage* (ISU), *Fédération Internationale des Luttes Associées* (FILA), and *Fédération Internationale des Echecs* (FIDE).[22] The IAAF and the IOC kept Soviet officials waiting for a while longer.

The Soviet Union's entrance into several of the aforementioned international federations should not seem all that surprising. First, there was a general interest in their participation as early as 1946. Soviet athletes appeared at the European Track and Field Championships in Oslo, Norway, in 1946.[23] This incident was not an isolated one. The Soviet Union had already been competing with athletes from other countries, which were members of the federations, as well as with members of the IAAF and the IOC. Also, they had experience with international sports federations and groups, specifically noting the ones that the Soviet Union created to foster interstate socialist sport. Furthermore, it is important to recall that the Soviet Union, unlike in the period before World War II, was now actively interested in partaking in the international sports community. Finally, Sigfrid Edstrom, president of the IOC and the former president of the IAAF, took it on himself to garner Soviet membership by sending them regular invitations.

The difficulty for the Soviet Union joining the IAAF and the IOC was that it had been attempting to join without assenting to many of the rules and practices of both organizations.[24] On the contrary, Soviet officials wanted concessions made for them. The IAAF made huge concessions for the Soviet Union when Edstrom invited the Soviets to become members. The IAAF, like most international federations, did not send invitations to join or participate in its events or governing body. The established procedure involved a nation forming a committee and submitting a request for formal recognition. The very fact that invitations were sent was seen as a concession to Soviet interests and placed the Soviet Union in a position to make demands as conditions on their membership. This differed from the usual situation, where the IOC or the IAAF would place its conditions on the nation that was requesting membership. As it turned out, the IAAF, the IOC, and the Soviet Union all had demands that needed reconciliation before the Soviet Union could be brought in as a member of either organization.

The IAAF and the IOC were open with their demands: The Soviet Union had to formally accept the Olympic charter, its rules and its procedures, and pledge to abide by them. The Soviet Union had little difficulty agreeing to that. The IAAF and IOC, however, had major problems with the state of amateur sports in the Soviet Union. Both organizations had strict, complicated rules on amateur competition that were incompatible with the Soviet definition of amateurism.[25]

Simply put, the IOC and Soviet definitions of the terms *professional athlete* and *amateur athlete* were too different for Soviet athletes to legally compete in IAAF- and IOC-sponsored events. Eventually, and in a completely unexpected change of policy, the Soviets acquiesced to the demands of the IOC and changed their rules governing the definition of amateur and professional athletes. But there was still confusion because the status as an amateur athlete, as it is understood in the West, requires that athletes at the time not receive monetary compensation for training, competition, or performance. Professional athletes are those individuals that are paid a substantial amount of their livelihood due to their participation in any given sport. Because athletes in communist states were government subsidized, many nations argued that this constituted a professional athlete. While the Soviet Union realigned certain understandings of its internal sports policy to accommodate the issue of amateurism, allegations of state-sponsored sport being a violation of the prohibition against professional athletes in the Games remained an issue of significant confrontation for several decades.

Putting IAAF and IOC demands aside, the Soviet Union, as a condition for joining the IAAF and the IOC, had three demands of their own: the expulsion of Franco's Spain from membership, the placement of a Soviet representative on the Executive Council of the IOC, and the institution of Russian as an official language of the IOC.[26] It should come as no surprise that the IOC's official response in 1950 met none of these demands. In a completely unexpected turn of events, four months later in April 1951, the Soviet Union sent a telegram to the IOC. Petr Sobolev, who was the secretary of the newly formed Soviet National Olympic Committee (USSR NOC), wrote, "We inform you that an Olympic Committee was created in the URSS. This Olympic Committee examined the Rules of the IOC and declared them accepted. The Olympic Committee of the URSS requires its admission to the IOC."[27] The IOC had to accept the Russian claims at face value and accept the USSR NOC into its family. After sending its formal acceptance of the USSR NOC, the IOC then elected Constantin Andrianov as the IOC representative from the Soviet Union. Incidentally, this is the first time the IOC accepted, without question, a government appointee for membership into the IOC.[28] The outcome of these communications was the ascension of the Soviet Union to membership in the Olympic Movement. Yet we are still left asking why the Soviet Union's government completely changed its position on USSR participation. Why did the Soviet Union abandon all the demands it made previously just to ensure its acceptance into the Olympic Movement? The sudden change of policy has been the subject of considerable debate in the past. An in-depth study of this would unnecessarily sidetrack this book; however, one key factor relating directly to this shift in Soviet policy is worth mentioning as it also affected other Soviet sports policies pertinent to this study. Stalin, who died in the early part of 1953, was slowly losing power in the Soviet Union. His decline brought to an end the existence of a very powerful negative Soviet policy toward the Olympics. This was an antipathy that was mutual. Stalin's decision to pressure the IOC to move the 1936 Olympics left many, including Avery Brundage, bitter toward the Soviet leaders. The antipathy softened on both sides following World War II. By 1953, the IOC was interested in having the entire Soviet Bloc fully integrated into international sports, and Stalin's death led to complete changes in Soviet policy in several areas, including those that had previously made Olympic membership difficult.

SOVIET GOLD SEEKING

The Soviet Union, after Stalin's death, underwent a complete restructuring of their governing system. In the arena of sports, the All-Union Committee of Physical Culture and Sport was moved under the Ministry of Health and all local committees on Physical Culture and Sport were relocated under the appropriate departments within the Health ministry. This process of consolidation of sport within the Soviet Union cleared the way for a more integrated sports policy for competition in international sports. Additionally, several Stalin-era policies were rescinded as they reflected his antipathy toward the IOC and other international sports governing bodies. However, while the Soviet system was going through several changes, the consolidation of sports programs remained a constant.

Under Stalin's leadership, the Council of Ministers issued a resolution titled "On Remuneration of the Sporting Attainments of Soviet Sportsmen," in which athletes were rewarded for their success in representing the Soviet Union through sports.[29] A year later, another resolution "made it clear that improved proficiency could and should be based on mass participation,"[30] a sentiment that would later be echoed in the language of the Ninth Five-Year Plan of the Congress of the Communist Party of the Soviet Union.[31] The Party resolution also "outlined a specific programme for attaining the targets it had set; it entailed reinforcing the organization of sports collectives; ensuring the all-round expansion of all sports with particular attention given to Olympic sports; improving the sports amenities; bringing Master's and other ranking standards in line with international records; setting up sports schools."[32] Sports policy continued to grow during Stalin's declining years and continued when Nikita Khrushchev rose to power. Among Khrushchev's many changes to Soviet society, he further strengthened Soviet sports programs. Under his leadership, the Central Party Committee and the Council of Ministers, in 1959, adopted a joint resolution that ordered the complete restructuring of Soviet sport into a more effective institution.

The resolution called for fostering greater involvement of the public in sports programs and, in particular, to increase the level of performance of Soviet athletes. The resolution specifically stated that the goal of the new policy was to have Soviet athletes break more records and gain more victories in international competition. The last noteworthy line in the resolution calls for in-depth education of youth and athletes in the Communist Party, loyalty to the Soviet Union, and a devotion to the cause of socialism and communism.[33]

It was under this new system that the number of sports and the regularity of competitions increased in the Soviet Union and the number of memberships the Soviet Union had in international federations steadily grew. Later, particularly in the mid-1960s, many of Khrushchev's changes to the Soviet system would be removed, but the consolidation of sports would stay. In the 1970s, Soviet sport reached a new level of planning. At the Twenty-Fourth Congress of the Communist Party of the Soviet Union (CPSU), Chairman Alexei Kosygin summarized the successes of the Eighth Five-Year Plan and then called for several changes and highlighted areas for growth. While his summary makes no note of growth of sport or physical culture, he later calls for the Ninth Five-Year Plan.[34] In the documents of the Twenty-Fourth Congress's Ninth Five-Year Plan for 1971–1975, specific attention was given to the growth of physical culture and sports programs. Section 7, titled "Raising the Standard of Living," called for two changes in sports policy.[35] First, it stated, "Steps shall be taken to secure . . . the development of physical culture and sports."[36] It goes on to recommend an increase in facilities and education to broaden the number of Soviet citizens involved in the Soviet sports program.[37] To summarize, regardless of major shifts in direction of the Supreme Soviet during the period from World War II through the 1970s, there was in general a trend toward increased involvement, increased consolidation, and increased performance in sport in the Soviet Union.

Another key factor was that the growing number of nations trying to join the IOC after World War II left the Soviet Union with very few nations with which to compete.[38] As stated earlier, FIFA's policy of not allowing nations in the international federation to compete with nations outside of it (mentioned previously as the cause of the Soviet willingness to join FIFA) was not unique. With an increasing number of nations joining international federations with this policy, the Soviet Union was quickly finding itself isolated from international competitions. Even Soviet allies, including Czechoslovakia, Poland, and Romania, were in the Olympic Movement and unable to compete with the Soviet Union.

Years of policy adjustment, complex relations with sports governing bodies, and adjustments to Soviet sports infrastructure culminated in the first appearance of the Soviet Union in the Olympics. At the 1952 Helsinki Summer Olympics, the Soviet Union came in second place, winning 71 medals.[39] That was 29 more than the third place winner, Hungary, and five medals shy of the United States and first place.[40] This suggests that the Soviet Union had been quietly preparing for competition during the years of negotiation leading up to the eventual agreement on Soviet membership in the Olympic Movement. The performance also fits into a very standard rubric of Soviet sports competitions in which the Soviet Union opts to compete only in instances where their victory is likely. This aspect of Soviet sports diplomacy will play a recurring role in their history. It is an aspect that will prove very important for the history of Soviet involvement in the Olympics and for their boycott in 1984.

The lack of participation in other sports is partly due to the unwillingness of the Soviet Union to compete internationally unless they were confident they could effectively compete. Nikolai Romanov offered proof of this in his memoirs. Quoted earlier, Romanov explained that the Soviet Union would not participate in a sports competition in which he could not guarantee a victory.[41] In another part of his memoirs, he recalled that the Soviet Union considered joining the Olympic Movement soon after World War II had ended. He went on further to state that the Soviet Union had concluded that participation in the 1948 London Games was not possible because their athletes simply were not ready for them.[42]

Another sign of this attitude was the relative inconsistency of Soviet participation in the 1940s and 1950s. The Soviet Union strategically selected where to send their athletes. Considering Stalin's demands for victory, it is safe to assume that the Soviets only attended events in which they were certain they would perform well. On two occasions, the Soviet Union sent a group of athletes to participate in a competition to which they had not been invited: the Oslo European Track and Field Championships in August 1946 and a weight lifting competition in Paris October of 1946.[43] During this time, the IAAF had made several attempts to get an application for admission from the Soviet government. In most cases, the invitation to join was ignored, but a lack of membership did not stop appearances by Soviet athletes at competitions throughout Europe. Oddly enough, the opposite action occurred as well. In some cases the Soviet Union did not participate at a competition they had been expected to attend, as was the case in a major gymnastics competition in France in 1947. If any word could be used to describe Soviet participation in sport, it would be either *unreliable* or *selective*. Another example of this selective competition occurred in the Olympiad of 1952.

The Soviet Union's radical shift in policy in 1951 led to its full membership into the Olympic Movement in 1952. Nikoli Romanov explained that the postwar delay in applying for membership was due to the lack of preparedness of the Soviet athletes for the 1948 London and St. Moritz Games. Once the Soviet Union became part of the Olympic Movement, it was assumed that it would participate in the Games of 1952. When the 1952 Olympics arrived, the Soviets appeared in Helsinki for the Summer Games but not in Oslo for the Winter Games roughly four months earlier. Even though the Soviets had already joined several winter sports international federations, skating being the first, they elected not to attend the Oslo Winter Games.

Some historians have claimed that the absence of a Soviet delegation in Oslo was due to a lack of normalized relations between the two countries. Any argument for the existence of a political motivation, however, must be dismissed when two facts are made clear. First, the Soviet Union attended the European Track and Field Championships that were in Oslo six years earlier in 1946. There were not any problems between Norway and the Soviet Union from 1946 to 1952 that would have impeded the attendance of the Soviet Union. Second, the Norwegians did not discriminate based on the postwar situation. West Germany was in attendance at the Games, as were the Soviet-sphere nations of Hungary and Czechoslovakia. The Soviets' lack of attendance therefore cannot be linked to a diplomatic decision, since Soviet satellites went to Oslo.

Politics and IOC rules were not factors in the absence of a Soviet team, or else they would not have appeared in Helsinki. Finances, political stability, or other domestic factors were not significantly different in the Soviet Union from 1948 to 1952. All that remains is a conscious decision of the Soviet government to not attend Oslo for reasons related to the competition or their expected performance. Evidence from decades of Soviet sports policy decisions supports the argument that they simply did not feel confident about their expected performance in Oslo. While this is hard to conclusively prove, with aforementioned statements by Nikolai Romanov[44] and the fact that the Soviet Union had no background in the largest sports event of the Winter Games—the ice hockey tournament—it is reasonable given Soviet sports history to contend that the Soviet Union was simply biding its time on participation in the Winter Games.

There is one final compelling piece of evidence to demonstrate that the Soviets appeared only in competitions in which they believed they were prepared to compete. A study of the results of Soviet participation in the 1952 Helsinki Summer Games and the 1952 Cortina D'Ampezzo Winter Games offers some surprising statistics. The Soviet Union, prior to their appearance in the Summer Games, had not competed domestically in several Olympic events within their borders. But by the time of their appearance in the Olympics, they had developed strong competitors in every sport but one: field hockey.[45] The Soviet Union in their inaugural appearance in the 1952 Summer Olympics placed second in the overall medal count. They won 22 gold, 30 silver, and 19 bronze medals for a total of 71 medals. The only nation to surpass them was the United States, which earned 40 gold, 19 silver, and 17 bronze for a total of 76 medals, just 5 more than the Soviets. For a nation that had never competed internationally in many of the Olympic sports, that was a phenomenal performance. And this was just four years after the London Olympics that the Soviets did not attend because they were, according to them, not sufficiently prepared. The results in 1956 in Italy were comparable. The Soviet Union, in their inaugural appearance in the Winter Olympics, took first place in the medal count. They won 7 gold, 3 silver, and 6 bronze medals for a total of 16. Austria won second place with 4 gold, 3 silver, and 4 bronze for a total of 11: 5 less than the Soviet Union. If there was ever any doubt about the Soviet Union preparing its athletes for victory in the Olympics, it can be answered finally by one event: ice hockey.

Ice hockey was not played in the Soviet Union before World War II. But, when their joining the Olympic Movement seemed guaranteed, they hired coaches from Czechoslovakia, a historic powerhouse of ice hockey, and began training. In Cortina D'Ampezzo, Soviet ice hockey, which became a very popular sport in the Soviet Union, was tested, and they achieved unbelievable success. They took the gold, defeating the United States in the final round. The Canadians took the bronze.[46] Regardless of all issues concerning amateurism and professionalism, it should be obvious that the Soviet Union had established that they could dominate the Olympics. Their government started sports programs and competitions in the Soviet Union simply for competition on the international level. It is obvious that the Olympics were the main focus of this, as the Soviets managed to compete in almost every Olympic competition, even in those sports in which they had absolutely no tradition of participation among their citizens.

The reasons behind Soviet sports policy are complicated, but they are linked to the effective uses of the Olympic Movement as a political tool. In their view, the competition between East and West could be reduced to an argument over whose system was better. Sports provided a great forum to test this hypothesis. In 1973, Soviet sports official I. Stoliarov stated, "The mounting impact of socialist sport on the world sports movement is one of the best and most comprehensible means of explaining to the people throughout the world the advantages that socialism has over the capitalist system."[47] Athletes became another means of waging surrogate warfare in the Soviet Union's quest to prove system dominance. In return for their efforts, the Central Committee handsomely rewarded their athletes for winning on their versions of the battlefield.

Initially, the Soviets had given cash bonuses for success. They gave 15,000 rubles to any athlete who broke a national record and 25,000 rubles to any athlete who broke a world record. This practice was eliminated and replaced with the presentation of medals and awards so as to not violate the IOC rules of amateurism, which would prevent Soviet athletes from competing. The degree of patriotism afforded to successful athletes was no more obvious than in 1956. When the Soviets returned from the 1956 Melbourne Summer Olympics, having broken the record for the most medals won by a nation in a single Olympics,[48] some of the athletes, coaches, and officials received even higher honors in the Soviet society. The Order of Lenin, the highest honor of the Soviet Union, was awarded to 17 members of the Soviet delegation to Melbourne.[49]

Unfortunately, the degree of praise for success was met with an equal amount of condemnation for failure. Soccer was a disaster for the Soviet Union in 1956. The Yugoslavs eliminated the Soviets in the first round. Yugoslavia and Russia had very difficult relations in the 1950s, so this loss was a blow not only to the Soviet Union's nationalist pride but also to their arguments that the Yugoslavs had perverted socialism. The seriousness of this failure in sport by the Russians was noted perfectly in this situation by the actions of Josef Stalin. Stalin immediately dissolved the team, calling it back to Moscow, and also dissolved the Army 11 military unit, which had made up the majority of the team.[50]

The Soviets wanted desperately to prove the superiority of their system. The sports world, through a surrogate war, allowed the Soviet Union a chance to engage nonsocialist states in contests every four years. The use of sports policy and diplomacy was not, however, limited to athletic contests between the ideological camps. Successes in foreign policy through the IOC, most notably in the appearance of a unified German team at the 1956[51] Summer Olympics and the two Chinas at the 1984 Summer Olympics, offered all sides the opportunity to claim a diplomatic victory regardless of the fact that neither side actually had a major role in the diplomacy. Still, this allowed all sides the illusion of success over the enemy. The Soviet Union's recurring victories at the Olympics, both sporting and nonsporting, created a degree of complacency in the socialist camp while American and Western victories, which were usually unexpected, allowed for surges of nationalist pride. The situation had actually "cooled off" to the state of a healthy rivalry both among the athletes and among the politicians. This period of a "cooler" rivalry in Olympic sports would heat up again quickly. Once the Soviet Union, the United States, and Canada entered into a bidding war to host the Olympics, the three would enter into a period of very heated sports diplomacy. This would lay the groundwork for the boycott era. In addition to the bidding process itself, other factors in Soviet Olympic sports history would contribute to the Olympic drama of the 1980s.

THE SOVIET SPORTS MACHINE

In the twenty-year period from 1952 to 1972, the Soviet Union consistently built up the role of sport in its society and diplomacy. There are numerous places to look for examples of this change. First, constitutionally, the role of sport went from being completely undefined to being defined and then redefined. The Soviet Union had constitutions ratified in 1918, 1924, 1936, and 1977. The first two constitutions make no statements on sport. The 1936 constitution would be the beginning of the emergence of policies relating to sport present in Soviet constitutional law.

Article 126 of the 1936 Constitution states that the "masses of the people . . . are ensured the right to unite in public organizations—trade unions, cooperative associations, youth organizations, sport and defense organization."[52] The government went even further in the 1977 Constitution, which states in Article 24, section 2 that "the state encourages cooperatives and other public organizations to provide all types of services for the population. It encourages the development of mass physical culture and sport."[53] The 1977 Constitution notes further in Article 41 that "[c]itizens of the USSR have the right to rest and leisure."[54] It goes on further to state that such a right is ensured through many measures, which specifically include "the development on a mass scale of sport, physical culture, and camping and tourism; by the provision of neighborhood recreational facilities."[55]

From 1960 to 1980, the year the Soviet Union hosted the Summer Olympics, the number of stadiums in the Soviet Union seating more than 1,500 spectators increased from 1,981 to 3,693. That is an increase of more than 100 percent. On a more grassroots level, the number of gymnasia increased from 15,000 to 74,000, and the number of swimming pools increased from 896 to 1,750. Finally, facilities such as courts and fields increased from 293 to 503.[56] Also, availability of information on sport was widespread. By 1973, there were 14 periodicals published by Soviet authorities in Moscow and there were 17 periodicals published in the various republics, Moscow, and Leningrad.[57] Other Soviet policies were enacted to foster sports in the Soviet Union.

Soviet athletes initially received monetary awards for success in competition, but IOC definitions of amateurism made the policy untenable if said athletes were to compete in the Olympics. Instead of simply eliminating the policy of recognition, the government replaced the monetary rewards with medals, official recognition, and even the title of "Master of Sports." Their awards program was actually quite extensive, with as many as eight separate meritorious classifications depending on the sport in question.[58] The Russians turned their successful athletes into heroes with household names. This had the dual effect of both rewarding good performance of current athletes and raising awareness and interest of sport among the general population.

The Soviet Union ran several physical training centers, sports schools, and other facilities for Soviet athletes. In addition to structural concerns, the Soviet Union was also steadily increasing the number of sports their citizens competed in. At the international level, the Soviet Union joined 15 international federations from 1946 to 1949. Their list of memberships increased to 30 in the 1950s, 33 in the 1960s, and 36 by the 1984 Summer Olympics.[59] The number of sports with national championship competitions also increased. The Soviet Union added nine new national championship competitions from 1950 through 1984.[60]

Studying the growth of sports programs in the Soviet Union as well as domestic policy designed to foster sports involvement by Russian citizens, it becomes clear that the Soviet Union was consciously increasing the role of sport in its society. Broadening programs is a typical strategy of states attempting to both attract competitions to host events in their states as well as foster the spirit of competition among their citizens. According to a Soviet Information Department publication of the USSR embassy, "the organization of sports training on a mass scale provides opportunity for those talented in sports to reveal themselves."[61] This undoubtedly explains the success of Soviet Olympic basketball, especially in the then Lithuanian Soviet Socialist Republic. Such programs and philosophy has resulted in the participation of numbers in the millions. For example, in 1988, the Soviet Union reported 7.4 million citizens participating in track and field, 6.3 million in volleyball, and participation in other sports totaling more than 30 million people.[62] The whole process was a success. By the time the Soviet Union hosted the Summer Olympics, they were competing in every type of sporting event held at the Games, including those sports only recently added to the list of competitions.

As it is now clear, there were several well-crafted attempts to change the face and form of sport in the Soviet Union during the 1950s through 1970s. Similar changes were also occurring in the diplomacy aspect of the Soviet Union's involvement in sport. Aleksei Romanov, in reference to the Olympic Movement, stated that "there is a continuous struggle of the new with the old, of the progressive with the reactionary, and, as a mass social movement, international sport is in our time an arena of sharp political and ideological struggles."[63] Romanov shows us that while Soviet policy became increasingly more compatible with IOC policies, it did not signal an end to occasional confrontation or animosity between the two.

What we have witnessed so far is a consistent and deliberate process of growth of sport in Soviet history from its emergence out of the Russian Revolution to the eve of the Moscow Summer Olympics. This period of more than sixty years saw stark contrasts in policy including isolationism, socialist sports systems, and eventual ascension into global sports organizations and the dominance of many of the sports competitions of these organizations. At the same time, a strengthening domestic policy that created a more conducive atmosphere for the growth of sport among Soviet citizens fostered increased interest in and political benefit from sports. Furthermore, the Soviet Union had also developed a series of goals for its sports policy and sports diplomacy. These goals would result in a consistent sports policy that emphasized the use of international sports to demonstrate the superiority of the socialist system, which would both broaden Soviet reach into the international arena by building their relations with many other states and also set clear requirements needed to be met before the Soviet Union would be allowed to enter into an international competition of any kind. This history sets the stage for a US-versus-USSR competition between athletes, host cities, and ownership of the title of "Best of Olympic Games ever," as Soviet success in sports is an inescapable metaphor for success of the Soviet system as a whole.

CHAPTER 4

MONTREAL, MOSCOW, AND LOS ANGELES
BIDDING FOR THE GAMES

AN INTRODUCTION TO THE COMPETITION OF BIDDING

Any discussion of the boycott of the 1984 Summer Olympics usually begins with the US boycott of the 1980 Summer Olympics, the result of a general belief among Western historians that the Soviet boycott was nothing more than retaliation for the 1980 American boycott. Indeed, it would be foolish on the part of anyone to dismiss the possibility that elements in the Supreme Soviet wanted a vengeance-oriented response to the US boycott of the Moscow Olympics. However, it would be equally (perhaps even more so) foolish to assume that there was no other explanation but tit-for-tat retribution. It is this latter assumption of Western historians and political scientists that this book seeks to challenge. By either ignoring outright or only cursorily considering the bidding process, researchers are skipping half the story. The events of the boycott of 1984 start in 1970, ten years before most other studies begin research. Tensions over Moscow and Los Angeles's selections for the Olympics were a decade old when Soviet military personnel crossed into Afghanistan.

The foundation of the conflict over the 1980 and the 1984 Olympics began at the sixty-ninth International Olympic Committee (IOC) session in Amsterdam, Netherlands, in May 1970. At this session, the IOC agenda included the selection of the 1976 Summer and Winter Games. The IOC selected Denver, Colorado, over close opponent Sion, Switzerland, for the Winter Olympics. The information in the minutes of the IOC's sixty-ninth session poses some very interesting questions and reveals significant facts. Three cities bid for the 1976 Summer Olympics: Los Angeles, Montreal, and Moscow. Of these, Montreal was selected. The story continued at the seventy-fifth session of the IOC, which took place in Vienna, Austria, in October 1974. At this session, the agenda of the IOC contained the selection of the 1980 Summer and Winter host cities. Since Lake Placid was the only city that bid for the Winter Games, it was not surprising that the Winter Olympics went to Lake Placid by a unanimous vote.[1] The Summer Olympics had two cities bidding: Los Angeles and Moscow. In this case, Moscow was selected. At the eightieth session of the IOC, the IOC members were to select the host city of the 1984 Summer and Winter Olympics. At this session, held in Athens, Greece, the Winter Olympics were awarded to Sarajevo, Yugoslavia, over Gothenburg, Sweden, and Sapporo, Japan. Los Angeles, which had the only bid for the Summer Olympics, was awarded the Summer Games.

On the surface, the host selection at the sixty-ninth, seventy-fifth, and eightieth IOC sessions seems straightforward. Two of the choices were simply rubber-stamped, as there was only one city bidding for those Games. Yet, instead of a simple decision process, complicated questions faced Los Angeles in 1978. The events of that decision, and the selection process for the previous two Olympiads, illustrated an already present and hostile atmosphere in the Olympics. One would assume that the dynamics behind this delicate and very argumentative process would have received more attention by academics. However, the fact remains that scholars investigating sports diplomacy and sports politics have primarily ignored the competition of the United States and the Soviet Union over the right to host the Olympics. What is even stranger is the fact that this competition has not been discussed in the context of the boycott problems of 1980 and 1984. This is especially surprising when there is evidence that the Soviet Union was against awarding the 1984 Olympics to Los Angeles from as early as 1978, two years before the actual US boycott that was, according to many historians, the "only cause" of the 1984 Soviet boycott.

To begin this investigation, we must first start with some background information on the actual process as well as a few notes on issues regarding the research for this question. First and foremost, bidding for the Olympics is not an exact science. It is impossible to completely describe the reason one city is selected over another, due to the fact that there is a degree of personal preference and opinion involved in the decision process. It is, for example, easy to point out failings in the transportation system and infrastructure in Osaka and

Istanbul's bids for the 2008 Summer Olympics as the reason they were not selected.[2] It is not as easy to explain why, in the final round of bidding, the IOC voted to place the 2008 Summer Olympics in Beijing, with Toronto in second place and Paris in third.[3] All three were what the Bid Committee referred to as strong bids by cities that could effectively host the Games.[4] Because of this, only generalizations can be made about any bid process unless all IOC members are asked to explain why they voted as they did. Currently there are no available reports of the voting rationales of IOC members. There is no doubt that some IOC member votes are politically driven, but to what extent that can be established and to what degree it affected the outcome of any given selection will have to fall to deductive reasoning based off of very limited resources.

The willingness of the IOC to put the Olympics in a particular area is important because the IOC has refused to consider a strong bid by some cities for no apparent reason. A good example is the recurring story of Sweden's attempts to host the Olympics. Sweden had numerous attempts, over a span of a few decades, to win the right to host, but they have been repeatedly refused with little public explanation. One possible explanation for Sweden's failures might rest in its neutrality during World War II and later during the Cold War. Sweden's decision to remain neutral meant that they lost the support of all sides. East and West supporters would vote for their respective allies, leaving very few nations to support Sweden. This would also explain the repeated failure of cities in Switzerland, most notably, Sion, which has had numerous bids to host the Winter Olympics. It should be noted that these more political decisions have been over which of two capable cities to give the Games to. There is no clear evidence to support any accusation that IOC members have *en masse* voted to support, for political reasons, a city that was incapable of hosting the Olympics.

Because IOC votes are not provable as objective and because there are political motivations attached to these decisions, we will not automatically assume the best city was chosen in each selection decision discussed in this book. Whether cities that were incapable to host were chosen is irrelevant, as the evidence will show that hosting the Olympics was well within the ability of Montreal, Moscow, and Los Angeles. What that will leave us with for analysis are the actual elements within the bids. Thus the emphasis of this chapter will turn to an evaluation and analysis of the bid process to host the Olympics of 1976, 1980, and 1984.

To accomplish this task, the most useful and interesting avenue of research turned out to be the actual discussions of the bids before the IOC. In these sessions, all information on each bid is formally presented to the members of the IOC. In the final session before a selection is made, the IOC members and the representatives of the international federations are given the opportunity to pose any questions and express their support or lack thereof. Once debate on the issue is finished, the IOC moves into voting procedures and makes their official selection. The minutes of the sessions cover the debating, question and answer periods, and the final announcement.

Among the events of the bid process, the analysis of the bid, through questions, helps to form a coherent understanding of the IOC's position on that city's preparedness. As the validity and viability of the Los Angeles Games are of particular interest, the terms and conditions of the Los Angeles Games are of critical importance. Therefore, this study must evaluate the responses of the IOC and the international federations to a city's bid, which means examining the minutes of the debates on the floor of the IOC becomes an excellent avenue of research. While some specifics on the plan to host, particularly matters relating to finance, security, and the Olympic program, are germane, the real focus is to determine the status of the Los Angeles bid, compared to Montreal and Moscow, while also gauging the position of several actors, most importantly the Soviet Union and the IOC, toward the Los Angeles Olympic Organizing Committee (LAOOC) and its bid.

This whole process will provide an overall understanding of the acceptability of the cities that are bidding as well as allowing for a sense of both how the elected city won and, more important, how and why the unchosen cities lost. Since this study primarily focuses on the Russian and American problems that led to the 1984 Soviet boycott, it will pertain mainly to bids for the Summer Olympics. The Winter Olympics will be discussed in a limited fashion here, only in reference to any impact the Winter Games had on the bid process for the Summer Olympics.

ROUND ONE: A CANADIAN SHOW STEALER?

The first critical step on the road to the boycotts was the selection of the hosts of the 1976 Games. In Amsterdam, in 1970, the IOC chose Denver, Colorado, and Montreal, Canada. Denver defeated the cities of Sion, Switzerland; Tampere, Finland; and Vancouver-Garibaldi, Canada. Three bid cities, Los Angeles, Montreal, and Moscow, presented their candidacy for the Summer Games.[5] The Los Angeles bidding committee, which consisted of John Kilroy, president of the 1976 Los Angeles committee; Sam Yorty, mayor of Los Angeles; and four others, received the most questions posed to the three delegations.[6]

Pollution was brought up as a problem, as was how the distribution of revenue would be handled. The Montreal team, which consisted of Montreal mayor Jean Drapeau; Pierre Charbonneau, president of the Canadian Athletics Federation; and three others, received only one question.[7] They were asked if the City of Montreal "would be ready to make a financial guarantee [deposit] of performance to the IOC."[8] As this question was, and still is, asked of all candidate cities, this does not indicate that there were any specific financial concerns.

The Moscow delegation, consisting of Constantin Andrianov, president of the Soviet National Olympic Committee (and IOC member), and four others,[9] also received a lot of questions. Several of these questions were previously fielded to the Los Angeles organizers, indicating similar concerns that threatened the Los Angeles bid. The sheer number of questions put to the Los Angeles and Moscow organizers shows there was a degree of concern about both bids. Specific questions to Moscow indicate that some of these concerns were enough to block Moscow's bid for the 1976 Games, such as Moscow's ability to handle a large number of spectators at its rowing and canoeing competitions. Questions referencing the financial viability of a Moscow Olympics were also a problem; there were direct concerns over the ability of the media market to generate revenue for the Moscow Games.[10]

From a brief look at this bidding process, two things can be gleaned immediately. First, the IOC and the international federations did not have noteworthy problems with Montreal's bid. This can be inferred from the lack of questions and the fact that the city won the bid. Furthermore, it can also be assumed that Moscow and Los Angeles both had problems with their bid. This is obvious since both cities were asked to justify the environmental and financial plans for their cities. At this point, a safe guess would be that Montreal would win and Moscow and Los Angeles would lose. When the votes of the two rounds of voting were tabulated, they were as follows:

Table 4.1   Balloting for 1976 Summer Games Host

Vote	Candidate	Ballots
Round 1	Moscow	28
	Montreal	25
	Los Angeles	17[11]
Round 2	Montreal	41
	Moscow	28
	Blank Ballots	1[12]

Montreal had been selected as the host in the final ballot, but there is more to the story than that. When the final vote was announced, the Moscow delegation was astonished. They had counted on winning the final ballot because the Soviets had won the first round of voting. To clarify, selection requires a majority in the vote, not a plurality. While Moscow got the most votes in round one, they failed to get the necessary majority that would constitute a victory. While Moscow received a plurality of the votes of round one, they would have to win in one more round in order to get the necessary majority. In this situation, the city that received the least number of votes, in this case Los Angeles, was dropped from the ballot and the second round of voting was held. So why did the Soviet Union fail to win in round two?

To understand why Moscow was able to come in first place in round one but only in second place in round two, you must understand the role state ideology can play in influencing the votes of IOC members. First, votes in the IOC were often split along ideological lines.[13] Some IOC members, when given a choice between a candidate that is an ally of their home state and one that is not, will select the candidate whose state has better relations with their state.[14] Building off this, when faced with the selection between two Western hosts, the better prepared of the two—Montreal—received more votes than Los Angeles. Therefore, Montreal comes in second place, and Los Angeles comes in third.

In round two, Los Angeles is no longer an option on the ballot. Therefore, every IOC voter that selected Los Angeles in round one now had to choose between Moscow and Montreal. It is not unreasonable to claim that Western-leaning IOC members, who split their votes between Montreal and Los Angeles, would now vote in favor of Montreal. In addition to this, it is worth noting that IOC members from countries with candidate cities are barred from voting. Since Los Angeles was no longer a candidate, IOC members from the United States were now eligible to vote, though as the vote totals are the same for both rounds, clearly the safest assumption is that the list of voters remained the same. In the event, however, there was a change in who voted, and IOC members from the United States were now among the votes cast. We can follow the previous logic and conclude that it is likely they would have voted for Montreal.

Considering the potential ideological motivations of the Los Angeles supporters and also considering Avery Brundage's recount of the successes of the Montreal bid in comparison to Moscow,[15] it should make sense why Moscow came in first place in the first vote and second place in the second vote. However, to eliminate any further doubt, let's consider the actual vote totals of each city in the two rounds. In round one, Moscow got 28 votes. In the second round, Moscow also received 28 votes. As Moscow remained on the ballot in both rounds, we will accept a simple assumption that everyone who thought Moscow was the best choice in round one did not suddenly change their mind with the absence of Los Angeles on the ballot. Moscow's second round vote total was the exact same as round one, so we can further state confidently that they did not gain a single vote when Los Angeles was removed from the ballot. Montreal, in round one, received 25 votes. In round two, Montreal earned 41 votes. The difference between the two, a total of 16 votes, is only one vote shy of indicating that 100 percent of the supporters of Los Angeles went for Montreal in round two, if you accept the aforementioned argument that none of Moscow's supporters voted differently in rounds one and two. Without knowing the actual the name and state affiliation of the voter who cast the blank ballot, there is no way to analyze or raise an argument with regard to that decision.

In short, whether it was because of the degree of preparedness of Montreal's bid or because of a love for Western ideology, a statistically significant number of IOC members that voted for Los Angeles voted for Montreal in round two. Montreal, as a presumably stronger bid, simply attracted more of its allies' votes than Los Angeles. When the second round of voting occurred, the Pan-American nations could no longer vote for Los Angeles and instead (assuming this ideological bias) sided with Montreal.[16]

In response to the decision, Constantin Andrianov stated that there were "no political, economic, or sporting reasons why Moscow should not be chosen."[17] Clearly, Andrianov would agree with my analysis that IOC voters were more likely to have been influenced by the ideology of the city's nation than being solely influenced by the character and strength of the bids of each city. This situation would not be repeated in 1974, when the host of the 1980 Games was chosen. Fortunately, with only two candidates for the 1980 Olympics, the added complexity of multiple rounds of voting was eliminated, and Moscow would not have to face two rounds of voting.

ROUND TWO: MUSCOVITE TRIUMPHANT

The 1974 IOC Session in Vienna was the location for the vote to place the 1980 Olympics in Lake Placid, New York, and Moscow, Soviet Union. Unlike the sixty-ninth session, the issue of host city selection was a lively debate. IOC members posed far more questions to the candidates than four years earlier. The questions that were posed to the candidates were also more in-depth than they had been at the sixty-ninth IOC session.

From an evaluation of the types of questions asked, it is clear that Moscow had an edge over Los Angeles. Philip O. Kruman, president of the United States Olympic Committee; Los Angeles mayor Thomas Bradley; and four others presented their candidate city.[18] It is important to note that this iteration of the Los Angeles bid was more carefully thought out than the previous presentation. The mayor announced the support of the Games by the US president, the California governor, and the people of Los Angeles. The bid also drew attention to Los Angeles's Olympic heritage. Regardless of its upgrades to the bid, Los Angeles's bid was not met with the enthusiasm that the Moscow bid received. The international federations questioned the existence of venues and warming-up/training areas.[19] In fact, the international federations were concerned with the overall plan of the layout of the venues. Taken together, the criticism of the international federations suggested that the Los Angeles bid was incomplete or at the very least lacking in some peripheral planning. Although none of the IOC members or the international federations outright dismissed the Los Angeles bid as a failure, none of them praised it either. To complicate matters for Los Angeles, the Moscow bid received the exact opposite response.

Constantin Andrianov, president of the Soviet National Olympic Committee (USSR NOC), introduced Moscow's candidacy. It also included Sergei Pavlov, chairman of the Preparatory Committee for Staging the 1980 Games, and four others.[20] Andrianov announced that Moscow was more than willing to stage the Olympics and expounded on the financial capacity of Moscow and the Soviet willingness to follow all IOC regulations and provisions. Even though Andrianov had addressed the major financial concerns that ended the Moscow bid four years earlier, the IOC members still had questions for the Moscow delegation, focusing primarily on the logistics of issues only indirectly related to the Olympics, such as currency conversion into rubles and how to facilitate the smooth arrival and departure of international media correspondence during the Games.[21] It seemed that the IOC members were content with the Moscow bid and saw no need to discuss the actual logistics of it. The international federations, on the other hand, did focus on the logistics of the Moscow bid.

The international federations openly praised the Moscow bid. The president of the *Association Internationale de Boxe Amateur*, Mr. Hogberg, stated that "his federation's Executive Committee supported Moscow's bid, since many other international sports competitions had been held in Moscow which assured them that their needs would be met."[22] The salutations continued. Even absentee international federations, for example FIFA, had sent their support of the Moscow bid through letters to the executives of the IOC.[23] This, of course, is not to say that support for Moscow was unanimous. Some international federations, especially the International Archery Federation (IAF), were not pleased with the planning. However, even with all their concerns, none of the international federations openly rejected the Moscow bid.

It was perfectly clear even before the vote had taken place that Moscow had the upper hand. Putting the actual bids aside, it is important to note that there were three other factors working against a Los Angeles bid for the 1980 Olympics. First, there was a great deal of support for Moscow to win solely because no socialist nation had hosted the Olympics before—not to mention that the Games were rarely held east of Athens.[24] Since Tokyo in 1964, Summer Games had been held in Mexico City, Mexico; Munich, West Germany; and Montreal, Canada. It had been 16 years since the Summer Olympics ventured eastward. This recent history of Olympic hosts added further justification to the Moscow bid.

Soviet grumbling and outright complaining that included accusations of collusion because the Olympics were awarded to two North American cities is the second factor.[25] Ever since the Olympic Movement started to grow during the 1960s, there have been attempts to share the Olympics. From the 1950s through the 1980s, the Summer Olympics were held in the following cities:

1952—Games of the XV Olympiad—Helsinki, Finland
1956—Games of the XVI Olympiad—Melbourne, Australia
1960—Games of the XVII Olympiad—Rome, Italy
1964—Games of the XVIII Olympiad—Tokyo, Japan
1968—Games of the XIX Olympiad—Mexico City, Mexico
1972—Games of the XX Olympiad—Munich, Germany
1976—Games of the XXI Olympiad—Montreal, Canada
1980—Games of the XXII Olympiad—Moscow, Soviet Union
1984—Games of the XXIII Olympiad—Los Angeles, United States
1988—Games of the XXIV Olympiad—Seoul, Republic of Korea

The Games were never held in the same continent for two Olympiads in a row. Montreal, a North American city, immediately weakened any other North American city's chances for the 1980 Olympics. The third and final factor had to do with the selection of the host city for the 1976 and 1980 Winter Olympics. The 1976 Olympics were awarded to Denver, Colorado. Later, the city of Denver would opt against hosting and the IOC held a special election to replace Denver with Innsbruck, Austria. In addition to this, it was a virtual guarantee that the Winter Olympics would again be awarded to the United States; Lake Placid, New York, was the only city to submit a bid for the 1980 Winter Games. The vote, more of a confirmation than anything, selected Lake Placid shortly before the IOC considered whether to give the Summer Olympics to Los Angeles or Moscow.

Whether Soviet claims of conspiracy were justified or not, it could not be ignored that putting the 1980 Winter Games in New York and the Summer Games in California would look suspicious, especially after the previous 1976 Winter and Summer Olympics were awarded to North American cities. All concerns of conspiracy aside, it is hard for the IOC to explain why it would bequeath such an honor on the same city twice,[26] while Moscow, in a nation that had yet to host the Olympics, was more than capable of hosting the Games. Also, it is worth noting that the IOC had not placed the Winter and Summer Olympics in the same nation since Germany held them both in 1936.

Taking all this into account, the Los Angeles organizers were fighting a completely uphill battle in their attempt to win the 1980 Olympics. Thus it should be no surprise that Los Angeles lost the Games to Moscow. Since there were only two candidates, the IOC only needed to hold one vote. Once the election was held, Lord Killanin, the IOC president at that time, announced that Moscow had won the election. He did, however, refuse to release the actual results of that election. The vote tallies were not placed in the IOC minutes and further inquiries into the results at that time were denied. This led supporters of the United States and its bid to question the validity of the decision. Such accusations were, however, largely dismissed due to the fact that Moscow had fared so well in the question and answer period of the IOC's inquiry earlier that day.

Inquiries made to the International Olympic Committee in 2001 resulted in the IOC opening the results of the election. The votes went as follows:

Table 4.2   Balloting for 1980 Summer Games Host

Vote	Candidate	Ballots[27]
Round 1	Moscow	39
	Los Angeles	20
	Abstentions	2

Since Moscow did get more than the simple majority required to win the election, there was only one round. Also, since there were no other rounds to compare votes with, and since the IOC does not record how specific IOC members voted, there is no way to further analyze these numbers. Furthermore, there is little point to comparing the results to those of sixty-ninth session, as there is no way to conclude whether specific IOC members voted for Moscow in two separate elections or if there were any other consistencies between the two elections. However, one observation is worth noting: nearly a two-thirds majority of the IOC ultimately voted in favor of Moscow.

Moscow received 39 votes in the 1974 election and received 28 votes in the 1969 election. Assuming that everyone who voted for Moscow in the first election voted for it again in 1974, then 11 supporters of Montreal or Los Angeles in 1970 voted for Moscow in 1974. Was this a sign that IOC members were being less ideologically motivated? Or was this a sign that Los Angeles's bid was plagued with enough problems that it was enough to keep some IOC representatives from maintaining an ideological stance in their vote? There is one piece of evidence—namely, the IOC's concerns with the Los Angeles bid four years later—that suggests that, regardless of what city Los Angeles was up against, it was likely to lose. At the meeting in 1978, the IOC placed conditions on Los Angeles's right to host. The IOC's decision to put the 1984 Games in Los Angeles was less than a confident endorsement. In fact, before even discussing the conditions, let's first explain why a bid with as many problems as Los Angeles was allowed to host.

ROUND THREE: THE LOS ANGELES GAME OF SOLITAIRE

At the eightieth session of the IOC, in Athens, Greece, in 1978, Los Angeles was the only city bidding for the Summer Olympics. The Montreal Olympics had been a financial disaster. Although historians now know that the financial failure of the Games and the near bankruptcy of the city were due to the ill-controlled expenditures of the Montreal organizing committee, the details of the cause of the financial mess were not known when cities were deciding whether to bid for the Summer Games of 1984. The Olympics had suddenly become a risky financial endeavor.

This was not a unique situation. The 1974 Vienna session considered only two Summer Olympic candidates and one Winter Olympics candidate because of other risk factors. In this case, the election took place two years after the 1972 Munich disaster, which saw a terrorist attack take hostage and then kill several Israeli athletes. This political turmoil, coupled with the fact that the bids from the Soviet Union and the United States were intimidating to smaller bidders and first-time bidders, kept the competition down for the 1980 and 1984 Summer Olympics. The lack of bidders, however, did not force the IOC to compromise on its expectations of hosts. Issues with the Los Angeles bid and challenges in negotiations between the IOC and the bid committee give us a compelling argument for why Los Angeles lost its bid to Moscow four years earlier. It also sets the stage for concerns with Los Angeles by the Soviet Union and other states.

A major issue that kept Los Angeles from winning the bid was that Los Angeles was unwilling to accept the contract as it was initially written between the IOC and the host city. At first, the Los Angeles organizers sent its own contract to the IOC, one that the IOC could not possibly sign. The fact that no other city was bidding to host the Olympics meant that Los Angeles was in a position to make demands on the IOC. Some IOC members, especially Soviet representative Constantin Andrianov, however, challenged their position. In the debate on the city selection, Andrianov remarked,

> Los Angeles' presentation the previous day had not confirmed that the NOC, in accordance with the IOC rules, guaranteed the organization of the Olympic Games; furthermore the candidature was submitted by the Southern California Committee for the Olympic Games, a philanthropic organization that had no legal right to represent the city or the NOC. As far as the technical organization was concerned, Los Angeles claimed that the games could be held tomorrow, yet there was no rowing course, no canoe course, no shooting range, no hockey pitch, and distances between some venues were too great. Altogether 17 IF's [international federations governing the individual sports competitions] had criticized the installations. The answers to the questionnaire were unsatisfactory and Los Angeles was exploiting the fact that they were the only candidate city to enforce their conditions.[28]

While a bit of an exaggeration, this statement contained some worthwhile facts. The Los Angeles committee did not present a very effective bid, and statements about the malcontent of the international federations were not exaggerations. Andrianov went on to propose the decision be postponed for three months so that Los Angeles could restructure its bid in accordance with IOC regulations and to give other cities the chance to submit a bid.[29]

Eventually, the IOC had to decide on the matter. The decision they made broke new ground, since it did not actually award the Games completely. The IOC announcement was as follows: "The Games of the XXIII Olympiad to be provisionally awarded to the city of Los Angeles subject to the city's entering into a contract in accordance with the Olympic rules and in the form prescribed by the International Olympic Committee, before 1st August 1978. In the Event of such a contract not being signed by 1st August 1978, the provisional award of the Games of the XXIII Olympiad to Los Angeles be withdrawn and new applications called for."[30] The decision was hardly a vote of confidence. It forced Los Angeles to find a reasonable degree of agreement with the IOC on a contract that was within the rules of the Olympic Charter. It was also the first time the IOC gave a conditional award and threatened, in writing, to revoke a city's selection to host. So what led the IOC to accept the Los Angeles bid as is in August of 1978 when it was not willing to do so several months earlier?

The main point of contention between the IOC and the bid team was the contract. All IOC philosophy on the process of hosting supported their assertion that the host city financially supports the Olympics in order to guarantee the extravagance of the Olympic Games. Building off this, Rule 34 of the 2004 version of the Olympic Charter explicitly requires a host city to assume financial liability of the Games.[31] The charter has been amended several times since then, but this requirement remains an integral part of the agreement to host by a state.[32] The LAOOC, which was formed between the original announcement of the IOC and the deadline for compliance with IOC rules, remained adamant on its stance that the Los Angeles Olympics be a private enterprise. Los Angeles Mayor Tom Bradley also proved unyielding on the issue. The IOC, even faced with this degree of adamancy, initially refused to give in.

The crisis reached its critical turning point when "a frustrated Bradley responded by recommending that Los Angeles withdraw its bid to host the 1984 Games."[33] This very staunch, almost antagonistic response, by the mayor surprised IOC officials. Since the IOC still had no viable alternatives to Los Angeles, and sensing the general membership of the IOC's lack of a continued effort to fight Los Angeles, IOC President Lord Killanin gave in. The agreement reflecting the spirit of the contract that Los Angeles suggested, including the provision for the Games to be privately organized without the financial liability of the city, was accepted by the IOC. In its decision, the IOC specifically had to exempt the LAOOC and the city of Los Angeles from Rule 34 of the charter.

Now able to move forward, the LAOOC defined its mission thus: "[T]o operate an Olympic games of the highest quality and to realize a surplus of revenues over expenditures at the time of final accounting."[34] Taken as a whole, there is a lot to analyze in this irregular selection process. The situation at the eightieth IOC session is an important piece of evidence to support Soviet assertions that there were rampant problems with the Los Angeles Games. Constantin Andrianov's aforementioned speech at the eightieth session will suffice as the most telling example of the concerns of the IOC and the Soviet Union over the selection of Los Angeles.

The city selection process of the 1970s turned the opportunity to host the Summer Olympics into a competition. The competitiveness in sport between the two superpowers now reached into the decision processes of the IOC. The Soviet Union's response to the selection of Montreal and Denver in 1970 shows that its government had taken the decisions personally and viewed the selections as a conspiracy. Allen Guttmann reported that "there were angry comments from TASS, the Soviet news agency, to the effect that the 'capitalists' had ganged up to deny the 'socialists' an opportunity to host the games."[35] The Soviet Union stepped up its efforts to host and put forth an even more impressive bid in 1974. The accusations of Andrianov and the clear increase in the quality of the Soviet bid justify statements that the Soviet Union viewed this effort as a competition. The response of American side of the competition also justifies this statement.

The Los Angeles delegation proved it was an issue of East versus West in a statement of Los Angeles mayor Thomas Bradley. He stated that Los Angeles could "ensure the success of the Games without propaganda, and . . . could guarantee free movement not only within the city but within the whole of the United States for all participants, officials, press, etc."[36] Most Olympic bids contain comments claiming that their city is the best prepared in some manner. These statements usually relate directly to issues in hosting the Olympics. There was not a previous example of one bid team attacking another. The comments by the Los Angeles mayor are nothing more than petty attacks on the ideology of the Soviet Union. Even if the statements by Mayor Bradley had merit, they were not germane to Moscow's capacity to host or why Los Angeles was a better choice.

Bradley's statements offer another piece of evidence that Los Angeles was not prepared to host in 1980 and likely were not prepared to do so in 1984. His statement was an attempt to discredit the Moscow bid, making it look like a dangerous choice for the IOC, and thus garner a victory for Los Angeles based on Moscow's "failures." This was in sharp contrast to the Moscow team's presentation that emphasized all the methods that Moscow was to implement in order to follow IOC regulations and successfully host the Olympics. Obviously, Los Angeles's strategy failed since the IOC was most impressed with Moscow's plans and gave no heed to Bradley's concerns.

It should come as no surprise that a rivalry among host cities existed. Each city tried to out-do the others in preparation, extravagance, and their overall ability to host the Games. In time, financial success would be added to the list. This, in fact, was part of the cause of the failure of Montreal's Olympics. The city overspent nearly every budget line in an attempt to create an extremely extravagant location. To Montreal's credit, the Expo Center is a fine example of architecture, featured in its leaned tower and removable roof. These excesses were all attempts to outshine the Munich Games of 1972.

Moscow had no difficulty in surpassing Montreal's success story (or lack thereof). But whoever followed Moscow would be in competition to out-do the Soviets. Los Angeles, the only city bidding at the 1978 Athens session, was being given the opportunity to show just how good they could have been in 1980 by giving them the chance to demonstrate that ability in 1984. Why else would Andrianov have been so critical of the Los Angeles bid? In his speech, quoted previously, he openly called for the IOC to give other cities the time to submit a bid to compete with Los Angeles. It is safe to state that Andrianov and the rest of the Soviet political and sporting hierarchy did not want Los Angeles and Moscow competing for the bragging rights of hosting "the best games yet held." A competition between Moscow and Los Angeles existed in 1970 and 1974. Neither city was able to claim a complete victory, and both accused the IOC of playing favorites in an attempt to discredit the choices of Montreal and Moscow.

There was no competition in 1978, but if Los Angeles had won the Games, the competition between the two cities would have started immediately after Los Angeles was awarded the Games and would have then continued until both cities had hosted the Olympics. The decision of which city was the most successful would then be up to the international community. They would judge, in a process that neither the Soviet Union nor the United States would have much control over, which system was more successful at organizing something as important and prestigious as the Olympics.

The entire situation functions as an excellent example of a surrogate war, as both states, and their respective political and economic systems, were pitted in discrete competition with each other where the rest of the world would be free to judge the winner. Not only was the competition itself a source of East-versus-West conflict and contest, but the bid process had become that as well, and with the confirmation of the IOC in August of 1978, the competition between host cities took on the flavor of all other Olympic competitions since 1952. This is the first of two likely reasons the Soviet Union had to boycott the 1984 Olympics. Their refusal to participate would short circuit any claim to host "the best Olympics" by the Los Angeles organizers by not allowing the United States to claim that an unboycotted Los Angeles Olympics was an ipso facto better Games than the boycotted Moscow Olympics.

Regardless of the clear advantage that Los Angeles now had in the comparison game, the Soviet Union was already committed to the surrogate war and now had to take those steps necessary to win. While the Soviet Union had a history of selecting when and where it would compete with the West, any understanding of their decision to host must be based on their assessment of the situation back in the 1970s and excluding the events of 1980. The Soviet Union was in unfamiliar territory, as they were engaged in a surrogate war in which the United States had the perceived upper hand. The competition between Moscow and Los Angeles would be out of the hands of the Politburo. Moscow and Los Angeles would be compared, and there was nothing either side could do but try their best to be judged above their rivals.

The whole world would judge these two cities on their organizational, political, financial, and other abilities. Taking into account both Soviet sports diplomacy to date and the facts of the bidding process, it is more than reasonable to assume that the Soviet Union would weigh the pros and cons of attending the Los Angeles Games. If they saw more risk in attendance than potential benefits, it makes perfect sense that the Soviet Union would boycott for reasons of their own well-established international sports policy.

CHAPTER 5

1980

AN AMERICAN WINTER AND A SOVIET SUMMER

PRECURSOR TO 1980

Once the International Olympic Committee (IOC) got past the complications of the bidding process for 1984, politics, especially Cold War politics, in the Olympics appeared to abate. It was a welcomed rest for the IOC. During the period from 1969 to 1978, the principle years of the bidding processes discussed in this study, the IOC weathered the boycotts, the massacre in Munich (1972), the dissolution of a unified German team in favor of teams representing the Federal Republic of (West) Germany and the (East) German Democratic Republic, and the continued problems with the two-China issue. This latter issue crescendoed at the 1976 Montreal Olympics, where the Canadian government made things even harder by refusing the admittance of athletes from Taiwan at the request of the People's Republic of China.

The IOC requires the government of the country containing the host city to admit all delegations recognized by the IOC. Prior to the Montreal Olympics, Canada had a one-China policy in effect. After the IOC selected Montreal as host, Canada opted against this policy by trying to block Taiwan's participation. While the IOC attempted to gain an equitable compromise between the three nations, Taiwanese officials felt insulted at the offer and boycotted, while the People's Republic of China withdrew because of Canada's approval of the IOC suggestion that Taiwan compete under that name.

The China issue was not the only one to complicate matters for the IOC. A foolhardy move by New Zealand to disobey FIFA's policies regarding the international sports ban of South Africa enraged a coalition of national Olympic committees and other international sports groups in Africa. As stated earlier, several African states boycotted the Montreal Games, in addition to the two Chinas who boycotted for their own reasons. Once the Montreal Games ended, however, most of the controversy went silent.

With the debacle in Montreal behind the IOC, and the decision to allow Los Angeles to host the 1984 Olympics also decided, the IOC only had two main issues with which to contend: to figure out the problems that led to the financial crisis of the Montreal Games and to continue to search for a solution to the China problem. Montreal overspent on the Games as well as poorly organized them in many respects. The result of these mistakes was a debt that broke $1 billion.[1] Financial issues were not a very pressing topic from 1976 to 1980, because Moscow and Lake Placid had more realistic financial plans in their initial bids. Lake Placid had a healthier financial plan for a smaller and less ostentatious Games. Moscow planned on having an extravagant event, and therefore the Kremlin was expecting to dole out a lot of money. In the end, they would spend more than $9 billion on the 1980 Summer Olympics.[2]

Lake Placid also had a fiscal responsibility plan. As a former host of the Olympics in 1932, Lake Placid already had facilities for the Olympics. Granted they were now more than forty years old, but many of the structures only needed to be updated or expanded. In short, the same privatization strategy that would make Los Angeles cost effective was implementable in Lake Placid four years earlier. Finances, while definitely a question the IOC would have to address, were not a pressing matter that needed to be solved by the 1980 Games in two years. China, however, remained an issue.

During the period between the Montreal Summer Olympics and the Lake Placid Winter Olympics, the IOC and many nations worked diligently to solve the problem of the official names of the two Chinese delegations. In the end, no one involved was able to solve the problem in a manner that would keep Taiwan from boycotting. The People's Republic seemed open to competition but inevitably would stay away from both Lake Placid and Moscow due to continued questions of the status of Taiwan and because of the boycotts that would eventually be raised against Moscow. Their nonparticipation, however, was not in support of the boycott. Instead, the ascension of the People's Republic of China was delayed as a result of the wealth of political issues and because the Chinese realized that any involvement in 1980 would be perceived as an act in support of either American or Soviet interests over the boycott.

While the two-China issue would continue to be a problem for a few more years, the South African issue was quickly coming to a close. The

IOC, the United Nations, and the Supreme Council for Sport in Africa (SCSA) worked to solve the problem. The Soviet Union, with every intention of avoiding an African boycott, worked directly with the SCSA to convince it not to boycott because of the attendance of states that had relations with apartheid South Africa. The Soviets proved successful at this endeavor. The final result was that African states overlooked the participation of states that competed with South Africa in return for South Africa's continued expulsion from the Olympic Movement.

Beyond these specific issues, the IOC had general concerns over the Moscow and Los Angeles Games. These concerns were only political, as the financial fiasco in Montreal was not expected to happen in either Moscow or Los Angeles. The official backing of the Soviet Central Committee for the Moscow Games and the present infrastructure and fiscal planning for the Los Angeles Games sufficiently allayed fiscal concerns in either city.

Focusing on the Moscow Games for now, the greatest concern was in the Soviet Union's political position vis-à-vis certain states, especially Israel.[3] The general concern, as IOC president Lord Killanin noted in his memoirs, was that the Soviet Union would seek grounds to not invite states it did not recognize.[4] Killanin also noted some general concern with the setup and design of a communist sports event, but he conceded that the Soviet Bloc had endured a capitalist design for so many years and that it was only fair that the Soviet Union presented itself, its state, and its identity just as previous hosts had had the right to do.

According to Killanin, none of these concerns came to any fruition, as the Soviet Union was more than diligent in guaranteeing they followed every IOC protocol. This is not to suggest that there were not issues with Moscow's planning. They are, however, irrelevant to the topic at hand.[5] The main goal of this chapter is to both turn attention to the facts of the Soviet Union's opportunity to host the Olympics (coupled with the American boycott) and to briefly discuss political matters at the Winter Olympics, both 1980 and 1984, to bolster the reader's understanding of the roles these events did or did not play in the Soviet boycott. Therefore, this chapter will continue chronologically, starting with the Lake Placid Winter Olympics.

LAKE PLACID: A RELATIVE CALM BEFORE THE STORMS

As painstaking as the bid process was and as disconcerting the potential Western boycott of Moscow became, the IOC and the Lake Placid organizers managed a successful Winter Games. The Games had a distinct aura of tension, particularly owing to the American-proposed boycott. Timing was the main issue, as the Soviet invasion of Afghanistan took place in the waning weeks of 1979 and the push for a boycott began in the first two weeks of January 1980. All this occurred before the Lake Placid Winter Olympics, which took place February 12–24, 1980. Because of the heightened political state of the Olympic Movement at that time, the Lake Placid Games were a delicate affair.

Regardless of the persisting international climate, the Lake Placid Games, much like every other edition of an Olympic Games, had its problems and surprises. Most of these matters turn out to be irrelevant to the drama that unfolded in Moscow and again in Los Angeles. One incident, however, is potentially relevant to this analysis: the outcome of the hockey tournament. At the Lake Placid Games, the Soviet Union, which had been favored to win gold, were upset in the aptly named Miracle on Ice, wherein the United States, who was not expected to place in hockey, took the gold.

The outcome of the hockey tournament is important for two main reasons. First, the match was very much an underdog story that was seen as pitting American youths against the Soviet sports machine. Second, the Iranian hostage situation and the situation in Afghanistan created an atmosphere that was very much ready for an opportunity that would rally Americans to their own flag. In short, the victory was important, not just because it happened, but because it was very well timed. Building off of that, the victory becomes important because of how it has been used in some scholarly circles. Certainly, the unexpected loss of the Soviet team rattled the Soviet National Olympic Committee (USSR NOC), but it left the Soviet Union no less transfixed on their main goal for 1980: the successful hosting of the Moscow Games.

It is an interesting suggesting that the loss rattled the Soviet Union enough to fear contests at the Los Angeles Games, but these theories prove unlikely. In addition to those arguments made elsewhere in this study, it is worth noting that the Soviet Union was back on track in 1984, taking gold in Sarajevo's hockey tournament. The loss in 1980 becomes a mere blip on the radar; Soviet sports continued as planned in the 1980 and 1984 Winter Olympics. Losing gold in hockey did not upset their eventual placement above the United States in final rankings, and there was no indication, in Soviet or American sources, that would suggest the Soviet Union was actually concerned enough to boycott an Olympiad.

To summarize, with the exception of the outcome of the ice hockey tournament, the Lake Placid Olympics were relatively uneventful and the outcomes of the medal totals were similarly unsurprising. While the politics of the Soviet invasion of Afghanistan began prior to these Games, there simply is no evidence that these Games were significantly affected by it. There is also little evidence that events at Lake Placid would have a significant impact on the next three Olympic Games. The United States began the whole Olympic crisis of 1980 when it decided to use the Moscow Summer Olympics as its platform to protest Soviet involvement in Afghanistan. Moscow, at least for Lake Placid, clearly resisted any temptation to do the same. While at a quiet growl in early 1980, politics and political abuses of the Olympics roared back to life and remained alive the remainder of 1980 up to and through the Los Angeles Olympics.

MOSCOW IN CRISIS

The predominant cause of the boycott of 1980 began in December 1979 when the Soviet Union sent troops into Afghanistan, reportedly at the request of the Afghan government. The Soviet Union occupied Afghanistan, forcing the United States to respond to what it felt was an illegal action by the Soviet Union. US president Jimmy Carter announced as early as January 1980 that the action taken by the Soviet Union was grounds for the United States to boycott the Moscow Olympics. The threat came rather quickly, and the Soviet Union was quick to respond with accusations that the United States was abusing the Olympic Movement with political maneuvers.[6] Whether to prove its point or because the issue seemed irrelevant to the Kremlin, the Soviet Union attended the Lake Placid Games while it continued to voice its opposition to American intentions to boycott five months later. By opposing an American politicization of the Games, the Soviet Union removed any future possibility of a similar boycott without invoking accusations of hypocrisy and prompted a more carefully crafted policy of official "noninvolvement" as part of Soviet sports nomenclature four years later.

Within the Soviet attendance in Lake Placid, and the rhetoric of both Moscow and Washington with reference to Afghanistan and the Summer Olympics, we find keen insights to the role the events of the Moscow Games would play four years later. Therefore, a better understanding of those events, especially the dialogue over the boycott, offers some insights into the Soviet decision four years later. President Jimmy Carter, in a speech to the nation on January 4, 1980, indicated that a boycott was a likely response to Soviet action in Afghanistan. He stated, "Although the United States would prefer not to withdraw from the Olympic Games scheduled in Moscow this summer, the Soviet Union must realize that its continued aggressive actions will endanger both the participation of athletes and travel to Moscow of spectators who would normally wish to attend the Olympic Games."[7]

Only a few weeks later, this decision turned from a threat to a reality and ushered in the boycott years. Unlike the following Soviet "nonparticipation," the US boycott was for reasons strictly not involved with the Olympic Games and as such was simply and tersely defined. Functionally, the Soviet Union only needed to pull out of Afghanistan to avoid an American boycott. US demands were not complex in their formulation or argument, yet it was unrealistic to expect the Soviet Union to reverse such a public and dynamic foreign policy action. While America's policy created very simple looking surrogate brinkmanship, it misconstrued the true complexity of the decision the Soviet Union had to make.

Surrogate brinkmanship becomes a useful term in this regard as it functions as an extension of our use of the term *surrogate war*. We can see this situation as a form of brinkmanship in which the United States handed decision-making power to the Soviet Union by binding its decision to boycott to a Soviet decision process. A true brinkmanship in this regard could have been a scenario where the United States threatens to declare war if the Soviet Union did not acquiesce to American demands for a withdrawal. The game of sports policy, through boycott, became its surrogate, and the United States was able to create a theoretically nonlethal brinkmanship whose escalation would avoid actual war but will still provide what the United States perceived to be a significant penalty for noncompliance.

Regardless of the justifiability of America's choice to link Afghanistan and the Moscow Olympics, the United States decided to do so and then turned to its allies in hopes of getting them to join the boycott as well. This was much harder than one might think. In the end, the US-led boycott would attract 62 countries to join its ranks. Absent from the boycott, however, was the elite of Europe. Of all Western Europe, only West Germany, Liechtenstein, Norway, and Monaco boycotted the Moscow Games.[8]

Interestingly enough, several of the European teams were able to circumvent the positions of the governments of their countries. The governments of Britain and France both indicated a lack of interest in attending. France went so far as to outright call for French withdrawal from the Games. However, both states competed at the Olympics, but not under their own national flags. The national Olympic committees of both states declared their intentions of going without the permission of their respective governments. British and French athletes arrived in the Olympic Stadium led by the Olympic flag during the opening ceremonies.[9] Officially, the governments of France and Britain were not represented in the affair—but their people were. To use the terminology of Chapter 2, the *states* of Great Britain and France boycotted, while the *nations* of the two were both competing in the Games. The United States Olympic Committee (USOC) and the US government also did not agree on the Moscow situation. The French, British, and other NOCs got away with challenging their respective governments because IOC rules, which governments had to accept to form a NOC, mandate that decisions on their involvement with the Olympic Movement be made by the NOCs. This rule also allowed the USOC to protest the boycott by the United States. The USOC, along with several athletes, challenged Carter's assertion. The result of which was a series of confrontations between the two organizations until such time as the USOC was swayed into accepting the terms of the US government. The USOC were asked to bring to the IOC a request to postpone, cancel, or relocate the Games.

The Soviet Union was less than pleased with the turnout for the Moscow Games: 62 nations boycotted, 14 NOCs sent athletes without the support of their governments, and 66 NOCs participated with their states' support. In total, 80 nations attended the Moscow Games. The Soviet Union made it no secret that they were looking forward to the opportunity to enhance the prestige of their state at the same time as trumpeting the value of the socialist system. While it is true that they were able to do both, its affect was much more limited. With 62 states boycotting, and therefore not receiving the telecast of the Games, the message of the Soviet Union only met its allies and those neutral states that were willing to ignore US pressures to boycott.

Beyond issues of pride, the boycott also meant economic problems for the Soviet Union. The mayor of Moscow stated that the anticipated attendance of tourists was dropped from 300,000 to 70,000.[10] Because of inconsistencies in the figures of how much Moscow spent to host 1980, as well as the difference between the expected and actual revenues of the Olympic Games, it is impossible to accurately express the economic losses incurred due to the boycott. But, with a reduction of more than 75 percent of expected attendance, we can surmise that the actual revenue was far lower than the expected revenue, regardless of whether that final amount meant the overall balance of the Moscow Olympics was positive or negative. My inclination is to think that the fact that the Moscow organizers were not announcing a profit on the Games suggests that they were either a loss or an insignificant profit.

Beyond economics and prestige, there were other political ramifications for the Soviet Union as a result of the boycott. In Chapter 2, we established that the Soviet Union placed a great deal of importance on their international sports involvement, and in Chapter 4 we established the importance they placed on the opportunity to host the Olympics. From this evidence, we can make statements on the Soviet view of the impact of the boycott against them. For the Soviet Union, the Olympics were an opportunity to further legitimize their political and economic system to many nations. With a wide-scale (nearly 50 percent of national Olympic committees) boycott of the Soviet Olympics, the ability of a socialist state, a command economy, and specifically the Soviet political system to handle a major international political event was not demonstrated. These issues led inevitably to a comparison between Moscow and Montreal.

Before the boycott happened, there was no comparison as to which city did a better job. Montreal ran a deficit that almost bankrupted the city and began opening ceremonies with the Olympic Stadium still not fully constructed. In addition, the situation with New Zealand and South Africa and the situation between the two Chinas resulted in a boycott of several states. The assumption was that as long as Moscow was well organized, it should have had no difficulty surpassing Montreal as an effective host. However, the unexpected events of the boycott eliminated that possibility.

Because of the US-led boycott, Moscow was no longer looked at as an unquestionable success. Montreal's political failures to avoid boycott pale in comparison to the magnitude of the boycott against Moscow. A 75 percent reduction in revenues due to absent spectators reduced financial expectations enough that Moscow was no longer able to demonstrate economic strength compared to Montreal. In fact, some states, especially in the United States and its allies, claimed that the Moscow Games were a failure. The IOC, wisely, stayed out of these comparisons between Montreal and Moscow, because they did not want to foster an even more competitive atmosphere surrounding the same question in reference to Moscow and Los Angeles.

LEGACY OF 1980

Soviet sports history and the competition between the Soviet Union and the United States both tell a story of continued efforts at showcasing the greatness of the socialist system. In this Olympic rivalry, the Soviet Union endured two humiliating defeats. While the Soviet Union could limit damages with selective press coverage to a domestic audience, it was powerless to influence interpretations in most of the international community. As a result, the Soviet Union simply had to act strategically when it came to 1984.

The authority of the Soviet sports machine, in competition, may have been shaken, but it was certainly not destroyed. Chapter 3 alerted us to Soviet tendencies of refusing to compete if victory was less than guaranteed. With a significant defeat in an American Olympics in 1980, there was a reasonable assumption that this could again be the case. Not the least of those claiming that the Soviets were intimidated to compete was Peter Ueberroth, president of the Los Angeles Olympic Organizing Committee. Ueberroth stated that he "believe[d] completely without question that before Sarajevo,[11] the week before, the day before, all systems were go for their [USSR] competing in the games . . . they didn't do well, and this is way underestimated in the eyes of the west. And they were severely criticized at home because they did so poorly."[12] Such a statement has no backing in the statistics of previous sports encounters between the United States and the Soviet Union. But the question still remains whether this is accurate. Did the events of 1980 so terrify the Russian government that they stayed away from Los Angeles in fear of defeat? While the Miracle on Ice, without doubt a classic David and Goliath story, was an embarrassment to the Soviet sports machine, suggestions that the Soviet Union's sports system was faltering are simply unsupportable.

Even though the Soviet Union lost gold in the ice hockey tournament, the Soviet Union still left Lake Placid with the largest number of medals. Soviet sports achievements in Lake Placid dwarfed those of the United States. The medal count for the top three states were as follows:

Table 5.1   Medal Count for the Soviet Union, the German Democratic Republic, and the United States at the Lake Placid Winter Olympics

State	Gold	Silver	Bronze	Total[13]
Soviet Union	10	6	6	22
German Democratic Republic	9	7	7	23
United States	6	4	2	12

Both the Soviet Union and East Germany nearly doubled the total number of medals that the United States won in Lake Placid. It was an across-the-board defeat, as the United States did not even win more medals of any specific type either. Therefore, while the US-versus-USSR hockey tournament was an unexpected success for the United States, it is impossible to suggest that the Soviet Union lost anything more than a symbolic victory in Lake Placid.

In fairness to the argument that a failing sports complex concerned the Soviet Union enough that ultimate defeat in Los Angeles was a reality, let us also consider the overall trajectory of Soviet competition in the Olympics. The Soviet Union had as strong a showing as in previous Olympiads as in Lake Placid. By examining the medal results of the Lake Placid Olympics, the performance of the Soviet Union would seem relatively consistent. If one had to argue a trend, then the following table would suggest a general strengthening of the Soviet Union's sports complex. The Soviet Union had the following medal counts at the following Winter Games:

Table 5.2   USSR Total Medal System (Winter Games)

Year	Gold	Silver	Bronze	Total	Rank*
1968	5	5	3	13	2
1972	8	5	3	16	1
1976	13	6	8	27	1
1980	10	6	6	22	1
1984	6	10	9	25	1

*Rank refers to the order of nations based on total number of medals. In 1968, Norway won 14 medals, taking first place, just one medal more than the Soviet Union.

Table 5.3   Winter Olympic Medals Point Scoring System*

Year	1st Place		2nd Place		3rd Place	
	Points	State	Points	State	Points	State
1968	32	Norway	28	USSR	23	France
1972	37	USSR	28	GDR	24	Switzerland
1976	59	USSR	38	GDR	28	USA
1980	48	USSR	48	GDR	19	USA
1984	51	GDR	47	USSR	30	Switzerland

*Many nations created a point-scoring system to show how one nation did better than another. No system was ever adopted by the IOC, for two reasons. First, the competitions were supposed to be between individuals or teams, not nations. Second, the differences in the system were irreconcilable. For this study, the simplest system—that of awarding three points for every gold, two points for every silver, and one point for every bronze—will be used, since the goal of this chart is to show the relative consistency of the Soviet Union's performance and not to attempt to accurately judge the level of accomplishment of one national team over others.

As the previous two tables suggest, the Soviet Union had been improving, albeit slowly, its performance level in each Winter Olympics. What is evident by Table 5.3 is that East Germany was also improving, but at a pace faster than the Soviet Union. The differences in the total medal count and the total points that the Soviet Union earned in 1980 and 1984 are not significant enough to suggest that there was need for a great deal of concern. Furthermore, in Table 5.3, the United States never placed higher than third place, and the only US ally on the list is France. Therefore, Ueberroth's comments on the failure of the Soviet Union's team in Sarajevo, or others' suggestions of failure in Lake Placid, are unsubstantiated by the data that reflects a strengthening Soviet sports system.

Before finally dismissing this argument, it is still possible to suggest that Soviet concerns were over direct competition with the United States instead of their overall success in the Olympics. Table 5.4 quickly looks at the only previous Olympiads where the Soviet Union competed in an American host city. In both cases, there is no evidence that "home-court advantage" was a significant influence in outcomes of medal totals for the United States and the Soviet Union.

Table 5.4   Medal Counts for the Soviet Union and the United States at US-hosted Olympiads.*

Olympiad	State	Gold	Silver	Bronze	Total
Squaw Valley, California (1960 Winter Olympics)					
	Soviet Union	7	5	9	21
	United States	3	4	3	8
Lake Placid, New York (1980 Winter Olympics)					
	Soviet Union	10	6	6	22
	United States	6	4	2	12

* St. Louis (1904), Lake Placid (1932), and Los Angeles (1932) are omitted because the Soviet Union either did not exist (1904) or was not a member of the Olympic Movement (1932) at that time.

Tables 5.5 and 5.6 chart the outcome of Soviet and American athletic efforts at the Summer Olympics from 1952, the first year the Soviet Union competed, up through 1976. The Moscow Games are excluded for the obvious reason that the United States was absent, making comparison impossible.

The outcome remains constant regardless of which table you analyze. The United States came in first place in 1952, 1964, and 1968. The Soviet Union came in first place in 1956, 1960, 1972, and 1976.

Table 5.5 Total Medal System (Summer Games)

Olympiad	State	Gold	Silver	Bronze	Total	Rank*
1952 Helsinki						
	USA	40	19	17	76	1
	USSR	22	30	19	71	2
1956 Melbourne						
	USA	32	25	17	74	2
	USSR	37	29	32	98	1
1960 Rome						
	USA	34	21	16	71	2
	USSR	43	29	31	103	1
1964 Tokyo						
	USA	36	26	28	90	1
	USSR	30	31	25	86	2
1968 Mexico City						
	USA	45	28	34	107	1
	USSR	29	32	30	91	2
1972 Munich						
	USA	33	31	30	94	2
	USSR	50	27	22	99	1
1976 Montreal						
	USA	34	35	25	94	2
	USSR	49	41	35	125	1

* Rank refers to the order of nations based on total number of medals.

Table 5.6   Point Scoring System* (Summer Games)

Year	1st Place		2nd Place		3rd Place	
	Points	State	Points	State	Points	State
1952	175	USA	135	USSR	84	Hungary
1956	201	USSR	163	USA	69	Australia
1960	218	USSR	160	USA	85	Italy
1964	188	USA	177	USSR	64	Japan
1968	225	USA	181	USSR	62	GDR
1972	226	USSR	191	USA	129	GDR
1976	264	USSR	197	USA	195	GDR

*See note on Table 5.3.

In terms of the spread of points for victory, the analysis is all across the board. The biggest victory belongs to the Soviet Union in Montreal, with 31 more medals and 63 more points than the United States. There is, however, very little consistency. While the two biggest spreads, 1972 and 1960, were Soviet victories, the next two, in terms of medals, are American victories (1968 and 1952). In terms of points, the next two are 1956, a Soviet victory, and 1968, an American victory. The outcome of Tables 5.5 and 5.6 suggest that the United States and the Soviet Union traded the top podium in terms of medal count and a simplified points system, sharing the victory a near equal amount of times.

Given that it appears Soviet and American athletes performed reasonably well, compared to each other, regardless of the host city, and also given that the Soviet Union had a strong showing at every prior American hosting of the Olympics, there is simply no evidence that would suggest the Soviet Union was concerned about their chances of victory in the sporting events. In fact, the Soviet Union's performance in two American Winter Olympics, as well as their successes in Munich and in Montreal, strongly suggests that the Soviet Union did not have any difficulty performing in significantly pro-Western environments. Munich, due to the continuing issue of a divided Germany, should have been the most hostile host from the period of 1952 to 1984 for a Soviet team. Yet Munich resulted in a strong appearance by both the Soviet Union and East Germany.

Beyond the statistics herein, there were opinions from within that the Soviet Union that reached a similar conclusion that attendance was better than boycott. Soviet IOC member Anatoly Smirnov said, "My opinion was that we should go to Los Angeles."[14] He continued, "If we don't go, we'll win nothing. If we want to achieve the political effect of sporting success, we should send our athletes. If we send six hundred young men and women, some of them will be heroes."[15]

Returning to our topic of 1980, there were two issues of contention to reconsider: first, Soviet inadequacies in competition, and second, the embittered attitude between American and Russian national Olympic committees and governments over the bid process. By this point it should be clear that Soviet sports performance ascended to a level where expecting a resounding failure in the athletic competitions is illogical. Certainly the surprise upset by the American hockey team rattled the Soviet Sports machine, but that defeat simply pales in comparison to its extensive successes in the prior thirty years. With questions relating to sports performance put to rest, the final question of the 1980 Games circulates around the adequacy of the Games themselves.

The conclusion of the US-versus-USSR clashes on the 1980 Moscow Games was clearly that no one won. The bidding wars ended with both cities getting the opportunity to host. As for the Soviet Games, there were both victories and defeats. The Soviet Union failed to attain their policy goals in hosting the Olympics, but the United States also failed to get a unified Western voice against Soviet actions in Afghanistan and against participation in the Moscow Games. Neither side could claim a victory, so the result was that both walked away from the confrontation disappointed, angry, and probably embarrassed as well.

However, as much as some policy aims of the Soviet Union were unsuccessful, others were still attained. No degree of boycott could affect the overall outcome of the planning and implementation of the Games. Moscow was successful in getting the Games off the ground and no one can suggest otherwise. American complaints on the Games did not challenge Soviet preparations. The United States never discussed publicly if there were concerns over the Soviet concept of hosting. There is also no significant evidence that the IOC was displeased with Soviet efforts to organize the Games. With the exception of some indications of discomfort with the concept of socialized sport, Lord Killanin's memoirs do not indicate the presence of IOC concerns.[16]

The Soviet Union, therefore, was able to pull off a major sports festival and, unlike Montreal, managed to do so without shortfalls in construction and money. The main failing in the Soviet-hosted Olympiad was in the number of participating countries: only 80 compared to 92 at Montreal and 121 in Munich. As a symptom of the lack of attending countries, the competitions were slimmer, in that athletes from traditionally strong Olympic delegations, notably the United

States, West Germany, and Japan, were absent. While the Soviet Union was no doubt disheartened by the weak attendance, the IOC, the Soviet Union, and others made it clear the fault in this aspect was due to the United States and its allies.

At this point, we can assess the events of the 1980 Olympics as being relevant in a limited manner to the 1984 Olympics. The events of the Afghanistan invasion and the US boycott took the already adversarial relationship between the United States and the Soviet Union and made it worse. What was initially a competition on many levels, including that of pride, was now exacerbated. At first, the competition was over who got to host. The Soviet Union lost round one and won round two. The United States, or more specifically Los Angeles, lost both in round one and two, but, because of the circumstances surrounding the conditional acceptance, they barely won round three against no competition except a belligerent IOC representative from the Soviet Union. The ground-work was already present for a rivalry between both host states, and both were vying for bragging rights as best host.

Now, thanks to the events of the period from 1978 through 1980, the situation was even tenser, more competitive, and more likely to result in political intrigue. It was on this stage that the Soviet Union needed to construct an international sports policy in preparation for the Los Angeles Olympics. American actions leading to boycott had severely weakened the Soviet Union's position in comparison to the forthcoming Los Angeles Olympics. In the previous two chapters, we established that the Soviet Union was known for using sports events for political ends and that they had vested a considerable amount of meaning into the relationship between political/economic system and successfully hosting the Olympics. Therefore, this comparison was more than just empty competition. The Soviet Union had vested the reputation of themselves and their political system on their ability to be a "better host" than capitalist America and Canada.

AFTERWARD: SARAJEVO IN BRIEF CONTEXT

Only the 1984 Sarajevo Winter Olympics separate the events of this chapter and the next. Before moving into the events of the Soviet boycott, a brief look at the Sarajevo Olympics will round out the history of this study as well as establish what roles Sarajevo may have played in this story. Given the events of the 1984 Winter Olympics, Sarajevo will remain mostly a footnote in this study.

A significant portion of the factors affecting the applicability of the Sarajevo Olympics is in relation to facts about Sarajevo and Lake

Placid. First, with very complicated and well-publicized controversies surrounding the Moscow and Los Angeles Olympiads, both the Lake Placid and the Sarajevo Winter Olympics were easily overshadowed. The second involves timing of both Olympiads and Winter Games. The first phase in the US-USSR boycotts was initiated by the United States only one month before the Lake Placid Games. As a result, the fallout was not really able to affect Lake Placid.

Certainly, the potential for a Soviet boycott in response to the US threat was possible, but that was not likely. First, it was very early in the crisis and there was real hope on the part of the IOC and the Soviet Union that the US boycott would fade away. Furthermore, in the discussions to avert the US boycott, the Soviet Union was able to use their presence in Lake Placid as a bargaining chip—a kind of claiming the high road. Lastly, and in keeping with Soviet sports policy, Soviet success in the Winter Olympics had been steadily increasing and was likely to not only continue but also potentially best the United States. The degree of success in Lake Placid only strengthens this argument for attendance of both states in Sarajevo.

Shows of good faith in attending the Winter Games by the Soviet Union in 1980 and the United States in 1984 were cards both sides played in attempting to avert boycotts of their respective Summer Games. Simply put, the possibility that the boycott would not occur remained a potential outcome well after the Lake Placid Games and, again, well after the Sarajevo Games four years later. So long as the option of retaliation against Moscow remained possible, the Soviet Union would not have significantly saber-rattled against the Lake Placid Games out of simple protection of their own. Similarly, the United States and the Soviet Union would have seen no purpose to making a stand in or over Sarajevo.

A little bit of luck, in terms of timing, and Soviet interests, which did not include boycotting Lake Placid, came together to minimize effects on Lake Placid. Sarajevo had a similar outcome, but other more important issues were at play in the winter of 1984. First, it is worth restating that, as the United States was also looking to avert the boycott, it was essentially in the same position the Soviet Union was four years earlier. Second, and in stark contrast to the Lake Placid example, neither the United States nor the Soviet Union were tied closely enough to Yugoslavia in order to draw them into the boycott.

Historically speaking, Yugoslavia and the Soviet Union had unfriendly relations. The Yugoslav government had, as a result, pursued an independent foreign policy for most of the Cold War.[17] Marshall Josip Broz Tito may have been dead for four years,[18] but that did not result in a major shift in Soviet-Yugoslav relations. Therefore, American threats against Yugoslavia would not have been a great bargaining chip for the United States.[19] Furthermore, Yugoslavia ignored the American boycott and looked likely to do the same in reference to the Soviet boycott. Because of Yugoslav refusal to stay in line with either side on several policy issues, the Sarajevo Games were not a likely pawn in the boycotts.

As a result of the timing of and the politics behind each boycott, the Winter Games were spared any degree of involvement in the boycotts. They were, due to outcomes of sports and of policy toward hosts and the Olympic Movement, similarly noncontroversial in that neither side used these two Winter Games as an opportunity for political grandstanding.[20] Furthermore, the appearance and performance of the Soviet Union was unsurprising at the Sarajevo Olympics, further weakening any impact they had on the events of the Summer Olympics of the same year. As a result, we are discovering that the possible motivations for the boycott are rapidly shrinking. Through an analysis of Soviet sports history, this study first eliminated traditional notions of tit for tat as outside the standard conventions of their sports policy.

In addition, by considering Soviet responses to the American call for boycott, we discover that a rigorous policy opposing politicization of the Olympics would ultimately restrict the Soviet Union's foreign policy options four years later. Any attempt at calls for a more or less similar boycott in 1984 would be openly attacked on the basis of their own policy four years prior. If nothing else, this bolsters not only the use of the terminology *nonparticipation* by the Soviet Union but also the principle argument of this study as seeking a more competent and policy-consistent Soviet reason for the boycott.

Within a consistent Soviet sports policy persists a tradition of avoiding competition where they could not succeed, but this fails to hold merit as a reason for the boycott. Soviet successes outlined in this chapter make it rather difficult to conclude that a fear of failure in athletic competitions was the underlying cause of the Soviet boycott. Other than the Soviet loss in ice hockey in Lake Placid, there is simply no evidence of a weak sports program. Even the hockey exception passes into irrelevance as the Soviet Union landed a gold medal in hockey after handily defeating silver-medalist Czechoslovakia 2–0, bronze-medalist Sweden 10–1, and fourth-place Canada 4–0 at the 1984 Sarajevo Winter Olympics.[21] Simply put, if the Soviet Union was in fear of embarrassment in Los Angeles, it was on a field other than athletics. I will argue that this embarrassment was most likely over the field of competition between hosts—the comparison of the Moscow Games to the Montreal and Los Angeles Games.

CHAPTER 6

THE LAOOC AND SOVIET REASONS FOR NOT ATTENDING

AN UPSET EAST AND AN ATYPICAL WEST

Having established that the bidding process and the 1980 US boycott set the stage for an adversarial relationship between the Soviet and American Olympic committees in the mid-1980s, we can move on to the events of that relationship. At first, this competition was waged over which city would host the Summer Games. This would become more adversarial as the Soviet National Olympic Committee (USSR NOC) representative attempted to block Los Angeles's chance to host the Olympics for a second time. The end of this short history is that Los Angeles was able to reach an agreement to host the 1984 Summer Games. In the analysis of this history, we discerned two issues that have bearing on the Soviet boycott of the Olympics.

First, Constantin Andrianov's statements suggest inaccuracies in the Soviet Union's concerns with the Los Angeles bid.[1] Second, we established that the Soviet Union had a history of avoiding competitions that would not cast a positive light on the socialist system. Third, the Soviet Union placed contingencies on their involvement in any international event on the state gaining some benefit from its participation. Avoiding Los Angeles for any of these reasons would be well within their established sports policy. The first and second reasons have already been dismissed by this study. The third reason is closely linked to the organization of the Games and how they would compare to the Moscow Games four years earlier.

In previous chapters, we established that Los Angeles's bid presented a series of problems. The Soviet representative on the IOC was vocally against the bid. If, by extension, the Los Angeles organizers had perceived flaws in the organization, then it may explain the reason for the Soviet boycott. If there were any merit to the actual statements from the Soviet government on why they chose not to attend, then there would be evidence to that fact in the process of organizing the Olympics and in the International Olympic Committee's (IOC) opinions of those efforts. In addition, the method by which the Los Angeles organizers chose to organize the Games must also be considered. We will therefore proceed by discussing the Los Angeles Olympic Organizing Committee's (LAOOC) organization and then following that with the documented Soviet point of view on that process.

The LAOOC did not go about the process of organizing the Games in the same manner as cities that came before it. The atypical organizing practices of the LAOOC and the Los Angeles Olympics began even before the city had been awarded the Games. The bid process, as discussed in Chapter 3, explained how the key weakness of the Los Angeles delegation's bid for the 1984 Olympics was the inability of the IOC and the city of Los Angeles to agree on a contract. The arguments between the two organizations ended with the city of Los Angeles assuming no financial liability. The contract actually absolved the city of any financial responsibility and formally recognized the fact that the Los Angeles Olympics would be organized privately. The Games had shifted from the responsibility of the government to the responsibility of a nongovernmental organization. This, as the very antithesis of Soviet organization and socialist thinking, would become the basis for several problems in negotiations between Los Angeles and Moscow.

The side effect of the structure of organizing the Los Angeles Olympics is that their methods of organization aggravated the Soviets' fears that the US government was involved at a level that they were not able to access. If there were going to be any problems, the Soviet Union wanted to work directly with the US government, not an independent organization. From the Soviet perspective, this international political competition must involve national governments. It was ludicrous, in the view of the Soviet Union, that the Reagan administration was not directly involved in the process of organizing the Games.

The Los Angeles Olympics did not involve the national government. In fact, it barely involved the government of the state of California. The only government directly involved with the LAOOC was that of the city of Los Angeles. The lack of trust between the two states fostered the belief that the federal government, and perhaps even Ronald Reagan (who had connections to California and Los Angeles), were secretly involved in the LAOOC. Soviet authorities refused to accept that Washington was not involved in the organizing of the LA Games when, in their perspective, an event like this could only be organized by direct government action. This viewpoint is compounded by the fact that both states have a history of utilizing the Olympics in their foreign policy objectives.

The Soviet Union viewed the Olympics as a competition, and it is more than reasonable to assume that they believed the United States held the same view. If the Reagan administration viewed the Los Angeles Olympics as a chance for competition between the United States and the Soviet Union, it is not unreasonable to surmise that the Reagan administration was helping to ensure that the Games would be a complete success. In 1998, President Reagan's former special assistant and speechwriter Peggy Noonan was quoted in *Time Magazine* as saying that Reagan viewed the Soviets as "not a people to be contained but a system to be defeated."[2] Reagan's position was not a secret, and, with California being his home state, it is likely that the president wanted to see the Los Angeles Games succeed. That being said, it is unrealistic for the Soviet Union to accept on face value that the Reagan administration was not involved. These concerns are not without some grounding. For example, as part of the effort to garner Romanian attendance, President Reagan negotiated new agreements with the Romanian government.[3]

Regardless of whether the government was involved with the LAOOC or not, the Soviets were not happy with the setup. They were being forced to negotiate with Peter Ueberroth, a private sector capitalist, and not with a government-level organizer. In short, the capitalist system that the Soviet Union was constantly fighting against was the very system they had to accept and work with in order to interact with the organizers of the Los Angeles Games. This also lends credence to the Soviet Union being unwilling to accept some claims of the LAOOC, since the Soviet system could not accept that the LAOOC had any jurisdiction to make any promises.[4] Whether this was paranoia or just good sense on the part of the Soviet Union, the fact remains that any claims of the LAOOC were shadowed by questions regarding the involvement and intentions of the federal government in the LAOOC, especially since some of these decisions involved foreign policy issues that must have had some degree of approval of Washington before the LAOOC could move forward. As if the situation was not complicated enough for the Soviet Union, the

LAOOC made it worse with stronger assertions against the involvement of local government officials.

The LAOOC stated publicly that no public officials—including the mayor—would have any authority in the decision making of the committee. Peter Ueberroth received the position of president of the LAOOC without confirmation by any government official. He was hired to head the LAOOC by representatives of the two previous bid committees and with advice from surviving members of the organizing committee from the 1960 Squaw Valley, California Winter Olympics.[5] Mayor Bradley supposedly had a veto power over the selection, but that was never confirmed. Moreover, since Ueberroth was the first choice to head the LAOOC, there was never an opportunity to prove if that check ever existed. From the beginning, the LAOOC was completely separated from the local, state, and national governments. This would later prove to be a benefit to the USSR NOC, since the LAOOC and Peter Ueberroth were far more willing to negotiate with them than US president Ronald Reagan and his administration would have been. In fact, during the boycott threats, Ueberroth was willing to visit Soviet Premier Konstantin Chernenko. This freedom from the federal government allowed Ueberroth to make many decisions that helped to make the Games as profitable as they were.

The financial success of the Los Angeles Games was not known for several months after the Olympics closed. This was common with Olympic Games. The many costs involved and the resulting revenue often didn't result in a clear understanding of the final balance of the finances of the Olympic Games for several months after the Games ended. Certainly, there was no way to do anything other than "project" the likely outcome of the financial aspects of the Games. Therefore, the outcome of the financial situation of the LAOOC would not have been known early enough to influence the Soviet decision. In spite of this, the Soviet Union would show concern over two financial matters: first, over how the LAOOC conducted its finances, and second, over how the LAOOC was announcing its financial position.

With regard to how finances were conducted, Ueberroth and his principle vice president, Harry Usher, exercised a tight control on the LAOOC purse strings. Almost every purchase, including those enumerated in the budget, had to be approved by him or Usher.[6] The financial workings of the LAOOC were well-kept secrets that Ueberroth and Usher shared with almost no one. Even when negotiating with major companies such as the ABC television network, the full story of the financial matters was never disclosed.

With regard to statements on the status of the financial situation, Ueberroth was more than happy to praise the LAOOC. As the Games got closer, the only information on money being reported by the LAOOC concerned how great their profit would be. As early as March of 1984, the LAOOC president was projecting that the Games would make a profit. His projection, made roughly two months before the announced Soviet boycott, was $183 million.[7] This was, in the end, a sizeable miscalculation. The LAOOC ended up with a net profit of $222,716,000.[8] As impressive as these figures are, they had little impact on the Soviet decision to boycott. First, the Soviet Union and others had not complained about the accuracy of financial statements during the threat of boycott. The Soviet Union did not even mention LAOOC financial reports in any statement regarding the Los Angeles Olympics or their intentions to either attend or boycott. This does not, however, totally remove financial matters from the discussion.

Even though the Soviet Union did not attack the financial dealings of the LAOOC, finances still may have played a role. The LAOOC made an important and impressive announcement on the financial situation of the Los Angeles Summer Olympics on December 20, 1983, at the Del Air Sands Hotel. At this meeting, Ueberroth announced a projected surplus of $15.5 million and revenues estimated at $513 million.[9] These figures, regardless of accuracy, had to be intimidating to the Soviet Union, which had hopes of discrediting the capitalist, private-enterprise Games as a complete failure. The fact that these figures kept rising during the period between December 1983 and the opening ceremonies had to be disconcerting, mainly because the United States and its allies would view Los Angeles a success if its capitalist system made a profit where other Games, regardless of ideology, had not.

So far, and with little effort or intention, the LAOOC had managed to aggravate the Soviet Union in several ways. The whole situation simply involved the fact that the LAOOC was organizing the Olympics without any form of government aid and was doing so in a fiscally successful manner. The organizational skill of Peter Ueberroth and his assistants guaranteed that the LAOOC was functioning at a fast and smooth pace to be able to show profits from interest on sales and contracts. In the early days of the committee, before the bulk of corporate sponsorship had arrived, the LAOOC sustained itself on the interest it was accruing—which in the final report totaled more than $76 million.[10] In many ways the LAOOC seemed more than suitably prepared for the Olympic Games. So one must ask, exactly what were the complaints of the Soviet Union?

SOVIET ACCUSATIONS AND
THE DIPLOMACY GAME

As it turned out, the Soviet Union made several claims that it eagerly debated and defended to the LAOOC, the IOC, the US government, and, later when the boycott became official, the Warsaw Pact nations and other Soviet allies. Peter Ueberroth and the LAOOC were focused on finding a solution to the Soviet Union's grievances. In retrospect, he made it clear that he believed that if Soviet Premier Konstantin Chernenko had accepted his request to meet with him, he would have been able to avert the boycott.[11] Why Chernenko would not meet with Ueberroth is a mystery. A possible explanation could be that Chernenko had given up on the Los Angeles Olympics long before Ueberroth sent his requests. Another possibility is that the Soviet premier would not meet with a private enterprise capitalist instead of a government official. Unfortunately for Ueberroth and the LAOOC, they would have to seek other means of convincing the Soviet Politburo.

During the period of time that the attendance of the Soviet Union was in question, a series of opportunities to convince the Soviets to attend presented themselves. One of the more important opportunities to garner Soviet attendance took place on April 24, 1984. On that day, a private meeting between representatives of the USSR NOC, the IOC, and the LAOOC was held in Lausanne, Switzerland. Present at the meeting were the following:[12]

Representing the Soviet National Olympic Committee

Marat Gramov—Chairman of the USSR NOC
Anatoli Kolesov—Deputy Chairman of the Committee for Physical Culture and Sport
Stanislav Belyayev—Interpreter

Representing the Los Angeles Olympic Organizing Committee

Peter Ueberroth—President of the LAOOC
David Simon—Vice President/Government Relations, LAOOC
Amy Quinn—Director of News Operations, LAOOC
Jerry Welch[13]

Representing the International Olympic Committee

Juan Antonio Samaranch—President of the IOC (Spain)
Ashwini Kumar—Vice President of the IOC (India)

Alexandru Siperco—Vice President of the IOC (Romania)
Louis Guirandou-N'Diaye—Vice President of the IOC (Côte d'Ivoire)

Minutes of the meeting either were not taken or have not been released to the public. However, David Simon wrote a letter on the meeting for his files, so the substance of the conversations was recorded, albeit only from the point of view of the LAOOC. The bulk of our knowledge on the Soviet complaints with the Los Angeles Olympics comes from this letter. With only the notes of one member of the LAOOC as evidence of the discussion in meeting, a valid question of their potential credibility can be posed. However, given the obvious motivations of Simon and the LAOOC representatives at the meeting, along with the rest of the LAOOC and the IOC, a few observations can be made.

The purpose of the meeting was to find solutions to the Soviet problem. The LAOOC wanted to bring the Soviet Union to the Games and earnestly approached the Soviet delegation. On a number of occasions, Ueberroth made it clear that in his mind Soviet and Eastern Bloc attendance was a requirement for the Los Angeles Games to be considered a success. If nothing else, we can emphatically state this was the goal of the LAOOC, and his notes can therefore be relied on as a reasonably accurate depiction of Soviet grievances as he and others on the LAOOC understood them. These grievances had to be addressed to the liking of the USSR NOC, if the LAOOC was to attain their goal.

Next, we must consider the validity of the information the USSR NOC representative brought to the meeting. Anatoly Smirnov, an IOC representative from the Soviet Union, was quoted as stating that the Soviet sports authorities also wanted to attend. Samaranch stated "that the decision of the USSR to participate would be a political decision."[14] He believed the USSR sports authorities were ready to go to Los Angeles and just needed to convince their government.[15] The lack of any official representation from the Kremlin as well as the lack of attendance of Soviet representatives to the IOC suggests that the delegation was there at the behest of the Olympic Movement in the Soviet Union and not specifically of Konstantin Chernenko or IOC representatives Smirnov and Andrianov.[16] This suggests that the Soviet National Olympic Committee members present had the same goals as IOC president Samaranch and LAOOC president Ueberroth. Also, the fact that the meeting was called by the IOC and was held on neutral ground (IOC Headquarters in Lausanne) adds even further credence to the statement that the USSR NOC officials viewed the meeting as an earnest attempt to address the concerns the political officials in Moscow had with sending a team to Los Angeles.

Finally, before continuing, we should address the IOC and its motivations. While it should be safe to assume that the IOC's only motivation at the meeting in Lausanne was to ensure the Olympic Movement, Olympic solidarity, and to bring to an end the era of boycotts before it lasted long enough to earn that title, it is best to not make the assumption and to quickly look at the IOC's delegation. The delegation consisted of the IOC president and three other IOC members. Samaranch chose the delegation wisely. On the committee was a representative from India, Romania, and Cote d'Ivoire. India and Cote d'Ivoire were officially democracies at this time in 1984, but neither one had glowing relations with the United States. One could question the attendance of a representative from Cote d'Ivoire, as that nation did boycott the Moscow Games. However, India was in attendance in Moscow, as was Romania. The most telling sign of the earnestness of the IOC's attempt to garner Soviet attendance was clearly in the presence of Alexandru Siperco.

Alexandru Siperco represented the IOC to Romania. Romania was a fellow communist state and member of the Warsaw Pact and was no doubt a welcomed presence in the meeting. Furthermore, Romania was also one of the few Eastern Bloc nations that had decided to attend. If any state in the world were likely to offer acceptable evidence for the USSR NOC to present to officials in Moscow, it would be Romania. It was the only Soviet ally willing to send a team to Los Angeles at the time of the meeting. The IOC contingency was wisely selected with the goal of balancing out LAOOC needs, Soviet interests, and for acting as a diplomatic channel between all parties. This committee roster implies a sincere effort on the part of the IOC to convince the Soviet Union to attend. As will be discussed in the remainder of this chapter, the IOC played an active role in trying to address every concern of the Soviet representatives at the meeting, and it continued to do so in the months that followed the meeting.

With LAOOC, Soviet, and IOC officials all in attendance and already in agreement that the goal of the meeting was to attain Soviet participation, the meeting progressed to a conversation of Soviet concerns and LAOOC responses to those concerns. It was clear that all three parties represented in the meeting were working toward identifying problems and providing solutions.

The meeting was conducted in two sessions and dealt with slightly different sets of grievances. The number of grievances from the first session was longer than the second and contained only Soviet complaints. The list from the second session was reorganized, having removed some issues (most notably concern over defections) and raised new issues, including explanations and LAOOC responses as well as some evidence to support what the Soviets and the LAOOC were claiming. The lists are summarized as follows:

Summary of Session 1 Grievances[17]

1. The "Ban the Soviets group"
2. Security issues and psychological pressure on athletes
3. Defections/requests for asylum
4. Authority of the State Department to refuse entry of specific members of the Soviet team
5. The Soviet vessel *Gruzia*
6. Access to all Olympic sites by USSR journalists and athletes
7. Radio Free Europe and Radio Liberty

Summary of Session 2 Grievances[18]

1. Security
2. Psychological pressure on USSR delegation
3. Visas
4. The *Gruzia*
5. Aeroflot charter flights
6. Access to Olympic sites by USSR athletes and journalists
7. Radio Free Europe and Radio Liberty

At this point, it is necessary to restate the fact that these are the grievances, as the USSR NOC understood and addressed them. As this study has been suggesting, there were "real" reasons for the Soviet boycott, which may or may not have been stated by the Soviet authority to its own NOC. If this statement is true, it means that this document contained only issues that the USSR NOC was aware of as problems. There are copious examples of the Soviet Union making statements on sports policy that it hoped would justify, to its allies and the international community as a whole, a decision such as a boycott. This is not to suggest that the USSR NOC was lying about the reasons behind the threatened boycott. They were simply working with what information the Soviet Politburo provided Gramov and other USSR NOC officials.

Samaranch was quoted earlier as saying the "decision would be a political one."[19] The problems discussed at that meeting were those problems that Politburo members had told the USSR NOC members. It does not matter if they believed them or not. These facts were the only ones the NOC had to work with in their attempt to placate the Politburo and get that body to approve Soviet participation. Whether or not the Politburo was creating a smokescreen to confuse the IOC, the LAOOC, and their own USSR NOC can only be speculated on. However, the East German NOC did tell the LAOOC that the government of the Soviet Union, in November 1983, contacted it about boycotting.[20] This would suggest that the Soviet authority had already contemplated boycotted five months earlier than the USSR NOC meeting with LAOOC and IOC officials. In summation, it appears that the USSR NOC and the Soviet Politburo had different expectations going into the April meeting. Therefore, it is reasonable to assume that the grievances brought to the LAOOC were only those that the USSR NOC knew and that there were still other motivations behind Soviet intentions to boycott.

DISSECTING THE BOYCOTT

At this point, we have redefined how to determine the actual reasons behind the Soviet boycott. For a study to be successful in this topic, it must first establish Soviet goals in participating in the Olympics, address the stated concerns of the Soviet Union with regard to their participation in Los Angeles, and analyze stated policy concerns provided by Soviet officials. In this process, many possible causes of boycott are removed due to evidence, logic, and Soviet and Soviet Bloc statements. Then we must compare what facts we have left to standard Soviet sports policy and other observable factors prevalent in the period of the boycott to discern the actual motivations behind the Soviet decision process. In some cases this is easy; in others it requires some careful analysis.

The simplest of the grievances will be discussed first to facilitate the discussion. First and foremost, the Soviet Union dropped the issue of possible defections. The Soviet Union could not have considered this a major issue, since the Soviet Union attended the 1980 Lake Placid Winter Olympics without fear of returning without its team. Another simple problem to answer was the issue raised in the morning session of the April 18 meeting regarding the State Department's intention to refuse entry of members of the Soviet team.

The LAOOC had to have an identity card policy to facilitate the large number of foreigners entering the United States for the Olympics. This is connected to the grievance, discussed in the afternoon session, over visas. In both cases, the situation was easily solved by the rules of the Olympic Charter. Since the IOC had confirmed that the plans of the LAOOC were not in violation of the charter, the Soviet Union simply had nothing to back up its claims. To facilitate matters even more, the LAOOC volunteered to handle all lists of athletes, officials, and family members coming from the Soviet Union instead of having them go through the US embassy. This effectively eliminated the State Department screenings from the process, a reality required by IOC agreements with the host city. Later in the meeting, the LAOOC and the USSR NOC agreed on a date for those lists to arrive, thus confirming Soviet accession to the compromise.[21]

In addition to entry visas, there was a question over radio licenses that was easily solved. At this meeting, the LAOOC agreed that any contracts with Radio Free Europe and Radio Liberty (regarded by the Soviets as propaganda arms of the US government) would have to be dealt with by the IOC and the USOC and not the LAOOC. In this case, the LAOOC agreed to let the IOC handle this, and the LAOOC would agree with whatever decision the IOC made. The Soviet Union had on several occasions asked for more oversight and policy implementation by the IOC, so this was more than amenable to them. In this issue, the Soviet Union got precisely what it wanted.

The question on free and unrestricted access of Soviet athletes and journalists was also easily explained. The USSR NOC representatives asking about free access for athletes and journalists at the Olympics caught LAOOC and IOC representatives by surprise. The issue, more of a nonissue in the eyes of the LAOOC, was easily resolved. The LAOOC already had a plan and official documents guaranteeing the rights of all nations and athletes to have free, unrestricted, and equal access to all venues and the Olympic villages. Initially, this issue was unresolved at the meeting, since Gramov requested to see the policy in writing.[22] Not expecting this to have been an issue, the LAOOC representatives did not have the requisite paperwork with them. This, however, could not have been a possible cause of the boycott, since the Soviet Union was also concerned about unrestricted fraternization of its athletes with others.

The Soviet Union wanted its athletes to stay on the *Gruzia*, a Soviet ship they wanted to dock in Los Angeles's harbor, so they would not be subjected to interference. The LAOOC later provided the requested documentation, which, one might add, did meet the established requirements of the IOC. Therefore, free access of Soviet personnel was no longer an issue. The issue of the *Gruzia* is more complicated and will be handled later in this chapter.

The final simple question to deal with was the question of the Aeroflot flights raised in the second session. The Soviet Union requested

25 flights to bring its team and other representatives to and from Los Angeles.[23] The LAOOC had approved only a "reasonable number."[24] This, as it turned out, was simply a communications error. The LAOOC had actually meant to explain that the number of Aeroflot flights would depend on the size of the delegation the Soviet Union was bringing and only at that time would the parties agree on the actual number of flights. Since the Soviet Union chose to boycott before it submitted any number of athletes to the LAOOC or the IOC, this simply never developed into an actual problem.

Aeroflot access was the simpler of the two grievances of the Soviets that involved transportation. The *Gruzia* posed a more difficult situation that would not be as easily settled as the Aeroflot issue simply because of security issues involved with having a Soviet ship docked in the harbor. The Soviet Union planned to dock the ship in the harbor near Los Angeles and to have a percentage of its delegation stay on board the ship. To handle the *Gruzia* situation, several compromises were made. The IOC regulations allowed athletes to stay outside of the Olympic Village as long as the NOC accepted that (1) the NOC still had to pay the fee for the Olympic Village and (2) the host's responsibility for safety was not extended outside of the sphere of the Olympic Village. This meant that the *Gruzia* was not a location where the LAOOC would need to guarantee the safety of the athletes. To the surprise of many, the LAOOC offered to pay for security at the *Gruzia* and was open to the idea of having Soviet athletes visit the ship freely. The discussion broke down on two issues.

First, the Soviet representatives wanted their delegation to stay, in part or in whole, on the ship. Because of Olympic protocols, this was not as simple as having the LAOOC approve the request. At the conclusion of the meeting, Gramov formally asked that the LAOOC consider this request.[25] The second was the question of guaranteeing the rights of the ship and that international regulations would be strictly followed. The actual situation was that the Soviet Union feared there would be an overzealous amount of inspecting done on the ship by the US government. As these were questions outside of the domain of the LAOOC, it was unable to comment on this issue as well. Regardless of the impasses involved with the *Gruzia*, Gramov seemed satisfied that the LAOOC was open to resolving the issues and he therefore seemed confident that they would be solved. The LAOOC indicated that they merely needed to process the request and check the figures involved in both security of the ship and the numbers of athletes likely to be embarking and disembarking the ship daily. There was no reason to believe that if an agreement over the

Gruzia could not be reached that the Soviet team's safety would be jeopardized.

Considering the importance of sport diplomacy and Soviet participation, it is impossible to believe that the Soviet Union would be unwilling to find a better solution to this situation than losing the chance to compete solely for issues of transportation. This and the Aeroflot confusion were really logistical issues that merely needed to be hammered out. Both of these were also connected to the concern that the United States would not follow international regulations when dealing with Soviet ships and planes.

The question of international regulations could not be dealt with in any other manner than to offer the USSR NOC representatives a guarantee. All the LAOOC and the IOC could do was to guarantee that the regulations and agreements would be followed. The LAOOC handled this as best it could, but it would not have been able to fully resolve Soviet complaints unless Washington was willing to back up LAOOC guarantees with federal authority. With no federal officials either present at the meeting or on staff in the LAOOC, nothing else could be done. This lack of a government presence would plague the LAOOC on many issues, notably security, while negotiating with Soviet Bloc states.

So far this chapter has dealt with all but three of the Soviet grievances. These three all have the question of security as a common thread. Two of the security-related issues can be rather simply dismissed. The first of these is the "Ban the Soviets Coalition," a reactionary group formed in response to a Soviet attack on a passenger airline. In the summer of 1983, Soviet military personnel shot down a South Korean plane over the Sea of Japan, claiming the lives of 269 people. In response, four California businessmen announced the formation of the "Ban the Soviets Coalition." This was a collection of right-wing political factions that wanted to block Soviet participation in pre-Olympic competitions and the Olympic Games.[26] It was a small but loud organization. The Soviets claimed that the coalition had some connections to the State Department. Although these assertions were denied at the time, and no research after the fact has shown any connection whatsoever, there was little that could be done to get the Soviet Politburo to accept the word of the LAOOC on this issue. This is understandable since the Soviet Union had no way to prove to itself that the US federal government was not covertly involved in the LAOOC. Claims that organizations such as the "Ban the Soviets Coalition" or even the LAOOC were covertly supported by the federal government could, therefore, be justifiable, especially when the American government guarantees such organizations the right to voice their opinion. Fortunately for the LAOOC, this very fact allowed the LAOOC to address the planned protests and actions against Soviet participation.

What would turn out to be the solution to this problem was that the freedom of speech and freedom of assembly that this and other groups were using to protest Soviet participation would not be revoked but instead displaced. Peter Ueberroth and the LAOOC planned to solve the problem by designating specific locations for protesters to exercise their constitutional rights. They planned for this situation well in advance and set up areas that were a suitably safe distance from the athletes, venues, and the Olympic Village. The Soviet Union was correct that this group might constitute a threat even if for no other reason than its vocal harassment, but the LAOOC maintained the demonstrations were not going to be near any athletes.

The LAOOC addressed the protester issue, and even went further to guarantee the safety of athletes from the Soviet Union and other Socialist states. When you factor in protest locations, offers to provide security for the *Gruzia*, and even offers to provide security escorts for teams, the LAOOC security protections and guarantees should have been enough to handle the situations that the Soviet Union allegedly feared. This isolation of the Soviet Union's athletes—and other athletes around the world—should also have satisfactorily addressed the issue of psychological pressure on the USSR delegation that Gramov was claiming caused serious damage. Unfortunately he was correct. The Soviet Union was the target of accusations and insults in previous years and was likely to receive them again. Sources of such harassments were not restricted to militant groups or overly patriotic and zealous fans. Marat Gramov's allegation that "talks of spies among the USSR delegation or of possible terrorist activities aimed at the Olympics, amounts to harassment of the USSR NOC,"[27] and the California legislature's short-lived "ban" of Soviet participation[28] offers an example where governing officials contributed to the general anti-Soviet atmosphere that the Soviet Union was objecting to.

The past instances of trouble with Soviet athletes, especially in the water polo match against Hungary in the 1956 Melbourne Summer Games,[29] suggests that a Soviet athletes would necessarily be prepared for negative treatment at any international sport competition. There is simply no way around the adversarial nature at some international competitions, causing anyone studying Soviet involvement in sport to wonder, "Was possible verbal harassment really a major issue?" Soviet officials did not see any danger in sending athletes to Lake Placid, New York, four years earlier, even with rumors of US boycotts of the

Moscow Olympics already being whispered throughout the international community. Furthermore, Soviet and East German athletes were in attendance at the 1972 Olympics in West Germany, clearly not a comparable ideological environment. Verbal harassment, a likely expectation in several pro-Western hosts, had not been enough to deter Soviet participation in the past, so it would not likely have been enough to keep the Soviets from coming to LA. In fact, unless there were significant other risks to security that East-West verbal relations would have exacerbated, then the problems the Soviet Union posited would have been minimal. In spite of this, the security issue would still remain a main issue for the Soviet Union.

It was the issue of security, in fact, that would continue to plague the LAOOC and eventually would be the principle explanation the Soviet Union would announce to justify Soviet boycott. But how true was this statement? It is clear that the Soviet Union and its allies had logical concerns over security. However, it is also clear that the LAOOC had been addressing the concerns and did develop plans to resolve the problem. There is very compelling evidence that shows the assertions of the Soviet Union on the issue of security were excuses. In other words, they were not the actual reasons for the Soviet Union's refusal to attend.

SOVIET HOCKEY AND THE SECURITY QUESTION

To completely understand the subterfuge, we have to start with competition in ice hockey in 1983. There was a very strange series of events surrounding the 1983/1984 ice hockey tour of the United States by a Soviet hockey team. In October 1983, under pressure from groups like the "Ban the Soviets Coalition," the California legislature passed a resolution that called for a ban on Soviet sports participation in its state. This legislation was rescinded shortly thereafter.[30] The Soviet Union responded to the threat by canceling the planned tour and series of games against the US Olympic hockey team. The tour was to take place in December.

When the California legislature and President Reagan made it clear that nothing would occur at any level of government of the United States to prohibit Soviet participation in any sports competition in the United States, the "Ban the Soviets Coalition" lost influence. This assertion by the California legislature and the president came after a 1983 resolution endorsing the attendance of athletes from every country (including the Soviet Union) passed unanimously in the US House of Representatives.[31] The dwindling of the influence of the

"Ban the Soviets Coalition" alleviated Soviet concerns, and the Soviet Union reinstated the ice hockey tour.[32] If the Soviet claims of unsafe conditions in the United States were true, then this tour would never have taken place. Furthermore, since the "Ban the Soviets Coalition" had failed in attempts to stop Soviet participation in 1984, and since there is no evidence of them gaining any influence since the US-Soviet hockey series, how could this be an issue four months later? In short, either there were no grounds for Soviet accusations on security, or Soviet officials were, at least at one time, willing to risk the safety of their hockey team.

At the April 1984 meeting in Lausanne, the LAOOC was able to address successfully all the issues the Soviet Union raised with the exception of security. Just to reinforce this argument, the Bulgarian NOC emphasized security matters as a continuing problem in their statement on Bulgaria's status as not attending. Trendafil Martinski, the vice president of the Bulgarian NOC and the President of the Central Council of the Bulgarian Sports Federation, noted that several issues had been solved by the time of their decision to boycott. In the formal announcement that Bulgaria would boycott the Los Angeles Games, Martinski remarked that "some of the questions raised by some NOCs were solved."[33] The Bulgarian statement notes the issues pertaining to application schedules, Olympic identity cards and visas, athletes' accommodations, transportation, training facilities, necessary services, and other logistical matters. The Bulgarian NOC affirmed that, with the exception of security, every issue discussed in this chapter was solved to the satisfaction of the socialist states.[34]

In summation, we are able to reasonably conclude that the majority of concerns raised by the Soviet Union and the Eastern Bloc were adequately solved. Remarks of LAOOC members, who described Samaranch as appearing visibly relieved, further enforce this conclusion.[35] This does, however, leave the Soviet Union's security issues as a potential concern for analysis. Ultimately, the safety of athletes and spectators outweighs all other issues and, if valid, lays the groundwork for a new explanation of the Soviet boycott.

As the security issue became the eventual main focus of Soviet statements on the boycott, it bares particular consideration. In this chapter, the rest of the list of Soviet concerns was nullified and the security dilemma was introduced as having its beginnings in the rhetoric of anti-Soviet organizations in the United States. The next chapter delves deep into the nature of security concerns, the response of Soviet allies, and the truth about the state of LAOOC security and the safety of Soviet athletes at the Games.

CHAPTER 7

SOCIALIST INCONSISTENCIES AND THE SECURITY ISSUE

SOVIET SECURITY CONCERN

The single most important concern of the Soviet Union, it claimed, was security. This can easily be found in the language of the Soviet National Olympic Committee (USSR NOC) statement announcing the official position of the Soviet Union on its team's attendance at the Los Angeles Summer Olympics:

> The National Olympic Committee of the U.S.S.R. made an all-around analysis of the situation around the Games of the 23rd Olympiad in Los Angeles and studied the questions of participation of the Soviet sports delegation in them.
>
> As is known, in its statement of April 10, 1984, the National Olympic Committee of the U.S.S.R. voiced serious concerns over the rude violations by the organizers of the Games of the rules of the Olympic charter and the anti-Soviet campaign launched by reactionary circles in the United States with the connivance of the official authorities, and asked the International Olympic Committee to study the obtaining situation.
>
> At its meeting on April 24 this year, the IOC found the stand of the U.S.S.R. National Olympic Committee to be just and substantiated.
>
> But, disregarding the opinion of the IOC, the United States authorities continue rudely to interfere in affairs belonging exclusively to the competence of the Los Angeles Olympic Organizing Committee. It is known that from the very first days of preparations for the present Olympics, the American administration has set course at using the Games for its political aims. Chauvinistic sentiments and an anti-Soviet hysteria are being whipped up in the country. Extremist organizations

and groupings of all sorts, openly aiming to create "unbearable conditions" for the stay of the Soviet delegation and performance by Soviet athletes, have sharply stepped up their activities. Political demonstrations hostile to the U.S.S.R. are being prepared, undisguised threats are made against the U.S.S.R. National Olympic Committee, Soviet athletes and officials. Heads of anti-Soviet, anti-socialist organizations are received by U.S. administration officials. Their activity is widely publicized by the mass media. To justify this campaign, the U.S. authorities and Olympics organizers constantly refer to legislative acts of all kinds. Washington has made assurances of late of the readiness to observe rules of the Olympic charter. The practical deeds by the American side, however, show that it does not intend to ensure the security of all athletes, respect their rights and human dignity, and create normal conditions for holding the Games.

The cavalier attitude of the U.S. authorities to the Olympic charter, the gross flouting of the ideals and traditions of the Olympic movement are aimed directly at undermining it. This line that was manifested clearly earlier is conducted now as well.

In these conditions, the National Olympic Committee of the U.S.S.R. is compelled to declare that participation of Soviet sportsmen in the Games is impossible. To act differently would be tantamount to approving of the anti-Olympian actions of the U.S. authorities and organizers of the Games.

Adopting this decision we have not the slightest wish to cast aspersions on the American public, to cloud the good feelings linking sportsmen of our countries.

The National Olympic Committee of the U.S.S.R., the sports organizations of our country, will further support the efforts of the International Olympic Committees, international sports federations, the international association of sports writers directed at strengthening the international Olympic movement struggle for preservation of its purity and unity.[1]

The head of the USSR NOC, Marat Gramov, delivered the announcement on May 8, 1984. But Gramov had been trying diligently to alleviate the concerns of the Central Committee so the boycott could be averted. His assistant Anatoly Smirnov voiced the NOC's opinion that the athletes should be sent to Los Angeles.[2]

The USSR NOC statement itself presents three concerns: anti-Soviet groups, political expressions of those beliefs, and Olympic security. The first, the issue of "anti-Soviet extremist groups" and the possibility of intensification of their activities, is simply unsubstantiated. The Soviet Union's participation in the ice hockey competitions in the United States in 1984, after the abatement of the actions of groups such as the "Ban the Soviets Coalition," shows that these groups were not as much of a threat as the Soviets were claiming them to be. The second issue is in reference to freedom of speech, press, and assembly in the United States. This was effectively dealt with by the Los Angeles Olympic Organizing Committee (LAOOC) when it said that demonstrations would take place only at specified areas that were a safe distance from the Olympic facilities and that security officials would keep protestors at that distance. The Soviet statements that "political demonstrations hostile to the USSR are being prepared"[3] and "heads of anti-Soviet, anti-Socialist organizations are received by U.S. administration officials"[4] are issues related directly to US constitutional law and classical liberal ideology, not to mention being completely in line with the kind of layered political language for which the Soviet Union was famous. The Soviet Union could not have had the actual existence of such rights in the United States as an issue or they would not have been able to compete in any events in the United States.

Soviet attendance at the 1980 Lake Placid or 1960 Squaw Valley Winter Olympics, as well as the track and field competitions between the United States and the Soviet Union during the 1950s and 1960s, could not have occurred if the American political system was an actual issue. Recall that the track meets took place at the height of anticommunist hysteria and McCarthyism in the United States. These facts strongly question any validity in fears that localized protests in Los Angeles were enough to scare the Russian bear out of competition in the United States. In short, Soviet concerns over this issue in the past plus the attention the LAOOC had given to this issue, which did appear to settle concerns of the International Olympic Committee (IOC) and the USSR NOC, leads us to the conclusion that this either was not an issue or was a very small one.

The third issue in the statement, which is a facet of the first two issues, was the state of overall Olympic security. Claiming that the LAOOC was not willing or able to ensure the security of all athletes is simply false. The LAOOC had agreed, at its meeting with the USSR NOC and the IOC on April 24, 1984, to supply security for the *Gruzia*, which is not required by the IOC. Since the LAOOC went beyond the IOC's requirements for security, it is difficult to accept Soviet claims that security was not going to be guaranteed for all athletes, especially their own. These facts discredit the security issue because they absolve the LAOOC and the United States from accusations that they intentionally did not provide protection for Soviet athletes. This lack of information provided to the general public in

1984 also harmed any Soviet claims, further bolstering the retribution arguments of scholarship.

Interestingly enough, the Soviet Union's position on Olympic security at the Los Angeles Games would be discredited by some of its own allies. When the boycott was no longer speculation, the Soviet Union turned its efforts to making it as widespread as possible. The Soviets pressured several socialist and communist countries in Europe, Africa, Asia, and Latin America to boycott, thereby hoping for as wide a boycott as possible. The following states took part in the Soviet boycott:

Table 7.1 Nations that Boycotted the Los Angeles Summer Games

Africa and the Middle East	Asia	Europe	Americas
Angola	Afghanistan	Bulgaria	Cuba
Ethiopia	Laos	Czechoslovakia	
South Yemen	Mongolia	East Germany	
	North Korea	Hungary	
	Vietnam	Poland	
		Soviet Union	

Fifteen countries took part in the boycott, which was far fewer than the Soviet Union had wanted and far fewer than the boycott of the Moscow Games. The Soviets failed in their attempts to get support from African nations, convincing only two states to boycott. When the Springbok rugby team from apartheid South Africa toured the United States in September 1981,[5] the African sports community quickly raised questions about a pan-African boycott. The Soviet Union used antiapartheid sentiment and claims of the security risk to their athletes as motivation to convince the African nations to stay away, believing that the Springbok rugby team's tour would ensure an African boycott. Congo (Brazzaville) officials echoed the sentiment of the Supreme Council for Sport in Africa by explaining that the Soviet Union did not support its boycott of the Olympics in 1976, so Congo, in the words of Congolese NOC director Suzanne Kakou, "would return that favor."[6] Of the African states, only Angola and Ethiopia, both closely allied to the Soviet Union, joined the Soviet boycott. Libya also boycotted the Los Angeles Games, but its reason for doing so was caused by the state of Libyan-US relations in 1984 rather than by any political alignment with the Soviet Union.

Given the political realities and consequences of the boycott, the Soviet Union had to manage its official statement on the boycott, convince its allies, convince states not directly allied to the Soviet Union, and manage any political fallout from the IOC and other elements of the international sports community. All this required careful planning not just in the statement itself but also in managing its relations with the rest of the Warsaw Pact and strategizing the best time to make the official announcement.

THE ANNOUNCEMENT

In addition to reasons, justifications, and assertions on the boycott, the Soviet Union also had to determine when to announce it. This could be done in one of two ways. Either the Soviet Union had to come up with its decision as quickly as possible and then announce immediately and contact its allies or it would choose to wait to make the announcement at the most advantageous moment. The Soviet announcement was made by the Soviet TASS News Agency on May 8, 1984. It seems odd that the Soviet Union would boycott the Olympics on the grounds of danger to socialist athletes and then delay its announcement a full week. If it were truly a decision made for the sake of the safety of athletes and to remain true to the ideals of sport, why wait? The only answer can be for political reasons. The Soviet announcement was delayed so it would have the most impact on the Los Angeles Games—the actual reason for the boycott. May 8, 1984, was the day the Olympic Torch arrived in the United States to start its tour of the country en route to Los Angeles.[7] The informal start of festivities of the 1984 Summer Olympics was darkened by the threat of boycott becoming a reality. The decision, much like the timing, was politically driven and aimed at undercutting the level of success of the Los Angeles Olympics. To add to the political context, the Soviet Union insisted it was "better" than the states that boycotted in 1980 because the decision in the Soviet Union was not made by the government. Soviet officials repeatedly claimed that the national Olympic committee, and not the government, made this decision.

It is odd that the national Olympic committee would meet with the LAOOC and the IOC on April 24, during which they would seem optimistic that all concerns would be solved and even make agreements on many issues, only to then decide less than a week later that attendance was impossible. The USSR NOC, constantly trumpeting the values of sport, waited another week to announce their decision to boycott on a day of great celebration for the Olympic Movement.

Regardless of any motivations in reference to the 1984 boycott, for the leadership of the USSR NOC and even two Russian IOC members to deceive the IOC with nothing more than lip service in a meeting would do more damage to Soviet-IOC relations than anything else.[8] Once the decision was made and announced, the Soviet Union moved on to convincing its bloc to boycott. Using "excuses" well documented in their meetings with the LAOOC and expressed in domestic public media, the Soviet Union quickly attracted the majority of Eastern Europe and a few other states to their "nonparticipation." Unfortunately for the Soviet Union, the explanations they offered would be discredited by several of their allies. Thus far, we have seen how Romanian attendance and Czechoslovak and East German lackluster support of the boycott offered weak, at best, support to their ally. The general sense is that Romania simply wanted to go and Czechoslovakia and East Germany boycotted out of alliance solidarity.

SOVIET ALLY POSITIONS

While the Soviet Union had little success garnering the support of states outside of its traditional bloc, they had even more trouble with their closer allies. The most serious problems for the Soviet Union came from states in Eastern Europe as well as Cuba. The positions of the Soviet Union's closest allies on the boycott varied greatly, and that provides us with a wealth of information. The positions of the Soviet Bloc can be broken into several groups.

The response of the Soviet Union's European allies, plus Cuba, ranged from full support to an outright challenge of their position. Some states simply toed the party line and supported the boycott, such as Bulgaria. Most states in the boycott, especially Cuba and East Germany, openly supported the boycott but made official or unofficial statements that were not in line with the Soviet position, proving that on some level that the Soviet position was problematic even to its closest allies. The most damaging state position came from Romania, which outright refused to support the boycott and had also sat on the IOC committee that mediated between the LAOOC and the USSR NOC. While there were other communist or communist leaning states that did not support the boycott, notably China, Yugoslavia, and several African states, these state's foreign policies were often distant from Soviet foreign policy aims, thus a statement of defiance by them would be less effective. In short, the most damaging position on the boycott, to the Soviet Union's positions, was undoubtedly Romania's.

Yugoslavia will also be eliminated from the list of countries being analyzed. Two facts will suffice to justify that decision. It is no secret of history that the Soviet Union and Yugoslavia had strenuous friendly relations at best. The plan in this study is to conduct a comparison between Soviet policy and that of its allies. Soviet and Yugoslav policies, both foreign and domestic, did not always coincide, and Yugoslav attendance in Los Angeles is not an exception to that standard. Therefore, any comparison would be plagued with accusations of typical Yugoslav obstinance in placating the socialist bloc or other factors that afflicted the ability of these two states to cohabitate internationally. Second, Yugoslavia hosted the 1984 Winter Olympics just months before the Los Angeles Games. Since Yugoslavia had its own Games to worry about, and since they were less likely to make a policy decision on the Olympics that went counter to IOC desires, it is easiest to eliminate the country from consideration in this study. Yugoslav interests to have both Russian and American athletes in Sarajevo also add a complicated dynamic to any action or decision that Yugoslavia would undertake in favor or against either state.

The People's Republic of China will not be examined for two reasons. First, there was never a strong relationship between Beijing and Moscow foreign policies; therefore any comparison between the two would require a lengthy study of prior Sino-Soviet relations in sport as well as to see if there were any advantages behind Chinese participation over Soviet nonparticipation. Second, the process of getting China into the Olympics was now more than twenty years old. Circumstances involving the two-China issue (both Chinese Taipei and the People's Republic of China attended Los Angeles, for the first time simultaneously attending an Olympic event) and the long history of Chinese noninvolvement, near involvement, and then finally involvement are too convoluted to draw clear and meaningful circumstances without conducting a major analysis of Chinese sports policy, culture, and their own set of goals for their participation in the Olympics.[9]

With a sense of the types of positions taken by Soviet allies, and having restricted our analysis away from a few irrelevant states, we are able to turn to the actual positions of the Soviet allies we will analyze in this chapter. Our emphasis will be on challenges to the Soviet stated position, focusing on the stated policies of four states: Bulgaria, Cuba, East Germany, and Czechoslovakia. These four states were chosen because of several reasons, all of which are rooted in their position in the Olympic family and their relationship with the Soviet Union.

First, and foremost, they were chosen because these governments were more vocal about their reasons to boycott than the others. This resulted in more statements and other paperwork of the official governments and their national Olympic committees to analyze. Furthermore, these states, particularly Czechoslovakia and East Germany, were selected because of their respect in the international sports community. Both states were renowned for their successes in Olympic competition and, like the Soviet Union, their attendance automatically guarantees a modicum of prestige because of the sheer number of medals they would undoubtedly win. Table 7.2 quickly demonstrates:

Table 7.2 Medal Totals for Bulgaria, Cuba, Czechoslovakia, and East Germany Combined[10]

	1968	1972	1976	1980
4 States	51	103	133	201
All Medals	525	600	613	631
4 States (%)	9.7	17.2	21.7	31.9

As you can see, these four states have an impressive history in the Olympic Movement. These four states took 9.7 percent of the medals in 1968, 17.2 percent in 1972, 21.7 percent in 1976, and 31.8 percent in 1980. Obviously, that last percentage is rather misleading, since the United States and many others did not attend the 1980 Games, but the other three figures do show a general trend of increased excellence by these teams. As a result, the actions of these states were carefully watched by LAOOC and IOC officials and by other states, as their decision would definitely affect the Games.

Bulgaria was also selected because their national Olympic committee published a booklet on their position to not attend, offering an abundance of information to analyze. Finally, these four states were also chosen because, while they did boycott, their statements on the decision as well as their reaction to Romania's attendance raise some very compelling questions on Soviet explanations and therefore must be considered in order to effectively discern the actual reasons behind the Soviet boycott.

Romania and Czechoslovakia

Romania is the best place to start this analysis, as much of the evidence from the other states, particularly Czechoslovakia, involved statements in response to the Romanian decision. The events behind Romania's refusal to boycott are complicated and involve political, economic, and sports issues that were all extremely important to Romania, the poorest and least influential of the Eastern Bloc nations. Romania's refusal to boycott kept the action from being a unanimous decision of the Soviet Bloc. Much in the way that England, France, and Italy's participation in the 1980 Moscow Olympics had undermined the US boycott, Romania denied the Soviet Union the chance to claim unanimous ideological support for their decision, keeping the Soviet Union from being able to claim complete victory in their "nonparticipation." Romania's decision also helped to discredit the boycott of the Soviet Union and Soviet Bloc nations by refusing to accept Soviet accusations: namely, that there was a risk to Eastern Bloc athletes, that the Games had been mismanaged, or that undue pressure from being in the United States would undermine the performance of their athletes.

Czechoslovakia was not happy with the Romanian decision because it called into question the decision of Czechoslovak government. On May 24–25, the sports officials of 11 communist countries met in Prague, Czechoslovakia, to discuss the boycott issue.[11] All the attending states except Romania complained about security for communist athletes. When Romania announced its decision to attend in spite of the bloc's pressures, it was naturally met with displeasure. According to a diplomatic source at the meeting, Czechoslovakia's representatives complained to the Romanian representative because "their [Romania's] decision to participate would make it more difficult to explain Czechoslovak non-participation to their own people."[12] Czechoslovakian sports officials were concerned that the Romanian decision would discredit their explanations for boycotting and make it very difficult to justify to anyone.

By attending, the Romanian government made a few critical statements. First, attendance meant that the benefits for participating, regardless of what those benefits were, far outweighed the risk to their athletes. Second, it also meant that the Soviet Union's explanation, and by *explanation* I mean what they told Soviet allies and not just what they told the LAOOC and the US government, was not compelling enough for the Romanian government to stay home, thereby willingly embarrassing the Soviet Bloc by attending when the rest of them did not.

Harold Edwin Wilson demonstrated specifically what Romania had to gain in attending and what risks were involved.[13] He showed that Romania was using the Olympics in an attempt to strengthen ties with non–Warsaw Pact states. He also pointed out that Romania did not believe there were any risks to their athletes. This is strengthened by Czechoslovak complaints that Romania was making it harder for them to convince their athletes of the necessity of the boycott and the dangers therein.[14] Bill Shaikin also pointed out three factors allowing a greater autonomy of Romania on this issue.[15]

First, Romania had a long history of being more independent of the Kremlin than other Eastern European states. Romania conducted its own foreign policy and domestic policy, often taking positions either completely or somewhat contrary to those of other socialist states.[16] Second, the Romanian government was the only Eastern European state under the Soviet sphere that forbade the placement of Soviet troops within its borders.[17] As much as the Soviet Union was losing in having Romania participate, the government was also clearly not confident enough in its position to force Romania to comply, nor did it have the ground troops in Romania to allow for instant retaliation. Regardless of other issues limiting the Soviet response, every one of Romania's allies were upset with the Romanian government on this issue, but none of them were confident enough in the issue to either force Romania to boycott or to even discredit the Romanian position to any extent beyond claiming further risk.

A third force helping the Romanian government was economics. Romania was by far the poorest state in the Warsaw Pact. As a result, the Romanian government was not always financially able to participate in international events without the assistance of its closest allies. Without Warsaw Pact support, the LAOOC and the IOC had to economically assist Romania. Romanian attendance was now feasible, as the LAOOC and the IOC each paid one-third the costs involved in bringing the Romanian team.

In the end, the Romanians attended, much to the chagrin of all its allies. Once the Games were over, the Romanians even further discredited the socialist position. Romania disproved all accusations that socialist athletes would be unable to function amid the hate, slander, protests, and threats by taking 20 gold medals, 16 silver medals, and 17 bronze medals.[18] It put them in second place in the overall medal standings. Romanian attendance defied the will of its ally and Romanian performance denied the validity of one of its ally's primary justifications for the boycott.

While most of the Soviet Union's allies were unhelpful in their support of the boycott, Romania was the only one that demonstrated that lack of support through participation. Several other Soviet allies, notably, East Germany, Cuba, and Bulgaria, remained loyal to the boycott but undermined the Soviet position in other ways.

East Germany

The Democratic Republic of (East) Germany supported the boycott almost immediately. Its support, however, was only for the boycott and not for the Soviet Union's position on the issues. Initial news reports in East Germany merely announced the Soviet position but did not show much support for it. According to East German sources, "the GDR was forced to follow the Soviet lead and . . . the GDR would otherwise have participated in the Games."[19] The East German government never made a clear statement as to what the LAOOC or the US government did to prompt a boycott by the German Democratic Republic beyond Warsaw Pact alliances. What was most useful from the East Germans was the information they supplied LAOOC officials on the timing of the Soviet boycott.

The decision to boycott had been made on April 30, 1984, but the discussion started in November of 1983.[20] This is important for two reasons. First, it shows that the Politburo did not expect (or possibly not want) the LAOOC or IOC to offer adequate solutions to allow Soviet participation. Even more important is that it shows the decision process was begun before the death of Soviet Premier Yuri Vladimirovich Andropov. Some historians have put forth the argument that the boycott threat emerged as a possibility only after Andropov's death on February 9, 1984, and the transfer of power to Konstantin Chernenko.[21] A brief history on Chernenko explains Chernenko's assumed role in this story.

Konstantin Chernenko was a close confidant and friend of Leonid Brezhnev. Brezhnev, premier during the 1980 Moscow Games, was both delighted by the Games and honored to have been the head of state to open them. The boycott was very disheartening to the Soviet administration, specifically Brezhnev. Chernenko, a top lieutenant under Brezhnev, was infuriated by the boycott and what it did to Brehznev, himself, and the Soviet Union. Therefore, the logical conclusion many historians have made was that Andropov's death, followed by the ascension of Chernenko, resulted in a Soviet leadership that was bitter and vengeful and would naturally boycott out of spite—tit for tat, as so many other historians have put it.

The timing of Soviet complaints on Los Angeles, in comparison to the dates of ascension of Andropov, Brezhnev, and Chernenko, offers a significant challenge to arguments that the current Soviet administration was inordinately angry toward the United States or the Los Angeles organizers. According to the East Germans, the decision to boycott was already on the table and being advertised to Soviet Allies four months before Andropov's death. East Germany's statement to the LAOOC that the Soviets had contacted them about the boycott roughly three months before Andropov's death proves that the change of power in the Soviet Union was not a significant factor.[22] Furthermore, the timing is enlightening about the meeting between LAOOC, USSR NOC, and IOC officials. The decision, according to East Germany, was made roughly one week after the April 24, 1984, meeting. It appears that the Soviet Politburo was willing to wait on a decision until after the meeting but gave almost no time for LAOOC, USSR NOC, and IOC officials to work on final details that were not resolvable in person. If anything, it suggests that the Soviet Union was more interested in how the LAOOC would respond to demands than the actual outcome, especially since so many of their demands were agreed to or resolved.

Regardless of whether the LAOOC and the IOC had been successful in dismissing announced Soviet concerns, the Soviet Union was already set on boycotting. Allowing representatives of the national Olympic committee to bring complaints of the Soviet Union to the LAOOC and the IOC must have been a strategy. Once again, we find useful information from the East Germans. Another important fact from the brief exchange between the LAOOC and the East German NOC is its statement "that the Soviets indicated then [November, 1983] that they would launch a campaign of complaints in their press about the plans for the Games, see which arguments were the most effective, and then come to a final decision on the boycott sometime in the spring."[23] According to this, the East Germans told the LAOOC that the Soviet Union had decided to boycott and only needed to find the best excuse to make part of the public statement. Taking the East German claims into consideration, we can now see that the meeting in Lausanne between the LAOOC, IOC, and USSR NOC gave the Soviet Politburo the opportunity to test its complaints on all three organizations and select the one that was the hardest to address—namely, security.[24]

Cuba

Only Bulgaria's statements seem to be a more-or-less full support of the Soviet position. East Germany, and to a more limited extent Czechoslovakia, posed minor problems, but ultimately were manageable compared to Romania. Cuba's Fidel Castro, who participated in the boycott, ultimately undermined the Soviet excuses for not participating the most of all boycotting states. Cuba had joined the boycott, but that did not stop Peter Ueberroth from visiting Castro in Havana to see if he could be convinced to reconsider. His trip took place on June 7–8, 1984.[25] The goal was to address Cuban concerns and alleviate any of Castro's reservations about participation.

Cuban nonparticipation had nothing to do with Soviet claims, with Los Angeles safety, or anything else related to the Olympic Movement. Cuba stayed away simply to support its allies. The Soviet Union and the Eastern Bloc nations had been Cuba's only allies since the 1960s, and that was an obvious deciding factor for Castro. But Cuba's comments on the boycott proved to be very damaging to the Soviet position. During their meetings in Havana, Castro "agreed that security at Los Angeles was not a problem and allowed the point to be made for him at a press conference, after which the Soviets never again used the security excuse."[26] Castro exposed the Soviet accusations concerning security at the Los Angeles Games as a mere smokescreen. Arguably, as this information came through Ueberroth, instead of Castro, it could be challenged. However, had the information been false, the Soviet Union should have challenged it themselves, or through Castro, instead of backing down on their security claims.

The Soviet abandonment of its position on security is telling; however, it was too late to rescind the threats to boycott. The Summer Olympics in Los Angeles started on July 28, less than two months after Castro's revelation to Peter Ueberroth. Castro's words may not have come early enough to change the course of events surrounding the Soviet boycott, but the legacy of his comments do more than simply vindicate the Los Angeles Olympic Organizing Committee.

Bulgaria

Where Romania provided some of our best evidence as a state in attendance at the Los Angeles Games, our second best source of information on the reasons behind the Soviet boycott came from Bulgaria. Of all the states that did choose to boycott, none provided a more well thought out and complete statement on the boycott than Bulgaria. Official representatives of sport in Bulgaria, specifically Ivan Slavkov, president of the Bulgarian Olympic Committee, and Trendafil Marinski, president of the Central Council of the Bulgarian Sports Federation and vice president of the Bulgarian Olympic Committee, released a collection of official statements and opinions of Bulgarian athletes to the Sofia Press. The Sofia Press then published them in a small booklet titled "Why Will Not Bulgaria Participate in the 1984 Olympic Games," which gave the official reason behind Bulgaria's boycott.

This publication consists of four sections. The first two sections include the declaration of boycott and an accusation that the Games were devoid of an Olympic Spirit. Ivan Slavkov authored both sections. The third section was a longer and more detailed explanation of several complaints of Bulgaria. Trendafil Marinski authored this section. The fourth section, which we will not focus on, was a nine-page collection of opinions of select athletes. Even though this source was a government publication, we cannot confirm that the opinions of the athletes represent the specific and detailed positions of the Bulgarian government or its Olympic committee.

The Bulgarian government was quick to announce several allegations to support the Soviet position. The overall tendency of the Bulgarian Olympic Committee statements suggested two things: first, that the Soviet Union was justified in its position on the Los Angeles Olympics and, second, that there were many key failures or problems with regard to the organization of the Los Angeles Olympics. As such, the position of the Bulgarian government was broken into two categories of complaints. Their accusations in support of the Soviet Union can be listed as such:[27]

1. The US government disregarded agreements made between the LAOOC, the USSR NOC, and the IOC.
2. The LAOOC was unable to orchestrate a ban on demonstration and propaganda activities.
3. The extremist and anti-Bulgarian groups, coupled with anti-Soviet groups, present in the United States constitute a threat to all socialist states.
4. The California legislature voted a resolution to ban the Soviet Union from the Games.[28]
5. The high crime rate in Los Angeles makes it an untenable host.

The second category of complaints focused around systemic violations of the Olympic Charter and a belief that the main responsibility for these problems rested with US state authorities.[29] These complaints of the Central Council of the Bulgarian Sports Federation can be listed as such:[30]

1. Security and the use of the Olympics for overt political ends, including as leverage during the 1984 presidential election, remained the main issues.
2. These problems are the direct result of the politically motivated actions of the Reagan administration.

3. The LAOOC made declarations that promised adequate security for socialist states, but then notes how several organizations were planning "large scale actions."[31]
4. The selection of Los Angeles was suspect and should have included the opinions of other officials, including the national Olympic committees and the international sports federations.
5. The accusations included anticapitalist rhetoric that charged Los Angeles with the overcommercialization of the Games.

The Central Council's assertions then suggest that a far more careful process of choosing hosts of the Olympics must be drawn and that the Games must not be given to any city on the grounds of political consideration.[32]

In addition to these statements, the Bulgarian publication also indicates that the LAOOC had solved many issues. Specifically, they state that the LAOOC had resolved several matters, which "were pertaining to application schedules, the refusal to recognize the validity of the Olympic identity cards . . . the athletes' accommodation, their transportation, training facilities, the necessary services, and the like."[33] In short, had there been any question left of the issues put forth by the Soviet Union (as stated in Chapter 6), the Bulgarian NOC dismissed most, if not all, of them, as they outright stated these issues had been solved.

Focusing on the Bulgarian accusations, we are able to point out several things that support this study's assertions about the Soviet boycott. First, items 1 and 2 on the first list and item 2 on the second list are irrelevant, as they lack factual accuracy. One of the main complaints of the Soviet Union, and a fact illustrated in numerous publications,[34] was the separation between the LAOOC and the US government. Whether the Soviet Union or Bulgaria was fully willing to believe this is a valid question, but neither state was effective in presenting evidence of the government's involvement.

In fact, Soviet examples (also discussed in Chapter 6) indicated their displeasure with not being able to work with the federal government. With a lack of evidence of American governmental involvement (from anyone) and an admission in both Soviet and Bulgarian statements of the capitalistic and business aspects that they opposed, these accusations are not credible. The lack of a concerted focus on the nongovernmental status of the LAOOC is also suitable evidence that this was not a major issue so much as an annoyance for diplomatic purposes.

Issues of factual accuracy may also dismiss issue 4 on the first list. While it is true that the legislature at first passed a motion to ban the Soviet Union, it is also true that the California State Legislature rescinded that action and the US House of Representatives passed legislation guaranteeing the invitation of all countries. The Bulgarian statement, which came out in 1984, was after these 1983 legislative actions. Therefore, the Bulgarian accusation is misinformed at best and misleading at worst. The issue of the ban revolved around the "Ban the Soviets Coalition," which is also connected to the second and third Bulgarian issues from the first list and the third from the second. As explained in Chapter 6, Soviet reinstatement of hockey tours, which were initially cancelled because of the aforementioned legislation and the "Ban the Soviets Coalition," offered suitable evidence that the concern over the direct influence and actions of extremist groups was marginal but still influenced the concerns over security. As the Soviet Union seemed willing to dismiss the coalition as a direct cause and attend its schedule hockey competitions, it seems odd that the Bulgarian government was not. As for anti-Bulgarian groups, I was unable to discover any such organizations, and Bulgaria's published statement lacks specificity to indicate exactly what they concerned.

My assumption is that, had the Bulgarian government had specific anti-Bulgarian groups in mind, they would have been directly referenced as was the "Ban the Soviets Coalition." The lack of this specificity, while not outright evidence, does supply suitable suspicion of the accuracy of this accusation. I will not, however, outright dismiss security as a concern because of this lack of exactitude. In addition, the third issue on the first Bulgarian list—security—is tied to second and fifth as well as the third from the second list. Basically, the Bulgarian government was arguing that Los Angeles's high crime rate, coupled with an antisocialist atmosphere and the refusal to ban protests, constituted a threat to the security of athletes.

Bulgarian accusations on security are certainly in line with Soviet accusations, and they are therefore challenged by the responses of Romania, East Germany, and Cuba. In reference to protests and "large scale actions," the matter is resolved simply. Such issues were to be contained by the Los Angeles security forces, and therefore the specifics of such accusations are less important than the general concern over security.[35] As the Bulgarian statement does not offer new evidence to challenge Los Angeles security systems nor respond to security statements that are in conflict with the Soviet and Bulgarian position, those statements made earlier in this chapter will suffice. In summation, the Bulgarian statement does not add to Soviet accusations on security; it merely reiterates them. It is interesting to note that the Bulgarian statement does mention that the LAOOC did make declarations promising security, but it notes that there was also an increase in planning on the part of those wishing to harm socialist athletes.[36]

The Bulgarian statement on crime rates as justification for concern over security requires special attention. Among the many issues in the evaluation of bid cities are crime rates and other matters owing to safety. The fourth issue of list one is somewhat irrelevant, as it states that the crime rate makes it an untenable host. Obviously, the IOC did not agree. This issue suggests that a new selection process must be implemented that is devoid of political considerations and involves the opinions of the NOCs and the international sports federations. This is an odd statement, as both the NOCs and the international federations (IFs) have the opportunity to question bidders, make statements on the bids, and discuss them in general (see Chapter 4). Bulgarian complaints on the bid process appear to be somewhat misinformed. Clearly, the Bulgarian Olympic Committee wanted the NOCs and the IFs to have a stronger role in host selection, but they already played an influential role in the selection process. Case in point, Los Angeles was only awarded a "conditional" right to host as a result of concerns of the IFs, some NOCs, and IOC members, notably Constantin Andrianov.

Lastly, the Bulgarian response made an interesting accusation that the Los Angeles Olympics lacked an Olympic spirit. Most other issues were objective, and in some cases quantifiable, but this latter accusation is quite interesting in that it deals with the definition of the Olympic Movement: its spirit. While each NOC is entitled to its opinion on the nature of Olympic spirit, its interpretation is ultimately the domain of the IOC. Since the IOC would most likely agree that the definition of what is Olympic is theirs to decide, accusations about whether a host was in keeping with that would be more their discretion than Bulgaria's. The Bulgarian government still maintained a position on the Olympic Movement, however, and went so far as to note that "the moral and humane principles and ideas of the Olympic Movement correspond to the nature of our socialist system."[37]

The Bulgarian statement on Olympism, which was in response to a question as to how to strengthen the Olympic Movement, states quite clearly that Bulgaria does not agree with the capitalization of the Olympic Movement. The fundamental truths about their definition of Olympism are, in fact, their reason for not being able to participate in the Games. Todor Zhivkov's statement was utilized by Martinski to justify Bulgaria's boycott on the grounds of violations of the Olympic Charter and the ideas of the Olympic Movement. As stated earlier in this book, because the interpretation of the charter is at the discretion of the IOC and because they accepted, albeit with some discord, LAOOC organizing efforts as within the charter, this statement is bothersome.

The venue for Bulgarian complaints over issues of the charter is IOC sessions, the same venue that approved Los Angeles's initial plans to host the Olympics. Such an argument held no sway during the Los Angeles selection process, so the current Bulgarian policy can be seen as railing at the wrong venue against a policy that already received broad acceptance within the IOC. This relegates the Bulgarian position to a complaint on the interpretation of the charter and on IOC-approved security matters. As these were both issues the IOC expressed no serious concerns over, Bulgaria's position held no weight beyond its allies.

Bulgaria's statement on the boycott can easily be seen as partially, if not totally, congruent with Soviet justifications. However, these statements did not expand on Soviet reasons for boycott by offering more evidence. Instead, the statement was more of a rallying cry behind Soviet reasons for boycotting and therefore offered nothing more than public support. We can therefore conclude that the Bulgarian statement is by and large an act of loyalty to the Soviet Union.

FINAL THOUGHTS ON SECURITY

Security ultimately turned out to be the stalling tactic that guaranteed Soviet nonparticipation. It was an effective choice. No matter how much the LAOOC planned, how much money they spent, or how many security forces they deployed, there would never have been a guarantee of total security. As a result, the Soviet Union was able to always return any LAOOC security plan as "needing more." While the IOC was able to accept security plans as adequate, the Soviet Union's concern for its citizens could not be abated so long as the Soviet Union insisted it was a problem. Unfortunately for the LAOOC, this meant that there was simply no way of garnering Soviet attendance.

Soviet attendance turned out to be an impossible goal for the LAOOC because they never had the opportunity to address the actual problem. Security, capitalization of the Games, the noninvolvement of the Reagan administration, and other Soviet issues were all distractions from the actual motivation of the Soviet Union. Whether Bulgaria and other states accepted security as an issue believed the

Soviet statement or whether they were simply supporting an ally, as was Cuba, is another debate, irrelevant for this study. The collection of policies put forward by Soviet allies did more to discredit the Soviet position, and LAOOC and IOC efforts outright dismissed most of the concerns on the table.

The simple fact of the matter remains that Romanian, East German, and Cuban statements and actions offer suitable evidence to prove that the Soviet Union's statements on security were unfounded. The actions of the LAOOC, the USSR NOC, and the IOC, as discussed in this chapter and the last, coupled with statements from Romania, East Germany, Cuba, and Bulgaria, are suitable evidence to effectively dismiss Soviet statements on why they boycotted. There must be a hidden reason that was never openly discussed by the Soviet Union. From start to finish, we have managed to establish many possible reasons and demonstrated the unlikely nature of all of them. This includes stated reasons, Cold War presuppositions, and the position of its allies. The final chapter of this study will provide an answer not found in any scholarly work to date: the theory that the Soviet Union was in the midst of a nested game, acted out through a surrogate war, with the United States.

CHAPTER 8

CONCLUSIONS ON SURROGATE
WARS, NESTED GAMES, AND
SOVIET SPORTS POLICY

THE NESTED SURROGATE WAR

Given historical and political analysis in this study, the most likely explanation of the Soviet boycott is contingent on analyzing the multiple layers of Soviet policy. George Tsebelis's study on nested games reminds us that the actual observed outcome is not always the main goal of action.[1] This is especially the case when analysis of the observed outcome does not fit into the overall rubric of the decision making of the actor. Having eliminated the obvious outcomes, the answer to the cause of the Soviet boycott must instead be a more nested game that would seek the long-standing goals of Soviet involvement in sports and surrogate wars.

Through careful analysis, we have dismissed the argument that the surrogate war between the United States and the Soviet Union in 1984 was one of athletics. We have also dismissed all Soviet concerns over the Los Angeles Games as being without merit. All current explanations and statements on the boycott simply do not hold water and do not result in outcomes consistent with Soviet interests to establish their system as superior. Frankly put, passing on the sports competitions, being vengeful over the 1980 American boycott, and passing on participation because they were unhappy with Los Angeles's version of Olympism do not meet any rational goals of the Soviet Union as established in their historical involvement in surrogate wars. What remains is to look deeper, as Tsebelis recommends, for a motivation behind the boycott that is not as obvious and still fits into the rationale of Soviet policy aims.

From all reasonable accounts of boycotts in the past, boycotts can cause enough harm to the success of the Games that the host will reconsider the policy or action that caused the initial threat. The logical next step is to ask whether the Soviet Union gained something more than vengeance in harming the success of the Los Angeles Games. In this question, we find the most likely truth about the cause of the Soviet boycott.

All actors involved in the politics of the 1976, 1980, and 1984 Olympics were aware that a weak performance by a Western host (Montreal), followed by a stronger performance by an Eastern host (Moscow), created the opportunity for a very natural and simple comparison between the successes and failures of the two hosts. If the Los Angeles Olympics have less positive and more negative moments, the Soviet Union is handed the perfect comparison between the East and the West. It was therefore in the best interests of the Soviet Union to do everything reasonably possible to guarantee that outcome.

This analysis suggests that the Soviet Union's interest in the Los Angeles Games was not in the actual sports competitions, the upholding of Olympic ideals, or in vengeance. Soviet interests were instead keenly interested in the comparison that would be made between the Los Angeles and Moscow Games. This goal fits squarely into previous Soviet policy interests in East-West competitions, as all of them have had the shared goal of showcasing the socialist system as superior to the capitalist one. Of all possible causes discussed in this study, this motivation is the only one that clearly meets Soviet interests with the sole exception of the claims they feared embarrassment in the actual sports competitions.

Looking for a policy-consistent outcome from the Soviet Union, we discover that a clear nested game was under way in 1984 in which the actual game was the fight to host the best Olympic Games and was not related directly to any aspect of Soviet participation and performance as a main goal. Previous understandings of the boycott, while focusing on Soviet performance or responses to the brinkmanship over the 1980 Games, have failed to see the underlying game of successfully hosting the Games.

CAPITALIST NONGOVERNMENTAL GAMES

Earlier chapters established Soviet distaste for the Los Angeles Olympic Organizing Committee's (LAOOC) structure of and planning for the Games. The bulk of these complaints are logically derived from the Soviet Union's antipathy toward the private organization of the

Games. Under the Soviet Union and all previous hosts, the government played a key role in the organization of the Games, primarily due to the fact that an event of such cost and logistical complexity was presumed beyond the capabilities of a private organization. The fact, however, is that public disdain for public funding of the Games in Los Angeles was so significant that the Los Angeles organizers opted for a privately funded effort.[2]

The California government was particularly interested in LAOOC plans for an Olympics that received no public funds. In 1981, the Special Committee on Legislative Oversight convened a hearing on holding the Olympics without cost to taxpayers.[3] From a financial perspective, the focus of LAOOC organization was structured as a private and inherently capitalistic system. At the heart of this planning was the need for the Games to be financially solvent without taxpayer money. The only two methods of securing that financial reality were to curb spending and establish profits.

Previous hosts of the Olympics have mostly seen financial losses in an Olympiad. According to Mark Brace,[4] only two Olympiads as of 1984 had posted profits: the 1932 and 1984 Summer Olympics, both held in Los Angeles. All others saw varying degrees of loss, primarily attributed to the need to build numerous facilities with short-term uses that would not independently produce enough revenue to cover their costs of production and operation. The secret to avoiding this financial pitfall was to build as little as possible and get funding for the venues that had to be built.

Los Angeles organizers planned on using sports stadiums built for the 1932 Games as well as facilities for professional sports in the area and facilities at universities in the region. Ultimately, only two venues had to be built from scratch,[5] though the LA Coliseum, the stadium used in 1932, needed significant repair and renovation. Los Angeles organizers succeeded in raising $5 million as a matching donation to funds supplied by the LAOOC for renovation of the Coliseum.[6] In addition to this gift, 100 percent of the costs to build the swimming stadium and the velodrome were financed by the Southland Corporation and the McDonald's Corporation, respectively.[7]

Building expenditures are typically the most expensive aspect of hosting the Games. Since the LAOOC had these costs easily covered, they were able to focus on avenues of revenue for the Games. LAOOC plans focused on primary sources of revenue being sales of television rights, commercial sponsorships, and ticket sales. They planned on raising 90 percent of all revenue from these three categories.[8] The brilliance of their fundraising schemes focused on shrinking the number of corporate sponsors as a means of creating an increased sense of demand for and value of sponsorship rights.[9] In the end, the LAOOC used simple market indicators driven by supply and demand to outpace Lake Placid sponsorship revenue. With 29 sponsors, the LAOOC raised $126 million compared to Lake Placid's revenue of $9 million from 381 sponsors.[10]

As for television rights, the LAOOC employed a vigorous negotiation strategy with potential American broadcasters. Passing on costs for broadcasting facilities and access for foreign broadcasters to the highest bidder resulted in minimal costs and maximum revenues from the television contracts.[11] In the end, ABC agreed to pay $225 million to be the sole broadcaster of the Games in the United States.[12]

Given the degree of success of anticipated revenue by 1981, the LAOOC was projecting a surplus of $21 million, and its executive vice president Harry Usher conceded that it was likely a conservative estimate.[13] In his testimony, Usher demonstrated that LAOOC plans resulted in a zero tax liability for the city, county, and state governments.[14] The only question that remained was whether the LAOOC's plans were fiscally stable in case of a major boycott by the Soviet Bloc, African nations, or others.

In a moment whose irony would not be appreciated for several more years, Harry Usher and other LAOOC representatives predicted that there would be no Soviet or other boycott of the Los Angeles Games. Usher stated, "I think the world including the Soviet Union and the Soviet bloc and we are accord in at least one particular etiological area. And that is that boycotts don't do any good and that they really only hurt one particular aspect and that's the athletes."[15] Usher's remarks, while wise ultimately, were nonpredictive, as Los Angeles fell victim to the same boycotts that plagued the previous to Summer Olympiads. Even though it was deemed unlikely, the LAOOC wisely planned for the event of a boycott.

Financially, sponsors were contractually banned from withdrawing support for the Games in the event of a boycott.[16] Contracts for television rights only allowed ABC a rebate of $70 million in the event of a Soviet boycott if the boycott resulted in a drop in audience rating.[17] The LAOOC exhibited great resiliency in its financial planning and as such made it difficult to financially harm the Games. The reality of this resiliency is that it is rooted in the LAOOC's business orientation and its focus on finances as a question of profitability and tax neutrality. All this is directly tied to the private nature of the LAOOC.

Several individuals, notably Kenneth Reich (1986), Peter Ueberroth (1985), and Richard Perelman (1985), attribute the success of the Los Angeles Olympics to the private sector status of the LAOOC and its managerial style that focused on a streamlined, economical, and efficient Olympic Games.[18] With the LAOOC squarely focused on running a profitable business instead of a government-funded public organization, they were able to capitalize on strategies for financial growth that previous hosts simply ignored. The outcome of this structure was that the LAOOC and the Los Angeles Olympics were about to outperform Moscow, Montreal, and many others on a financial level. As a recipient of a percentage of profits, the International Olympic Committee (IOC) was naturally happy with the financial planning and did not see complaints on this aspect of preparations as having any merit.

From this consideration of the financial and private sector realities of the Los Angeles Olympics, we have gleaned two important facts. First and foremost, the LAOOC easily outperformed every prior Games on financial gains, and its privately (capitalist-oriented) funded strategy was the primary reason for this success. Second, it is obvious that by 1981 the resiliency of financial plans eliminated any possibility of the Soviet Union undermining the financial success of the Games. As a result of this latter reality, the Soviet Union's ability to undermine the Los Angeles Games and justify their belief that the socialist system organized the "best Games ever" rested squarely on structural, symbolic, philosophical, and athletic grounds.

With the Soviet Union locked out of any meaningful comparison on financial grounds, Soviet rhetoric focused squarely on the spirit of the Olympics, the majesty of the Games, and the value of its spectacle. The official announcement of the Soviet boycott referred to "anti-Olympian actions,"[19] and the grievances presented by the Soviet National Olympic Committee (USSR NOC) in meetings with the IOC and LAOOC alluded to charter violations (see Chapter 6). LAOOC planning, expected financial success, and determination to outperform the Soviet Union all resulted in a very complicated and symbolic comparison game between socialist and capitalist hosts.

THE COMPARISON GAME

Soviet sports diplomacy, the competitive nature of the international community during the latter decades of the Cold War, and the competitive atmosphere among the host cities that was instigated by the bidding process in the 1970s all contributed to the Soviet boycott. The Soviet desire to demonstrate its supremacy through sport and the politically competitive atmosphere that the two superpowers fostered in the Olympics turned hosting the 1976, 1980, and 1984 Summer Olympics into a competition larger than sport. This reality was only exacerbated by a beleaguered Olympiad in Montreal and by Los Angeles, representing capitalism and private enterprise in its purest and most visible form, hosting a non-government-assisted Olympics in 1984.

The Montreal debacle and the new organizational structure of Los Angeles posed a great opportunity for the Soviet Union. Montreal's inability to finish key infrastructural needs before the start of the Games, coupled with a huge deficit as a result of the Games, all but guaranteed that the Moscow Games would look better organized from a structural and financial point of view. The African boycott of Montreal also helped ease any comparative pains by allowing Moscow to claim that Montreal in many ways suffered the same failure to host the entire Olympic family that Moscow suffered. While a complex comparison of the two Games goes beyond this study, this is enough to at least suggest with confidence that no one could argue Montreal outperformed Moscow. This would change if the Los Angeles Games were so successful that they could demonstrate financial and logistical success of a capitalist system while Montreal and Munich showed success in other sectors, such as larger Games in terms of spectators, athletes, and participating nations.

In the Munich Olympics, 121 nations participated.[20] At the Montreal Games, it was 93;[21] absent was almost the entire African continent due to boycott. Moscow hosted 81 nations in competition,[22] but of that number 15 nations[23] were present under the Olympic flag with varying degrees of support from their home governments and 1 of them[24] competed under the flag of their national Olympic committee.[25] Munich and Montreal clearly won the numbers game in attendance. The Soviet Union, in order to avoid unilateral failure in comparison to three Western hosts, was out of luck on attendance, as the Soviet Union simply did not have enough allies to bring down the total number of attending nations in Los Angeles to below Moscow's numbers.[26]

The Soviet Union had lost the numbers game with regard to participation, but the most important infrastructural and financial comparison before 1984, both with Montreal, was clearly a victory for the Soviet Union. In considering the Los Angeles Games, the functional reality is that the organizational and economic structure of the LAOOC and the 1984 Summer Olympics was the antithesis of Soviet organization, planning, and governance. Ultimately, it creates the perfect comparison for the Cold War: Who hosts a stronger Olympics? Is it the socialist, government-centered, government-controlled Games of the superpower of the Eastern Bloc or is it the capitalist, nongovernmental, private-sector Games of the superpower of the Western Bloc? As previous chapters demonstrated, the comparison now under way had its beginnings in the competition between Moscow and Los Angeles to host the 1976 and 1980 Olympics. After Moscow won the 1980 Games, Soviet IOC member Constantin Andrianov tried to block the selection of Los Angeles for the 1984 Summer Olympics. Sports competition went from the fields to the congressional sessions of the IOC and then to the world of public opinion where Montreal, Moscow, and Los Angeles all attempted to host the "best Games ever."

The Soviet Union was placed in a difficult situation by this competitive nature of the Olympics. On the one hand, they had their athletic prowess, and on the other, their financial, organizational, and infrastructural prowess in hosting. The Soviet Politburo had to decide which method of its sports diplomacy would have best handled the situation. The Soviet Union's system allowed it to display its supremacy by building athletes able to represent successfully the Soviet Union on a global level, but that required it to tacitly support the Los Angeles Olympics by sending a team. The Soviet Union's system of operations attempted to take a leadership role in the world and demonstrate how socialist organizing skill would outperform capitalist skill, but that would have required the Moscow Olympics to outperform the Montreal and Los Angeles Olympics.

The Moscow organizers had already proven to their satisfaction that Western ideology, in the hands of the Montreal organizers, had failed miserably when compared to the Moscow Olympics. Financial bankruptcy, unfinished venues, and a failing international diplomacy diminished the success of the 1976 Summer Olympics in Montreal. The Moscow Games were clearly better organized, better displayed, and simply more successful than the Montreal Games, in spite of so many countries boycotting the event. But were they willing to have that success challenged in 1984 without any efforts on their part to hinder Los Angeles's attempts?

Displaying their excellence in athletics was not the answer. The Soviets outperformed the competition in the 1972, 1976, and 1980 Summer Olympics. They outperformed in the Winter Olympics in 1972, 1976, and 1980, and almost did in 1984.[27] The success of the socialist system in sports was not in question, but the organization and economic aspects of the system had yet to be unequivocally proven— at least in the realm of major international events. In addition to these facets, the Soviet boycott allowed for the argument that the boycotted competitions were hollow because of the absence of three of the top medal winners in 1980 (Soviet Union, East Germany, and Czechoslovakia) and the top two medal winners in 1976 (Soviet Union and East Germany). The Soviet Union now had to prove itself better by having Los Angeles fail to upstage the Moscow Olympics.

The Soviet Union had two options before it. First, it could pressure the LAOOC to either admit to direct government management from behind closed doors or significantly involve the Californian and American governments. The outcome of this effort would be to suggest that a fully privatized Olympics was unsustainable and therefore an organizational structure similar to the Soviets was the only path to "save the Games" from the mess the Soviet Union insisted they were in. Soviet complaints pointed to a belief that the Reagan administration was secretly involved in the planning and wanted not only for the truth of this matter made public but for the government to take a stronger role in the organization so the USSR NOC could negotiate with a government instead of a business.

The second option would be to expose every possible failure of the LAOOC while attempting to undermine the Games through nonparticipation, accusations, and propaganda. Evidence of this effort can be found in every chapter of this study and speaks to the fact that the Soviet Union appeared desperate to discredit the Los Angeles Olympics. At the heart of this effort was a strong belief that the LAOOC organized the Games in a method that was inappropriate. Constantin Andrianov, in his 1978 speech at the IOC's eightieth Session in Athens, Greece, referred to the California Committee for the Olympic Games[28] as "a philanthropic organization that had no legal right to represent the city or the NOC."[29] He also stated that Jimmy Carter "had made no reference as to whether the Government would provide financial support" for the Los Angeles Olympics.[30] The California committee and the LAOOC both divested the government out of the process, an idea antithetical to Soviet thought.

From the perspective of attendance as legitimization, the Soviet Union could not dignify (or justify) the actions of the LAOOC by attending the 1984 Summer Olympics. The Soviet Union did turn out to be partially correct in this regard. Los Angeles commentators made many assertions of the symbolism behind the participation of socialist nations. The most important of them was the arrival of the team from Romania into the Olympic stadium. Its members received a standing ovation at the opening ceremonies solely for, according to the commentators, their defiance of the boycott and acceptance of the organization of the Los Angeles Olympics.[31] In other words, socialist

Romania validated the relationship between the Olympics and private enterprise by attending the Los Angeles Olympics. The Los Angeles Olympics presented a series of problems for the Soviet Union that not only would have resulted in a justification of the organizing practices of the LAOOC but also would have only added to the success of the Los Angeles Games. The political and economic systems of the two superpowers were being tested against each other, in a competition in which the Soviet Union wanted stronger guarantees of victory through their efforts to control or influence the outcome. Thus the Soviet Union had to compare its success to those of previous hosts and then determine its chances against Los Angeles. Given the outcome of their considerations, the Soviet Union then had to seek the most effective method of weakening Los Angeles's position, as compared to Moscow's.

The Soviet Union, having had its Summer Olympics boycotted, failed to break Munich's record for the largest number of attending countries and geographic regions, and fearing its triumph over Montreal being trumped by Los Angeles, had no choice but to boycott the 1984 Summer Olympics. Security issues, the *Gruzia*, the "Ban the Soviets Coalition," anti-Soviet hate, possible attacks, and terrorist threats were nothing more than red herrings and excuses in an attempt to justify the Soviet Union's own unwillingness to risk ideological competition in the Olympics and its desire to damage the success of the Los Angeles Olympics.

Thus we return to the standard explanation of the Soviet boycott: retaliation. The term *retaliation* suggests no purpose beyond an intentional harm to "pay back" for a harm perpetrated by the responder's victim. No doubt this, as should be apparent, had some bearing on the Soviet decision. But the question remains as to what is the most compelling argument for the actual motivation of the Soviet Union. The vested interest of the Soviet Union to use sports policy as a fitting venue to establish the viability of the socialist system, in comparison to the capitalist system of complete amateurism, is our answer. And within that answer, we find calculated strategies to augment their position as host of the 1980 Summer Olympics while diminishing the position of Los Angeles as host of the 1984 Summer Olympics.

Soviet actions during the boycott period, as a willful attempt at undermining the potential success of Los Angeles, suffice as yet another example of conflict between the two superpowers of the Cold War. This surrogate battle featured Soviet attempts to claim the more effective and efficient system at both sports competition and sports hosting. The simple conclusion of this competition was the bragging rights associated with having hosted the "best Games ever" and of having the "best" political and economic system. Saving face at minimal, besting at most, the Soviet Union sought an opportunity to remind its allies of the greatness of its own state, the expected result of which was continuation of Soviet prestige within its economic and security networks.

THE COST BENEFIT GAMES

So far, every effort to respond to potential causes of the boycott have demonstrated the logic of each possible motivation to boycott, and they have all worked on the simple premise that the boycott would have a positive outcome for the Soviet Union. That assumption, while convenient, only helps to encourage outdated notions on the boycott by luring analysts into accepting that the boycott was in itself an *ipso facto* benefit for the Soviet Union. If retaliation is the sole motivation, then the sole benefit of the boycott is the emotional satisfaction of that vengeance—satisfaction that comes at a very high price.

Unless we are inclined to assume that the Soviet Union was completely irrational in its decision-making process in 1984, we have to concede that Tsebelis offers the best explanation when he argues that "if with adequate information, an actor's choices appear to be suboptimal, it is because the observer's perspective is incomplete. The observer focuses attention on only one game, but the actor is involved in whole network of games."[32] The benefits of the boycott are related to a nested game between hosts of the Olympics. The multitude of benefits that result from proving the superiority of the socialist system in organizing a mega event provides a convincing benefit to outweigh the potential costs in boycotting the Games.

The benefit to proving superiority of political and economic systems through hosting "the best Games ever" provides a significant motivation for boycott. The "tit-for-tat" retaliation explanation provides a minor and ultimately superficial motivation for the boycott. This latter explanation is still viable so long as the cost in boycotting is not too significant so as to dissuade this motive. Bruce Bueno de Mesquita's 1981 study on the causes of war poses this scenario in his theory on the expected utility of war. He points out that a state would only go to war if the expected gains from the war were greater than the expected costs. This rational choice framework on decision making can be applied in several scenarios that involve state action, including war and surrogate war.

The expected utility of war remains true for a surrogate war for all the logical reasons it is valid in an actual war. In the surrogate war, the decision to take any action or participate must have the same positive expectation by the initiator of the conflict, otherwise the state would not seek to partake. Soviet decisions to compete, as noted in Chapter 3, fit this rubric but are modified from the aforementioned cost-benefit analysis. In this study, the question is a comparison between the likelihood of victory and defeat.

If this victory or defeat comparison holds true and is also established as a common logic in Soviet foreign policy, then by extension we can continue Bueno de Mesquita's logic to state the following must be true in order for the Soviet Union to opt out of the Los Angeles Olympics: The perceived benefits of boycotting the Olympics, in relation to the associated costs of said action, must have a positive expected utility.

The final step of this analysis is to simply ask what costs existed in the decision to boycott and then compare those costs to the benefit of boycott. As the decision to boycott the Los Angeles Olympics was not cost free, there is great value in understanding what the Soviet Union lost as a result of its decision. While it is important to note that the value of these costs is subjective and can only be understood from the perspective of Soviet officials, we can understand the general view of these costs when compared to Soviet sports policy as established in Chapter 3 of this book. Building off of that prior analysis, the most obvious cost involved in nonparticipation is the inability to showcase the continued dominance of Soviet, East German, and Czech athletes in the sports programs of the Games. By not attending, the clearest and most obvious source of socialist victory is simply lost.

In addition to the loss of sports victories, the domestic toll in disappointed athletes, athletes' families, and sports fans provided the same drawbacks that the Carter administration faced in the wake of the American boycott of the 1980 Summer Olympics.[33] Lastly, participation would have allowed the Soviet Union to put their defeat in hockey more clearly behind them by upsetting the host nation's athletes in dozens of other sports in 1984.

Another cost related to the boycott is the moral high ground in not politicizing sports. The Soviet Union was obviously concerned over the hypocritical decision of "not participating" four years after they blasted the United States for overt politicization of the Games. Insisting that their decision was a "nonparticipation" instead of a boycott and that it was a result of the host's desecration of the Olympic spirit was a clear attempt to avoid the political backlash of their own politicization of sport. Had the Soviet Union participated, they would have had a propaganda field day over the fair use of the Olympics.

In 1976, when President Carter was calling for the Games to be relocated from Moscow and the threat of boycott was growing louder, the Soviet Union still opted to compete in the Lake Placid Winter Games. This decision, coupled with the series of meetings on Soviet participation in 1984, created the impression that the Soviet Union was more committed to the Olympic Movement than the United States. That impression could have been strengthened with a decision to attend the Los Angeles Olympics. In participating, the Soviet Union would have seized the moral high ground, been able to embarrass the United States for its overt politicization of the Olympics, and easily demanded greater respect in the international sports community.

The decision to not participate functionally ended any opportunity to play the moral high ground during the era of the boycotts and damaged the Soviet Union in its own diplomatic circles (due to Romania's decision to participate) and in the international sports community. The decision also provided cover for the United States against any accusations that they cared less about the responsibility as caretaker of an Olympic Games than the Soviet Union.

Another potential cost is in relation to the threat of an African boycott of Los Angeles. Had the Soviet Union passed on a boycott, they could have offered their assistance on the threatened African boycott. Even though the boycott ultimately failed, the Soviet government could have easily accepted credit for African participation and then released statements to demonstrate that their willingness to support the movement transcended the East-West divide, a policy proven by their efforts to block a boycott against an American Olympics right after the host boycotted the Moscow Games. While on the surface this role in the African boycott appears to be just more uses of the "moral high ground," it is far more important, as it presents the Soviet Union as an arbiter in disputes with Africa and demonstrates diplomatic acumen in an area in which a Western host (Canada) failed eight years earlier. By not participating in Los Angeles, there was no feasible way for the Soviet Union to play a role in responding to the concerns of African nations.

In addition, numerous meetings and communication over security at the Games resulted in practical changes in LAOOC planning and IOC confirmation of the adequacy of security. Soviet participation could easily be justified as having been a result of their "significant" efforts to make the Los Angeles Olympics safer for all athletes. This could have also been tied to the Romanian position to boycott by simply arguing that Romania immediately joined the list of participating nations after Soviet concerns were effectively negotiated. Romania would then appear to be responding to efforts by both the United States and the Soviet Union in creating a safer Games, and the Soviet Union would have gotten to claim that their entire alliance followed their lead into participation as opposed to only a percentage of it following their lead in staying home.

Whether the benefit was in actual sports competition, in the moral high ground, or in carefully framed diplomatic discourse, the overall point of this section has been to illustrate the benefits of participation. It should not be seen as an exhaustive list but instead as an illustration of the possible opportunities the Soviet Union could have gained from participation. From here, we can pose two questions based on the expected utility of (surrogate) war. The first of these recalls prior explanations of the boycott. Does the satisfaction of a "tit-for-tat" boycott satisfy the expected utility of war by having a higher expected utility than participating in the Games? No form of logic or math, given all the benefits of participation, can result in a positive answer to that question.

Ultimately, any one of the potential benefits listed previously can be perceived as having greater value (and satisfaction) than the retaliation argument. Admittedly, these values are subjective to the Soviet officials making the decision, but as we add more and more benefits to the list it becomes increasing less likely that the Soviet Union would rationally lean toward boycott. This is in comparison to our second question: Does a strategic effort to weaken the Los Angeles Games by an organized boycott of the socialist states have a higher expected utility than participation?

Given the Soviet Union's propensity to prove the superiority of its system, we can accept that this has a high value in the Soviet Union's opinion. Can we without question assume to what degree this is true? No. But we can easily see the likelihood that the proposed explanation for the boycott is a high value option for the Soviet Union. Ultimately, the claim of this section is that the decision to boycott on the basis of retaliation is irrational because on the surface it neither meets any of the typical goals of Soviet sports policy nor has value in comparison to the likely value of participation. The only means of establish any logic in the decision to boycott is if we can find a value in nonparticipation that is related to a nested game occurring in the story of the boycott.

The only logical nested game present in the boycott years is the combination of the initial battle to host the 1976, 1980, and 1984

Olympics followed immediately by the competition to be declared the best host of the three if not of all Olympic history. As these interests are well established in many aspects of the Soviet Union's involvement in the Olympic Movement from 1971 to 1984, this proposition provides the only argument grounded in historical and political evidence that explains the Soviet decision to boycott. It does not, however, dismiss all previous explanations on the boycott.

In this analysis, I am willing to concede that Soviet authorities were bitter over the damages the American boycott did to the success of the Moscow Games. My principle argument is that the Soviet Union did not make decisions that are against its best interests. This does not preclude the following possible explanation for the Soviet nonparticipation: that the expected utility of boycotting the Los Angeles Games with the goal of weakening an American-organized Olympics plus the satisfaction of a retributive boycott clearly has a higher value than the benefit of participating in the 1984 Summer Olympics. There is no need for the Soviet boycott to be a result of a simplistic or singular motivation. I am willing to concede that the satisfaction of retaliation is an additional benefit to the decision to boycott, but it only becomes a compelling answer when, as illustrated before, it is tied to other motivations that present a real potential for symbolic gain in the Cold War.

LESSONS FROM THE BOYCOTT

In their decision not to participate in the Los Angeles Olympics, the USSR NOC made several arguments in support of their boycott. In their final meeting, the LAOOC, to the satisfaction of the IOC, negotiated solutions for the concerns of Marat Gramov and his assistants but would ultimately be unsuccessful in wooing the Soviets. Less than a month later, as the official reason its athletes would not attend, the Soviet Union announced that the Americans do "not intend to ensure the security of all athletes, respect their rights and human dignity and create normal conditions for holding the games."[34] Cuban president Fidel Castro, in his meeting with Peter Ueberroth and other LAOOC representatives, openly criticized this assertion and stated "that security at Los Angeles was not a problem."[35] The LAOOC could not have received a better response to the Soviet Union from any nation, especially one of its allies and one so opposed to the United States. Considering that the issues raised by the USSR NOC (in meeting on April 24, 1984) were satisfactorily addressed and the formal reason of the USSR NOC was discredited, there must have been other reasons behind the Soviet boycott.

With stated reasons for the boycott failing the test of the IOC, Soviet allies, and American allies, we turned to more commonly accepted arguments established prior to the publication of this study. Political and scholarly claims that the Soviet Union feared a poor athletic performance in 1984 have little merit given the history of Soviet performance in sports. While in line with traditional Soviet sports diplomacy, statistical evidence on Soviet performance at recent Olympic Games, summer and winter, and specifically at American-hosted events simply do not offer any evidence to support these claims. Quite the opposite, Soviet athletes were out performing every country in attendance but the United States and the German Democratic Republic. Against these states, the Soviet Union posted either regularly winning performances or respectable performances that would dismiss any statement that they were trounced.

Lastly, the same sports policy that supported, without merit, arguments of fear to perform outright challenges claims of mere retaliation. Soviet rhetoric against Los Angeles has been demonstrated to have started prior to the American boycott and merely became much louder in the post-1980 boycott rhetoric. Soviet objections were therefore more clearly focused on the entire effort of the Los Angeles Olympics and not simply an exercise akin to a postboycott tantrum. The balance of evidence in this study shows more weight behind challenges to the retaliation argument than weight backing it. Furthermore, there is no way to prove that vengeance was the only reason rather than a single (minor, in the opinion of this author) argument that was part of a far more complex Soviet strategy.

Instead, we find our answer in the history of the Soviet-US sports rivalry, the events of the 1970s, and Soviet sports history. We find that the challenges of hosting the Olympics became the clearest indicator of the motivations to "not participate" in the Los Angeles Olympics and that the Soviet Union was more deeply involved in the world perception of who hosted the best Games than in the American slight against the Moscow Games in 1980. The outcome of this study demonstrates that Soviet policy on the boycott was highly complex and exhibited multiple layers, including at least one nested game, and that all layers of this policy relate to the Soviet Union's desire to outpace the American system through surrogate wars.

BOYCOTTS AND SURROGATE WAR THEORY

As Carl von Clausewitz stated, war and politics go hand in hand. The interaction of all states, when in conflict, is conducted as a facet of war. Each state, which has a set of capabilities to structure its conflict with, must choose the appropriate means of conducting its conflict. For some states, this results in a traditional concept of war, including all the necessary equipment, troops, and likely destruction. In some cases, a traditional war becomes untenable and states instead must seek alternative venues for conflict, the result of which is a surrogate battlefield on which states settle disputes in a manner that, while structurally distinct from more traditional concepts of war, is no less valid and no less theoretically bounded.

The 1980 and 1984 Summer Olympics cycle was indeed a surrogate war. Both states were required to utilize the components of their political and economic systems in an attempt to organize their respective Summer Olympics. Because the IOC does not sponsor any official competition between host states—beyond the president stating "these are the best Games yet," if appropriate at the closing ceremonies—both the United States and the Soviet Union were left to draft their own concept of "success." In that endeavor, several challenges between the two led to a complicated sports diplomacy for all sides involved.

We have, therefore, a clear and simple example of a surrogate war between the Soviet Union and the United States. In this scenario, both sides concluded that the "better" system was the one that could be the most effective host of the Olympics. Both appear to consider the size of the attending nations to be a significant part of this competition. Both also appeared to consider efficient management, architectural wonderment, and success in the actual sports competitions as part of this challenge. It is also clear that finances were seen differently and the emphasis on a privately funded versus a government-funded event opens the question as to the efficacy of a financial comparison.

There is very little evidence that this surrogate war included financial profitability or efficiency as part of the Soviet definition of victory. Several proud announcements about the financial conditions of the LAOOC suffice to suggest that the American hosts considered this part of the conflict. While there were complications on how victory was determined and even on rules by which this competition was conducted, it is clear that both sides were "playing the game." Thus we can see that this example fits all the conditions of a surrogate war as defined in Chapter 1, while possessing clear assertions by both sides of their respective victories. In summation, within the current understanding of international conflict, we find a necessary expansion of the concept of conflict to include war, sports, diplomacy, and other "competitions" as the same in theoretically terms, differing only in the rules, tools, and processes by which they are contested. Furthermore, the scope of political analysis in terms of states in conflict must be broadened to include any venue in which a state vests a higher meaning, in terms of international politics, than it inherently possesses. Thus avenues of interstate inquiry that have been only limitedly considered, especially those with questionable assumptions, may be reexamined to establish their actual place in the international relations of the applicable states.

INTERSTATE COMPETITION AND CONFLICT STUDIES

In this analysis, we find that the well-established and theoretically robust methods of inquiry into state action and their plausible reasons and outcomes become the appropriate tools of analysis of many types of international events. The result of which is the reinterpretation of international competitions, such as sports, arms races, and technological races (the so-called Space Race, for instance) as having a purpose beyond the surface objective of attainment of victory. Instead, states engage in a complicated game of interests and objectives in these alternative venues of interstate conflict. These venues of competition can then be effectively analyzed through the same processes, theories, and philosophies on the international system as they are rationally and cognitively the same as conventional forms of conflict.

Too often in the field of political science, occurrences of political phenomena are grouped together on the basis of the type of conflict as opposed to the logic or decision process undertaken by political actors. Here, this logic is irrevocably challenged and political inquiry is expanded to include alternative forms of conflict. Events such as sports, chess competitions, the lunar landing, and other nontraditional forms of conflict have been treated as sideshows in international relations, a status that cannot be justified within any rational and open-minded political discourse.

Functionally, the only difference between the arms race between the Soviet Union and the United States and the Space Race between the same is the immediacy of the relationship between the former and national security. Both challenges featured economic, technological, infrastructural, and intellectual challenges. Both featured a similar logic that the participant states perceived great value and need in being ahead of the other in the race. The proximity of the issue to security does not significantly change the goals of the state nor does it change the sociopolitical benefits of declaring victory in the race.

I suspect that realist preoccupation with security has contributed to a general assumption in the field that theories on conflict, war, and diplomacy are best reserved for manifestations of conflict that are closely related to security and state survival. While I find no value in challenging this notion, I do have issue with assumptions that relegate all other manifestations of conflict as being sideshows where nonsensical or flippant responses of states are easily assumed to be right. These assumptions lure us into accepting irrational responses motivated by ideology as valid. The danger of such an assumption is twofold.

First, such a response fails to add any wisdom to our understanding of the international system because it dismisses many potential avenues of scholarship on the relations of states in the international sphere. These avenues can provide valuable insight into bilateral and multilateral relations and therefore broaden our overall understanding of international relations. Second, these assumptions lure us into repeating the mistake in more traditional areas of analysis. If we can accept that petty bitterness moves the foreign policy of the Soviet Union in sports, then it is possible for us to continue this logic to presume that the same attitude informs Soviet policies on security, economics, and other critical areas of analysis.

If nothing else, this study has sought to validate the rigorous study of atypical political conflicts as sources of greater understanding of bilateral and multilateral relations between specific states and on international relations as a whole. By posing a unique series of questions on the Soviet boycott of the 1984 Los Angeles Olympics, we have discovered that Soviet concerns over the worldview of their political and economic systems heavily influenced their sports policy in the 1970s and 1980s. In the short term, this knowledge could have offered valuable insights for the LAOOC to frame a response to the Soviet Union in order to garner the attendance of the Soviet Bloc. In the long term, this knowledge provides the IOC and other international political institutions valuable information on state interests in their events and further provides those institutions with a more informed arsenal of options to protect their events from the complex relations of participating states.

NOTES

INTRODUCTION

1. In some cases, regional or continental tryouts (such as for soccer) out-right precluded their participation. In some other sports (such as cross-country skiing), minimum standards of performance shut out athletes from states with weaker athletic programs. Lastly, many of these states found their Olympic participation being the honor of qualifying but beyond that were unexpected to challenge for a medal. In this latter case, participation was a footnote and the state normally gained little to no political consequence from this participation.
2. Istanbul, Madrid, and Tokyo.
3. British Olympic Association, *The Times of London*, March 7, 1936, 13.
4. Christopher Hill, *Olympic Politics: Athens to Atlanta* (Manchester: Manchester University Press, 1997), 153.
5. Forthcoming chapters detail the statements, accusations, and actions of the Soviet Union in regard to their boycott. For now, it is only important to note the differences being drawn between Soviet and American policy.
6. Alan Guttmann, *The Olympics: A History of the Modern Games* (Chicago: University of Illinois Press, 1994); Hill, *Olympic Politics*, Alfred Senn, *Power Politics and the Olympic Games* (Champaign, IL: Human Kinetics, 1999); Bill Shaikin, *Sports and Politics: The Olympics and the Los Angeles Games* (New York: Praeger, 1988); and others.
7. The Space Race, international chess championships, and Olympic sports, to name a few.
8. *Normally* is intended to indicate that this fact is the standard reality of a surrogate war. The unfortunate truth is that accidents have happened. Athletes have died in practice (e.g., Nodar Kumaritashvili, a Georgian luge athlete who died at the Vancouver Olympics) and competition (Jörg Oberhammer, an Austrian doctor who died in a skiing collision at the 1988 Calgary Olympics). Accidents in the Space Race lead to the deaths of astronauts (the Apollo 1 disaster). In addition, emotionally charged encounters between participants of two nations in the midst of a dispute have resulted in sudden flares of violence (the Hungarian-Soviet water polo match at the 1956 Melbourne Olympics).
9. Tim Rice, Benny Andersson, and Bjorn Ulvaerus, *Chess*, 1984, A&M Records, CD.

10. The flag consisted of the entire Korean Peninsula centered in white on a blue background.
11. Their appearances in Grenoble (1968), Montreal (1976), Lake Placid (1980), Calgary (1988), Seoul (1988), and planned appearance in Albertville (1992) suggest that the 1972 appearance was not atypical of their sports policy or the result of events particular to that year.
12. Kenneth Reich, *Making It Happen: Peter Ueberroth and the 1984 Olympics* (Santa Barbara, CA: Capra Press, 1986), 222.
13. Hill, *Olympic Politics*, 143.
14. All these assume the nation has made the policy decision to participate, in some way, in the international sports community.

CHAPTER 1

1. Hans Morgenthau, *Politics among Nations: The Struggle for Power and Peace* (Boston: McGraw Hill, 1993).
2. Thomas Schelling, *The Strategy of Conflict* (Cambridge, MA: Harvard University Press, 2002).
3. Christopher Hill, *Olympic Politics: Athens to Atlanta* (Manchester: Manchester University Press, 1997).
4. Bruce Bueno de Mesquita, *The War Trap* (New Haven, CT: Yale University Press, 1981).
5. Ibid.
6. George Tsebelis, *Nested Games* (Berkeley: University of California Press, 1992).
7. Morgenthau, *Politics among Nations.*
8. Schelling, *The Strategy of Conflict.*
9. Kenneth Neal Waltz, *Man, the State, and War: A Theoretical Analysis* (New York: Columbia University Press, 2001).
10. Ira Katznelson, "Structure and Configuration in Comparative Politics," in Mark Irving Lichbach and Alan S. Zuckerman, eds., *Comparative Politics: Rationality, Culture, and Structure* (Cambridge: Cambridge University Press, 1999).
11. William Safire, *Safire's Political Dictionary* (Oxford: Oxford University Press, 2008), 584.
12. This should not be interpreted to preclude the use of military assets in nonmilitary ways. For example, the use of members of the Soviet military to form its Olympic hockey team is an example of the use of military assets but not military capabilities.
13. Carl von Clausewitz, *On War* (New York: Alfred A. Knopf Everyman's Library, 1993), Book 1.
14. Events such as the British Empire Games (Leyson 1997) and domestic intrastate competitions, such as in Italy in the 1890s and 1900s (Gori 1997), are good examples of this, as they demonstrate how these

events were used to instill or broaden a notion of pride and loyalty in empire and nation, respectively.

15. It is worth noting that *deliberate* does not exclude *spontaneous*, which will have little preplanning or structuring. In these instances, victory either has to be an *ipso facto* outcome of the type competition or the likelihood of having value in labels of *win* and *loss* becomes tenuous. This ambiguity is an issue that weakens the value of the outcome of the surrogate war.

16. As a result of the need to structure the rules of the contest, surrogate wars do feature a degree of cooperative behavior. The purpose behind said cooperation is simply to streamline the rules and procedures by which the conflict will occur. The more structured the nature of the conflict, and the more complicated the rules that govern it, the higher the level of cooperation required. The Olympics is an example of one of the largest and most structured of these cooperative endeavors. The IOC provides the umbrella organization and overall governing structure of the Olympics. Each NOC governs the participation of their respective states, in accordance with IOC regulations. Dozens of international federations set up the rules of competition, means of determining victory, and have provided all other necessary regulations. This entire structure requires the participation of all states in the cooperative effort at sustaining these institutions.

The degree of complexity is directly related to the degree of cooperation necessary. In terms of sporting competitions, the simpler the rules, the less cooperation is required. In some cases, cooperation can be as minimal as agreeing to a time and location for the event. As either the nature of the competition becomes more complicated or the path to victory more ambiguous or subjective, the cooperation becomes more and more necessary to establish the ground rules of these circumstances.

17. The Space Race is a great example of a nonsport, nonathletic surrogate war. Whether to prove scientific brilliance, to create further military opportunities, or simply to outbuild and outspend everyone else, the race to space originated as a surrogate war between the great powers of the Cold War. Today, achieving space exploration is seen as a prerequisite for superpower status.

18. This excludes cease-fires, armistices, and other cessations of conflict, as they are complex outcomes where victory is shared, undeclared, or postponed.

19. *Oxford English Dictionary*, s. v. "boycott," accessed July 16, 2012, http://0-www.oed.com.ilsprod.lib.neu.edu/view/Entry/271106.

20. In an effort to avoid the American and Western Bloc boycott of the Moscow Games, Soviet officials openly attacked the use of the Games for political purposes by focusing their rhetoric on boycotts being against the spirit of Olympism.

21. Schelling, *The Strategy of Conflict*, 5.

22. Ibid.
23. Ibid.

Chapter 2

1. It is worth noting that Antwerp, the site of the 1920 Games, was attacked directly in August 1914 and then remained in German control until the end of the war. As such, it was a fitting symbol of survival in Europe following World War I.
2. Alan Guttmann, *The Olympics: A History of the Modern Games* (Chicago: University of Illinois Press, 1994), 38.
3. Ibid.
4. Ibid.
5. The 1928 Winter and Summer Games were both held in states neutral during World War I. The second Olympiad of the Winter Games was held in St. Moritz, Switzerland, and the ninth Olympiad of the Summer Games was held in Amsterdam, Netherlands.
6. The Netherlands lacks the requisite geography to host alpine events, and the precedent for having a separate city host specific events would not be set for another 28 years when Stockholm, Sweden, hosted all equestrian events of the 1956 Melbourne Olympics due to strict Australian laws governing the importation of animals.
7. Summer Olympics were planned for Tokyo and Winter Olympics were planned for Sapporo.
8. Alfred Senn, *Power Politics and the Olympic Games* (Champaign, IL: Human Kinetics, 1999), 41.
9. There were 2,543 in Antwerp and 3,738 in Berlin (Senn, *Power Politics and the Olympic Games*, 41).
10. British Olympic Association, *The Times of London*, March 7, 1936, 13.
11. Christopher Hill, *Olympic Politics: Athens to Atlanta* (Manchester: Manchester University Press, 1997), 199.
12. Ibid., 207.
13. Senn, *Power Politics and the Olympic Games*, 126.
14. It is worth noting that several international federations have prohibitions against their members competing against nonmember or banned-member states. Therefore New Zealand technically violated these agreements by competing with an expelled South Africa.
15. Senn, *Power Politics and the Olympic Games*, 117.
16. Taiwan does not have recognition in the Olympic Movement under the either of the two names of the island: Taiwan or Formosa. They are formally called Chinese Taipei.
17. It goes without question that the murder of athletes is outside the spirit of the Olympic Movement. Black power salutes and other actions that imply racial/ethnic inequality go against statements in the charter on the equality of all men and women. Numerous statements and

policies of the International Olympic Committee have decried overt uses of the Games to advance the political interests of a member of the international community.

18. This presumes we use an understanding of diplomacy consistent with Hans Morgenthau's definitions of a new diplomacy in which mutual understanding of all sides of a diplomatic contest are understood and appreciated by all actors. In short, it is diplomacy that seeks an equitable solution for all parties while not compromising on those things that are absolutely critical to state sovereignty.

19. Alan Guttmann, *The Olympics*, 21.

20. Richard Pound, *Five Rings over Korea* (Boston: Little Brown Company, 1994), 4.

21. Walter F. Mondale, "Speech to the USOC House of Delegates," April 13, 1980, *Walter F. Mondale Papers*, Minnesota Historical Society.

22. Ibid.

23. Senn, *Power Politics and the Olympic Games*, 59–60.

CHAPTER 3

1. Victor Peppard and James Riordan, *Playing Politics: Soviet Sport Diplomacy to 1992* (Greenwich, CT: JAI Press, 1993), 61.

2. David Miller's (2003) history of the Olympic Games includes appendices on overall medal counts and outcomes in individual sports. In addition, the final reports of the Games provide detailed results. Both can be referenced for this and similar statistics throughout this study.

3. David Miller, *Athens to Athens: The Official History of the Olympic Games and the IOC, 1894–2004* (Edinburgh: Mainstream Publishing Company, 2003), 476.

4. Henri de Baillet-Latour never expanded on his position, but the most likely reason for his position rests with concerns that states with socialized sports systems present a significant challenge to amateurism as the Olympic Movement defined it.

5. Peppard and Riordan, *Playing Politics*, 62.

6. James Riordan, *Sport in Soviet Society* (New York: Cambridge University Press, 1977), 405.

7. Nikoli Romanov's memoirs, as quoted in Peppard and Riordan, *Playing Politics*, 63.

8. International Olympic Committee, *Official Bulletin of the International Olympic Committee, 1931* (Lausanne: International Olympic Committee, 1931), 5.

9. Barcelona was a particularly apropos choice, as Spain was an early dissenter against European fascist movements until the Spanish Civil war installed its own. Barcelona then continued to be the center of a populist antifascist resistance against Francisco Franco y Bahamonde. The

irony in its selection is that Barcelona was the city that lost to Berlin to host the 1936 Olympics.

10. Peppard and Riordan, *Playing Politics*, 32.
11. Ibid., 32.
12. Ibid., 28.
13. Ibid., 50.
14. Norman N. Shneidman, *The Soviet Road to Olympus: Theory and Practice of Soviet Physical Culture and Sport* (Toronto: Ontario Institute for Studies in Education, 1978), 24.
15. Ibid., 24.
16. Naslednikan Revolyutsii, as quoted in Shneidman, *The Soviet Road to Olympus*, 25.
17. Just to name a few: *Fédération Internationale de Football Association*, formed in 1904; International Association of Athletics Federations, formed in 1912; International Hockey Federation, formed in 1924; *Fédération Équestre Internationale*, formed in 1921; International Basketball Federation, formed in 1932; and the World Archery Federation, formed in 1931. (All dates are taken from the official websites of the respective international federations.)
18. Peppard and Riordan, *Playing Politics*, 30.
19. This is not to suggest, however, that sports competitions were nonviolent. In fact, they were often quite the opposite. Bitter rivalries spurred on by sometimes-brutal foreign policy led to many dangerous situations for athletes competing in international sports competitions, such as the water polo incident.
20. Shneidman, *The Soviet Road to Olympus*, 14.
21. Ibid., 14.
22. Official names of the sports federations can be found on the website for the International Olympic Committee. For your convenience, ISU governs skating, FILA governs wrestling, and FIDE governs chess.
23. Alfred Senn, *Power Politics and the Olympic Games* (Champaign, IL: Human Kinetics, 1999), 85–86.
24. It should be noted for the benefit of the reader that the IAAF was the largest international federation. If any nation could attain membership in the IAAF, it generally meant that the nation would be able to gain membership in most other international federations. Due to the number of summer Olympic sports governed by the IAAF and the longevity of relations between the IAAF and the IOC, membership in the IAAF normally led to membership in the IOC soon thereafter.
25. James Riordan (1977, 1979, and 1991) provides a lot of background in the formative years of Soviet international sports competition, including their early relations with the IAAF and the IOC.
26. Peppard and Riordan, *Playing Politics*, 67.
27. This acronym refers to the official French version of the USSR's name: *Union des Republiques Socialistes Sovietiques*. S. Sobolev, "Letter to

IOC, Moscow, April 1951," Avery Brundage Collection, No. 149, USOA NOC, 1947–69, 2.

28. Senn, *Power Politics and the Olympic Games*, 92. IOC members are not representatives of their states in the traditional sense of an international organization. While they are listed and titled as being from their state, they are officially IOC representatives to their state of origin. The importance of this distinction rests in the fact that the primary interest of an IOC member is promotion of the Olympic Movement and not the policy of a state with a recognized national Olympic committee.

29. James Riordan, *Sport under Communism* (London: C. Hurst, 1981), 30.

30. Ibid., 30.

31. Kommunisticheskaia, *Twenty-Fourth Congress of the Communist Party of the Soviet Union* (Moscow: Novosti Press Agency Publishing House, 1971), 293.

32. James Riordan, *Sport under Communism*, 30.

33. Communist Party of the Soviet Union, *O Kulture Prosveshenii Nauki* (Moscow: Government of the Union of Soviet Socialist Republics, 1963), 254–60, as quoted in Barukh Hazan, *Olympic Sports and Propaganda Games: Moscow 1980* (London: Transaction Books, 1982), 28–29.

34. Kommunisticheskaia, *Twenty-Fourth Congress of the Communist Party of the Soviet Union*, 131–54, 196.

35. Ibid., 293

36. Ibid.

37. Ibid., 288.

38. This list would include Eastern European nations under Soviet influence, especially Poland, Czechoslovakia, Hungary, and eventually East Germany.

39. Miller, *Athens to Athens*, 478.

40. Ibid.

41. Nikolai N. Romanov, *Trudnye Dorogi K Olympu* (Moscow: Fizkul'tura I Sport, 1987), quoted in Peppard and Riordan, *Playing Politics*, 57.

42. Senn, *Power Politics and the Olympic Games*, 90.

43. Ibid.

44. Nikoli Romanov's memoirs, as quoted in Peppard and Riordan, *Playing Politics*, 63.

45. Field hockey was never a sport of interest in the Soviet Union, so there was no history for the sport to grow out of. Furthermore, unlike ice hockey, which is the only team sport in the Winter Olympics and therefore a high profile sport every Olympiad, field hockey was part of a crowded field of sports at the Summer Olympics. Repeated dominance in many other sports in the Summer Games meant one additional team spot held less value in the eyes of Soviet sports bureaucrats.

46. For all medal counts in this section, see Miller, *Athens to Athens*, Appendix C.

47. Stoliarov, as quoted in Peppard and Riordan, *Playing Politics*, 72.
48. They won 98 medals, 24 more than the second place nation, the United States. See Miller, *Athens to Athens*, 478.
49. Peppard and Riordan, *Playing Politics*, 71.
50. Senn, *Power Politics and the Olympic Games*, 104–5.
51. This success would be fleeting, since a unified German team disappeared in 1964 and would not reappear again until after German unification in 1990.
52. *The 1936 Constitution of the USSR* (Moscow: Government of the Soviet Union, 1936).
53. *The 1977 Constitution of the USSR* (Moscow: Government of the Soviet Union, 1977).
54. Ibid.
55. Ibid.
56. Pamphlet from the Information Department, Embassy of the USSR, *Soviet Sport: The Way to Medals* (Moscow: Novosti Press Agency, 1988), 16.
57. Shneidman, *The Soviet Road to Olympus*, 166–74.
58. Ibid., 143–45.
59. Boris Khavin, *This is the USSR: Sports* (Moscow: Novisti Press Agency, 1988). Some information was obtained directly from the sports federations. These included the federations for badminton, baseball, and softball. It should be noted that information was unavailable for some international sports federations. Therefore these numbers should be looked at as minimums and not the actual final total of international federations the Soviet Union joined during the specified time periods.
60. Ibid.
61. *Soviet Sport: The Way to Medals*, 4.
62. Ibid., 15.
63. Aleksei Romanov, as quoted in Rob Beamish and Ian Ritchie, *Fastest, Highest, Strongest: A Critique of High-Performance Sport* (New York: Routledge, 2006), 37.

CHAPTER 4

1. Lord Killanin, "Minutes of the 75th Session of the International Olympic Committee" (Vienna, Austria: Comite International Olympique, October 21–24, 1974, photocopied), 11.
2. Evaluation Commission, *Report of the IOC Evaluation Commission for the Games of the XXIX Olympiad in 2008* (Lausanne: Comite International Olympique, April 3, 2001), 90–92.
3. Beijing Organizing Committee for the Games of the XXIX Olympiad, *Official Report of the Beijing Games*, Vol 1 (Beijing: Beijing Organizing Committee for the Games of the XXIX Olympiad, 2008), 64.

4. Evaluation Commission. *Report of the IOC Evaluation Commission*, 90–92.
5. Avery Brundage, "Minutes of the 69th Session of the International Olympic Committee" (Amsterdam, Netherlands: Comite International Olympique, May 12–16, 1970, photocopied), 12.
6. Ibid., 12.
7. Ibid., 13.
8. Ibid., 12.
9. Ibid.
10. Ibid.
11. Allen Guttmann, *The Olympics: A History of the Modern Games* (Chicago: University of Illinois Press, 1994), 141.
12. Brundage, "Minutes of the 69th Session of the International Olympic Committee," 14.
13. This point will be demonstrated as we continue looking at vote totals of several host city elections.
14. Earlier, I made reference to the difficulty of neutral states (i.e., Sweden and Switzerland) being selected. The neutral states had the smallest group of allies, therefore they were the least likely to attract votes from IOC members that voted with a degree of ideological bias.
15. Brundage, "Minutes of the 69th Session of the International Olympic Committee," 12.
16. Senn reports that the Pan-American vote shifted from Los Angeles. He does not, however, cite the source. See Alfred Senn, *Power Politics and the Olympic Games* (Champaign, IL: Human Kinetics, 1999), 145–46.
17. Ibid., 145.
18. Lord Killanin, "Minutes of the 75th Session of the International Olympic Committee," 8.
19. Ibid., 8–9.
20. Ibid., 9.
21. Ibid.
22. Ibid.
23. Ibid., 10.
24. The exceptions being the 1956 Summer Olympics in Melbourne, Australia; the 1964 Summer Olympics in Tokyo, Japan; and the 1972 Winter Olympics in Sapporo, Japan.
25. The Summer Games of 1976 were awarded to Montreal, Canada, and the Winter Games were awarded to Denver, Colorado. Denver would later turn the offer down and the Games would be moved to Innsbruck, Austria.
26. Los Angeles hosted the Summer Olympics in 1932.
27. Three IOC members did not vote. Maude Graeppi, Documentation Department of the Olympic Museum in Lausanne, Switzerland, correspondence, August 3, 2001.

28. Lord Killanin, "Minutes of the 80th Session of the International Olympic Committee" (Athens, Greece: Comite International Olympique, May 17–20, 1978, photocopied), 29.
29. Ibid.
30. Ibid., 31.
31. The charter has seen numerous revisions. According to Bill Shaikin (1987), financial guarantees were stipulated in Rule 4. The current text of the charter is supplied in note 31 in order to place the matter into perspective for the reader.
32. The September 1, 2004, edition of Rule 34, Bylaw 2.4 states that "each candidate city shall provide financial guarantees as required by the IOC Executive Board, which will determine whether such guarantees shall be issued by the city itself, or by any other competent local, regional or national public authorities or by any third parties." International Olympic Committee, *Olympic Charter* (Lausanne: International Olympic Committee, 2004), 46.
33. Bill Shaikin, *Sports and Politics: The Olympics and the Los Angeles Games* (New York: Praeger, 1988), 41.
34. LAOOC, *Olympic Countdown: 200 Days to Go* (Los Angeles: Los Angeles Olympic Organization Committee, 1984), 50.
35. Allen Guttmann, *The Olympics: A History of the Modern Games* (Chicago: University of Illinois Press, 1994), 141.
36. Lord Killanin, "Minutes of the 75th Session of the International Olympic Committee," 8.

CHAPTER 5

1. Alfred Senn, *Power Politics and the Olympic Games* (Champaign, IL: Human Kinetics, 1999), 164.
2. Bill Shaikin, *Sports and Politics: The Olympics and the Los Angeles Games* (New York: Praeger, 1988), 38.
3. The Soviet Union revoked its recognition of Israel during the 1967 Six Day War.
4. Lord Killanin, *My Olympic Years* (New York: William Morrow, 1983), 174.
5. The goal of this study is to postulate that the boycott was a result of the Soviet Union's desire to have Moscow perceived as a better host than Los Angeles. The focus, therefore, is on Soviet and global perceptions of the Los Angeles and Moscow Games. This study is not intended to be a rigorous analysis of the performance of both cities as host.
6. Barukh Hazan, *Olympic Sports and Propaganda Games, Moscow 1980* (London: Transaction Books, 1982), 129.
7. Jimmy Carter, "Military Intervention in Afghanistan: Actions to Be Taken by the United States," *Vital Speeches of the Day*, January 15, 1980, 195.

8. Derek Hulme, *The Political Olympics: Moscow, Afghanistan, and the 1980 U.S. Boycott* (New York: Praeger, 1990), 62.

9. Organizing Committee for the Olympic Games-80, "Opening Ceremonies of the 1980 Moscow Summer Olympics," July 19, 1980 (Lausanne: International Olympic Committee).

10. Derek Hulme, *The Political Olympics*, 80.

11. Sarajevo hosted the 1984 Winter Olympics. They were held from February 7 to February 19, 1984.

12. Kenneth Reich, *Making It Happen: Peter Ueberroth and the 1984 Olympics* (Santa Barbara, CA: Capra Press, 1986), 222.

13. Medal counts present in Tables 5.1, 5.2, 5.4, and 5.5 were taken from the appropriate pages of David Miller, *Athens to Athens: The Official History of the Olympic Games and the IOC, 1894–2004* (Edinburgh: Mainstream Publishing Company, 2004). Point scoring totals, in Tables 5.3 and 5.6, are based off of statistics on medals from the same source.

14. David Miller, *Olympic Revolution: The Olympic Biography of Juan Antonio Samaranch* (London: Pavilion Books, 1992), 92.

15. Ibid.

16. Lord Killanin, *My Olympic Years*.

17. Roland Renson, "The Cool Games: The Winter Olympics 1924–2002," in Larry R. Gerlach, ed., *The Winter Olympics: From Charmonix to Salt Lake City* (Salt Lake City: University of Utah Press, 2004), 65.

18. Lord Killanin, *My Olympic Years*.

19. This is even more likely when it is recalled that Yugoslavia was not among the list of states supporting the Soviet boycott.

20. This is with two obvious exceptions. First was the politicization of the American hockey team's success, which lent more to domestic appeal within the United States than to anything else. Second, and not relevant to this study, is the benefits Yugoslavia reaped from hosting the Winter Games. It is simply worth noting, for the edification of the reader, that these benefits did exist.

21. Organizing Committee of the XIVth Winter Olympic Games, *Final Report* (Sarajevo: Organizing Committee, 1984), 87–88.

CHAPTER 6

1. Lord Killanin, "Minutes of the 75th Session of the International Olympic Committee" (Athens: Comite International Olympique, May 17–20, 1978, photocopied), 29.

2. Peggy Noonan, "Ronald Reagan: He Brought Big Government to Its Knees and Stared Down the Soviet Union. And the Audience Loved It," *Time*, April 13, 1998, 176.

3. Harold Edwin Wilson, "The Golden Opportunity: A Study of the Romanian Manipulation of the Olympic Movement during the Boycott of the 1984 Los Angeles Olympic Games," PhD diss., Ohio State University, 1993, 97–99.

4. Recalling the words of Andrianov when Los Angeles was awarded the 1984 Summer Olympics, the Soviet representative in the IOC had already questioned whether the organizers had the authority to speak for the local and national government.

5. It is commonplace that the committee that organizes the official bid for the winning city and the organizing committee of the Games to have overlap in membership, but it is also common that the committees feature different rosters of members, as bidding and organizing require a lot of different expertise. It is also common to have the hosts of a previous Olympics, held in the same country, offer advice and consultation for a current organizing committee.

6. Kenneth Reich, *Making It Happen: Peter Ueberroth and the 1984 Olympics* (Santa Barbara, CA: Capra Press, 1986), 88.

7. Ibid.

8. Ibid., 87.

9. Ibid., 92.

10. Ibid., 93.

11. Ibid., 60.

12. David Simon, "IOC/LAOOC/USSR NOC Meeting in Lausanne on April 24, 1984," Los Angeles Olympic Organizing Committee, 1984, 1. The position/role of each individual was sourced from various IOC and LAOOC records, as well as Richard B. Perelman, *Official Report of the Games of the XXIIIrd Olympiad Los Angeles, 1984* (Los Angeles: LAOOC, 1984); Perelman, *Olympic Retrospective* (Los Angeles: LAOOC, 1985); and Kenneth Reich, *Making It Happen* (Santa Barbara, CA: Capra Press, 1986).

13. Jerry Welch's role in the meeting is somewhat unclear. He is not listed in any seen studies on the Games, nor is he listed in the final report. General research on his name and names that are commonly nicknamed as "Jerry" was similarly unproductive.

14. Simon, "IOC/LAOOC/USSR NOC Meeting," 1.

15. Ibid.

16. At this point it is worth recalling that there is a long history of Soviet sport officials going to great lengths to justify attendance to government officials in Moscow. Often times, sports officials needed to track down necessary information as a means of convincing the Kremlin of the value of attending. It is reasonable to conclude this was another example.

17. Simon, "IOC/LAOOC/USSR NOC Meeting," 1–2.

18. Ibid., 2–4.

19. Ibid., 1.

20. Reich, *Making It Happen*, 224.
21. Simon, "IOC/LAOOC/USSR NOC Meeting," 2.
22. Ibid., 4.
23. Ibid., 3.
24. Ibid.
25. Ibid.
26. It is important to note that my research on this group did not show any evidence that the "Ban the Soviets Coalition" was connected to the Reagan administration or any other politicians in the local, state, or federal government.
27. Simon, "IOC/LAOOC/USSR NOC Meeting," 2.
28. Wilson, "The Golden Opportunity," 67.
29. The 1956 Summer Olympics took place shortly after the Soviet invasion of Hungary that put down revolts in Budapest. The Soviet/Hungarian gold medal water polo match was so violent that it was ended early. Spectators commented that there appeared to be more blood than chlorine in the water.
30. Wilson, "The Golden Opportunity," 67.
31. Bill Shaikin, *Sports and Politics: The Olympics and the Los Angeles Games* (New York: Praeger, 1988), 50.
32. Wilson, "The Golden Opportunity," 67.
33. Bulgarski Olimpiiski Komitet, *Why Will Not Bulgaria Participate in the 1984 Olympic Games* (Sofia, Bulgaria: Sofia Press, 1984), 11.
34. Ibid.
35. Simon, "IOC/LAOOC/USSR NOC Meeting," 2.

CHAPTER 7

1. This is the text of the original press statement released by the Soviet Union to ITAR-TASS, Reuters, Associated Press, and others. The statement was widely covered in American and British press on May 8–9, 1984. In most cases, newspapers published the entire statement. Multiple newspapers were checked and the language compared to confirm accuracy of the language and that the statement was presented in its entirety.
2. David Simon, "IOC/LAOOC/USSR NOC Meeting in Lausanne on April 24, 1984," Los Angeles Olympic Organizing Committee, 1984, 1.
3. Kenneth Reich, *Making It Happen: Peter Ueberroth and the 1984 Olympics* (Santa Barbara, CA: Capra Press, 1986), 208.
4. Ibid.
5. Harold Edwin Wilson, "The Golden Opportunity: A Study of the Romanian Manipulation of the Olympic Movement during the Boycott of the 1984 Los Angeles Olympic Games," PhD diss., Ohio State University, 1993, 63.
6. Ibid., 87.

7. Bill Shaikin, *Sports and Politics: The Olympics and the Los Angeles Games* (New York: Praeger, 1988), 47.

8. With the next Summer Games in Seoul, South Korea, and socialist states expressing very strong interests in the bid process to host the 1992 Games (which would be chosen in 1986), the Soviet Union simply could not afford to damage relations with the IOC that carelessly.

9. The simple fact that the Chinese willingly attended an event in which Taiwan, titled Chinese Taipei, would have formal attendance suggests there is a lot more to study in this question than would fit in this chapter.

10. David Miller, *Athens to Athens: The Official History of the Olympic Games and the IOC, 1894–2004* (Edinburgh: Mainstream Publishing Company, 2004), Appendix C.

11. Wilson, "The Golden Opportunity," 93.

12. US Department of State, Briefing of the US Embassy in Prague, *Romanian Decision to Attend the Olympic Games*, June 1984, 2.

13. Wilson, "The Golden Opportunity."

14. US Department of State, Briefing of the US Embassy in Prague, *Romanian Decision to Attend the Olympic Games*, 2.

15. Shaikin, *Sports and Politics*.

16. Ibid., 58.

17. Ibid.

18. Medal counts taken from Miller, *Athens to Athens*.

19. US Department of State, Briefing of the US Embassy in Berlin, *GDR Treatment of Olympic Decision*, May 15, 1984, 2.

20. Reich, *Making It Happen*, 224.

21. Wilson, "The Golden Opportunity," 69.

22. Reich, *Making It Happen*, 224.

23. Ibid.

24. It is impossible to know whether the USSR NOC was aware of the strategy or just a pawn in the game. However, it is also irrelevant. Whether the NOC knew the list of complaints was sent in earnest or not really does not matter, as they would have had to proceed with the discussion candidly either way.

25. Reich, *Making It Happen*, 230.

26. Christopher Hill, *Olympic Politics: Athens to Atlanta* (Manchester: Manchester University Press, 1997), 57.

27. Bulgarski Olimpiiski Komitet, *Why Will Not Bulgaria Participate in the 1984 Olympic Games* (Sofia, Bulgaria: Sofia Press, 1984), 1–9.

28. The source actually states "the South California Legislature"; however, other sources (Shaikin, *Sports and Politics*) indicate it was the official state legislature and not something else.

29. Komitet, *Why Will Not Bulgaria Participate*, 5.

30. Ibid., 10–19.

31. Ibid., 13.

32. In making this assumption, the Bulgarian Olympic Committee even suggested that there would be similar issues regarding the 1988 Seoul Summer Olympics, suggesting that the Bulgarian position may have much larger ramifications for Olympic competitions beyond the 1984 boycott. Komitet, *Why Will Not Bulgaria Participate*, 14.
33. Ibid., 11.
34. See Reich, *Making It Happen*, and Shaikin, *Sports and Politics*.
35. It may be worth noting that no protests or other altercations with any politically motivated group affected the Games or its athletes. Although, in fairness, one could easily argue the counterpoint that with most of the Eastern Bloc boycotting and Romania considered the hero that stood up against the Soviet Union, the motivation for such protests and threats was no longer present.
36. Komitet, *Why Will Not Bulgaria Participate*, 12–13.
37. Todor Zhivkov, at the Olympic Congress in Varna, as quoted in Komitet, *Why Will Not Bulgaria Participate*, 16.

CHAPTER 8

1. George Tsebelis, *Nested Games* (Berkeley: University of California Press, 1992).
2. Mark L. Brace, "Revisiting Los Angeles: A Financial Look at the XXIIIrd Olympiad," *Southern California Quarterly* 83, no. 2 (Summer 2001): 173.
3. California Legislature, Senate, Special Committee on Legislative Oversight, *Olympic Organizing Briefing: Holding the 1984 Olympics Without Cost to Taxpayers*, November 23, 1981, 1.
4. Brace, "Revisiting Los Angeles," 162.
5. The LAOOC had no preexisting venue for an aquatic center (for swimming and diving events) or for a velodrome (for cycling events).
6. Peter Ueberroth, *Made in America: His Own Story* (New York: William Morrow, 1985), 86.
7. California Legislature, *Olympic Organizing Briefing*, 20. Brace, "Revisiting Los Angeles," 170, puts the cost for each project at $4 million, establishing a roughly $13 million corporate sponsorship for all sports-related building projects to host the Games and reducing LAOOC costs for all venues to $5 million.
8. Ueberroth, *Made in America*, 61.
9. Brace, "Revisiting Los Angeles," 171.
10. Ibid.
11. Ibid., 172.
12. California Legislature, *Olympic Organizing Briefing*, 21.
13. Ibid., 55.
14. Ibid., 57.
15. Ibid., 50.

16. Ibid., 52.
17. Kenneth Reich, *Making It Happen: Peter Ueberroth and the 1984 Olympics* (Santa Barbara, CA: Capra Press, 1986), 89.
18. Richard Perelman provides details on the LAOOC's "Approach to Management," which contained the governing principles behind staging a successful Olympic games. The seven tenets were architecture, commercialism, finance, government, protocol, provisions of services, and venue management. See *Olympic Retrospective* (Los Angeles: LAOOC, 1985), 34.
19. "Soviet Text Cites 'Rude Violations,'" *Washington Post*, May 8, 1984.
20. Pro Sport München, *Die Spiele: The Official Report of the Organizing Committee for the Games of the XXth Olympiad Munich*, vol. 1 (Munich: Pro Sport München, 1972), 40.
21. Le Comitee Organisateur des Jeux Olympiques je 1976, *Montreal 1976 Games of the XXI Olympiad Montreal 1976, Official Report*, vol. 1, 137.
22. Organizing Committee for the Olympic Games-80, *Games of the XXII Olympiad Moscow 1980, Official Report of the Organizing Committee of the XXII Olympiad, Moscow, 1980*, vol. 2, 191.
23. Andorra, Australia, Belgium, Denmark, France, Great Britain, Ireland, Italy, Luxembourg, Netherlands, Portugal, Puerto Rico, San Marino, Spain, and Switzerland.
24. New Zealand. The flag was of the New Zealand National Olympic and Commonwealth Games Association.
25. Organizing Committee for the Olympic Games-80, "Opening Ceremonies of the 1980 Moscow Summer Olympics," July 19, 1980 (Lausanne: International Olympic Committee).
26. According to the final report of the Los Angeles Olympics, 140 nations were present in the 1984 Summer Olympics. That is after the 14 members of the Warsaw pact boycotted. Even if the Soviet Union swayed the three remaining and noteworthy participating communist states (China, Romania, and Yugoslavia) to join and achieved a complete African boycott, the participating nations count (98) would still be over the number in attendance in Moscow.
27. East Germany came in first with a total of 24 medals, consisting of 9 gold, 9 silver, and 6 bronze medals. The Soviet Union placed second with a total of 25 medals, consisting of 6 gold, 10 silver, and 9 bronze medals. The United States placed a distant fourth with 8 medals, consisting of 4 gold and 4 silver.
28. The California Committee for the Olympic Games was the organizer of the Los Angeles bid and would help form the LAOOC. This was a nongovernment organization designed to further Olympic sports and heritage in California.
29. Lord Killanin, "Minutes of the 80th Session of the International Olympic Committee" (Athens, Greece: Comite International Olympique, May 17–20, 1978, photocopied), 29.

30. Lord Killanin, "Minutes of the 75th Session of the International Olympic Committee," 29.
31. LAOOC, "Opening Ceremonies of the 1984 Los Angeles Summer Olympics," July 28, 1984 (New York: ABC News).
32. George Tsebelis, *Nested Games*, 7.
33. Nicholas Sarantakes, *Dropping the Torch: Jimmy Carter, the Olympic Boycott, and the Cold War* (Cambridge: Cambridge University Press, 2010), and Jerry Caraccioli, *Boycott: Stolen Dreams of the 1980 Moscow Olympic Games* (New York: New Chapter Press, 2008), provide some background on the reception of the American boycott.
34. Reich, *Making It Happen*, 208.
35. Christopher Hill, *Olympic Politics: Athens to Atlanta* (Manchester: Manchester University Press, 1997), 157.

BIBLIOGRAPHY

Barcelona '92 Olympic Organizing Committee. 1992a. "Opening Ceremonies of the 1992 Barcelona Summer Olympics." New York: NBC News, July 25.
———. 1992b. "Closing Ceremonies of the 1992 Barcelona Summer Olympics." New York: NBC News, August 8.
Barnhart, Clarence, ed. 1949. *The American College Dictionary*. New York: Random House.
Beamish, Rob, and Ian Ritchie. 2006. *Fastest, Highest, Strongest: A Critique of High-Performance Sport*. New York: Routledge.
Beijing Organizing Committee for the Games of the XXIX Olympiad. 2008. *Official Report of the Beijing Games*, Vol 1. Beijing: Beijing Organizing Committee for the Games of the XXIX Olympiad.
Berlioux, Monique. 1970. *Olympic Review 32*. Lausanne: International Olympic Committee.
"Bolivia Going to the Games." 1984. *New York Times*, June 22. A21.
Brace, Mark L. 2001. "Revisiting Los Angeles: A Financial Look at the XXIIIrd Olympiad." *Southern California Quarterly* 83, no. 2 (Summer 2001): 161–80.
Bramson, Leon, and George W. Goethals, eds. 1964. *War: Studies from Psychology, Sociology, Anthropology*. New York: Basic Books.
British Olympic Association. 1936. *The Times of London*, March 7.
British Olympic Association Homepage. Accessed July 15, 2001. http://www.olympics.org.uk.
British Olympic Committee. 1980. *Sport: Official Report of the 1980 Games*. London: Epic Publishing.
Brundage, Avery. 1970. "Minutes of the 69th Session of the International Olympic Committee." Amsterdam, Netherlands: Comite International Olympique, May 12–16. Photocopied.
Bueno de Mesquita, Bruce. 1981. *The War Trap*. New Haven, CT: Yale University Press.
Bulgarski Olimpiiski Komitet. 1984. *Why Will Not Bulgaria Participate in the 1984 Olympic Games*. Sofia, Bulgaria: Sofia Press.
Burns, John. 1984. "Final Plea by Olympic President Turned Down in Moscow Meeting." *New York Times*, June 1. A9.

California Legislature, Senate, Special Committee on Legislative Oversight. 1981. *Olympic Organizing Briefing: Holding the 1984 Olympics Without Cost to Taxpayers.* November 23.

Caraccioli, Jerry, and Tom Caraccioli. 2008. *Boycott: Stolen Dreams of the 1980 Moscow Olympic Games.* New York City: New Chapter Press.

Carter, Jimmy. 1980. "Military Intervention in Afghanistan: Actions to Be Taken by the United States." *Vital Speeches of the Day,* January 15.

Chalip, Laurence, Arthur Johnson, and Lisa Stachura, eds. 1996. *National Sports Policies.* Westport, CT: Greenwood Press.

Chase, Jeffrey Scott. 1973. "Politics and Nationalism in Sports: Soviet and American Government Involvement in Amateur Sport as an Aspect of the Cold War." MA Thesis, California State University.

Clausewitz, Carl von. 1993. *On War.* New York: Alfred A. Knopf Everyman's Library.

Comitee Organisateur des Jeux Olympiques je 1976. 1978. *Montreal 1976 Games of the XXI Olympiad Montreal 1976, Official Report.* Volumes 1–3.

Comité National Olympique et Sportif Français Homepage. Accessed July 10, 2001. http://www.comite-olympique.asso.fr.

Communist Party of the Soviet Union. 1963. *O Kulture Prosveshenii Nauki.* Moscow: Government of the USSR.

Dorling Kindersley. 2000. *Olympic Games: Athens 1896–Sydney 2000.* London: DK Books.

Ducey, Kimberley Anne. 2000. *Nationalism and the Break-up of the Big Red Machine: A Study of the Importance of Olympic Sport in the Domestic and International Ideological and Symbolic Legitimization of the USSR.* Ann Arbor, MI: University Microfilms International.

Espy, Richard. 1981. *Politics of the Olympic Games: With an Epilogue, 1976–1980.* Berkeley: University of California Press.

Evaluation Commission. 2001. *Report of the IOC Evaluation Commission for the Games of the XXIX Olympiad in 2008.* Lausanne: Comite International Olympique. April 3.

Fédération Internationale de Football Association Official Site. Accessed July 10, 2001. http://www.fifa.com.

Findling, John, ed. 1996. *Historical Dictionary of the Modern Olympic Movement.* Westport, CT: Greenwood Press.

Gafner, Raymond. 1996. *International Olympic Committee—One Hundred Years: The Idea—The Presidents—The Achievements.* Lausanne: International Olympic Committee.

Gerlach, Larry R. 2004. *The Winter Olympics: From Charmonix to Salt Lake City.* Salt Lake City: University of Utah Press.

Glad, Betty, ed. 1990. *Psychological Dimensions of War.* Newbury Parks, CA: Sage Publications.

Gori, G. 1997. "Sports Festivals in Italy between the 19th and 20th Centuries: A Kind of National Olympic Games?" In Naul, Roland, ed. *Contemporary*

Studies in the National Olympic Games Movement. New York: Frankfurt am Main.

Government of the Soviet Union. 1936. *The 1936 Constitution of the USSR.* Moscow.

———. 1977. *The 1977 Constitution of the USSR.* Moscow.

Graeppi, Maude. 2001a. Documentation Department of the Olympic Museum in Lausanne, Switzerland, correspondence, August 3.

———. 2001b. Documentation Department of the Olympic Museum in Lausanne, Switzerland, correspondence, August 8.

Guttmann, Allen. 1994. *The Olympics: A History of the Modern Games.* Chicago: University of Illinois Press.

Hargreaves, John. 2000. *Freedom for Catalonia: Catalan Nationalism, Spanish Identity, and the Barcelona Olympic Games.* Cambridge: Cambridge University Press.

Hazan, Barukh. 1982. *Olympic Sports and Propaganda Games, Moscow 1980.* London: Transaction Books.

Hill, Christopher. 1997. *Olympic Politics: Athens to Atlanta.* Manchester: Manchester University Press.

Hoberman, John M. 1986. *Olympic Crisis: Sport, Politics, and the Moral Order.* New Rochelle, NY: A. D. Caratzas.

Houlihan, Barrie. 1994. *Sport & International Politics.* New York: Harvester.

Hughes, John. 1984. US Department of State Statement, May 14.

Hulme, Derick. 1990. *The Political Olympics: Moscow, Afghanistan, and the 1980 U.S. Boycott.* New York: Praeger.

"Hungary and Poland Expected to Join Olympic Boycott." 1984. *U.P.I.,* May 15.

Iams, John. 1984. "Soviets Announce Olympic Boycott." *U.P.I.,* May 8.

International Olympic Committee. 1931. *OfficialBulletin of the International Olympic Committee, 1931.* Lausanne: IOC.

———. 1984. *Resultats officiels: XIIIes Jeux Olympiques d'hiver, Lake Placid 1980: Jeux de la XXIIe Olmpiade, Moscou, 1980* [*Official Results: XIIIth Olympic Winter Games, Lake Placid, 1980; Games of the XXIInd Olympiad Moscow, 1980*]. Lausanne: IOC.

Katznelson, Ira. 1999. "Structure and Configuration in Comparative Politics." In Lichbach, Mark Irving, and Zuckerman, Alan S., eds. *Comparative Politics: Rationality, Culture, and Structure.* Cambridge: Cambridge University Press.

Keohane, Robert. 1984. *After Hegemony: Cooperation and Discord in World Political Economy.* Princeton: Princeton University Press.

Khavin, Boris. 1988. *This is the USSR: Sports.* Moscow: Novisti Press Agency.

Kifner, John. 1984. "Bulgaria Follows Moscow's Example on Olympic Games." *New York Times,* May 10. A1.

Killanin, Lord. 1974. "Minutes of the 75th Session of the International Olympic Committee." Vienna: Comite International Olympique, October 21–24. Photocopied.

———. 1978. "Minutes of the 80th Session of the International Olympic Committee." Athens: Comite International Olympique, May 17–20. Photocopied.

———. 1980. "Minutes of the 83rd Session of the International Olympic Committee." Moscow: Comite International Olympique, July 15–18. Photocopied.

———. 1983. *My Olympic Years.* New York: William Morrow.

Killanin, Lord, and John Rodda, eds. 1980. *Olympic Games, 1980: Moscow and Lake Placid.* New York: Collier Books.

Kommunisticheskaia. 1971. *Twenty-Fourth Congress of the Communist Party of the Soviet Union.* Moscow: Novosti Press Agency.

Krüger, Arnd, and James Riordan. 1999. *The International Politics of Sport in the 20th Century.* London: E & FN Spon.

LA84 Foundation Homepage. Accessed September 1, 2012. http://www.aafla.org.

"L.A. Insists Boycott Hasn't Hurt Ticket Sales." *San Diego Union-Tribune,* May. C9.

La Rochefoucauld, François de. 1959. *Maxims.* Translated by Leonard Tancock. London: Penguin Classics.

Lee, Jong-Young. 1990. *Sport Nationalism in the Modern Olympics.* PhD Dissertation, University of Northern Colorado.

Lensky, Helen. 2000. *Inside the Olympic Industry: Power, Politics, and Activism.* Albany: State University of New York Press.

Levi, Margaret. 1999. "A Model, a Method, and a Map: Rational Choice in Comparative and Historical Analysis." In Lichbach, Mark Irving, and Zuckerman, Alan S., eds. *Comparative Politics: Rationality, Culture, and Structure.* Cambridge: Cambridge University Press.

Leyson, G. A. 1997. "The First British Empire Games, Hamilton, Ontario, Canada, 1930." In Naul, Roland, ed. *Contemporary Studies in the National Olympic Games Movement.* New York: Frankfurt am Main.

Lichbach, Martin Irving, and Alan S. Zuckerman. 1999b. *Research Traditions and Theory in Comparative Politics: An Introduction.* In Lichbach, Mark Irving, and Alan S. Zuckerman. 1999a. *Comparative Politics: Rationality, Culture, and Structure.* Cambridge: Cambridge University Press.

Litsky, Frank. 1984. "Moscow Will Keep Its Team from Los Angeles Olympics; Tass Cites Reil, U.S. Denies IT; Major Effects Seen." *New York Times,* May 9. A1.

Los Angeles Olympic Organizing Committee. 1980. *First Official Report of the Organizing Committee of the Games for the XXIII Olympiad: Submitted to the Members of the International Olympic Committee in Moscow, July 16, 1980.* Los Angeles: LAOOC.

———. 1984a. "Opening Ceremonies of the 1984 Los Angeles Summer Olympics." New York: ABC News, July 28.

———. 1984b. "Closing Ceremonies of the 1984 Los Angeles Summer Olympics." New York: ABC News, August 12.

———. 1984c. *Programma Olimpico Ufficiale: Giochi della XXII Olimiade, Los Angeles, 1984.* Los Angeles: LAOOC.

———. 1984d. *Olympic Countdown: 200 Days to Go.* Los Angeles: LAOOC.

———. 1985. *Official Report of the Games of the XXIIIrd Olympiad Los Angeles, 1984.* Volumes 1–2.

Lucas, John. 1994. *The Modern Olympic Games.* New York: A. S. Barnes.

Machiavelli, Niccolo. 1992. *The Prince.* Translated by W. K. Marriott. New York: Everyman's Library.

McGeveran, William A. 2001. *World Almanac and Book of Facts 2001.* New York: World Almanac Books.

McPhail, Thomas L. 1989. *The Olympic Movement and the Mass Media: Past, Present, and Future Issues.* Calgary: Hurford Enterprises.

Mead, Margaret. 1964. "War Is Only an Invention." In Bramson, Leon, and George W. Goethals, eds. *War: Studies from Psychology, Sociology, Anthropology.* New York: Basic Books.

Miller, David. 1992. *Olympic Revolution: The Olympic Biography of Juan Antonio Samaranch.* London: Pavilion Books.

———. 2003. *Athens to Athens: The Official History of the Olympic Games and the IOC, 1894–2004.* Edinburgh: Mainstream Publishing Company.

Mondale, Walter F. 1980. "Speech to the USOC House of Delegates." April 13. *Walter F. Mondale Papers.* Minnesota Historical Society.

"More Countries to Join USSR in Boycott of Olympics." *Christian Science Monitor* 14 (May 1984): 2.

Morgenthau, Hans. 1993. *Politics among Nations: The Struggle for Power and Peace.* Boston: McGraw Hill.

Morrison, Ray L. 1982. *Government Documents Relating to the 1980 Olympic Games Boycott: A Contents Analysis and Bibliography.* Washington, DC: Educational Resources Information Center.

Mueller, John. 1990. "Retreat from Doomsday." In Glad, Betty, ed. *Psychological Dimensions of War.* Newbury Parks, CA: Sage Publications.

Naul, Roland, ed. 1997. *Contemporary Studies in the National Olympic Games Movement.* New York: Frankfurt am Main.

Noonan, Peggy. 1998. "Ronald Reagan: He Brought Big Government to Its Knees and Stared Down the Soviet Union. And the Audience Loved It." *Time,* April 13. 176–80.

Official Site of the International Olympic Committee. Accessed September, 2012. http://www.olympic.org.

Olympiad-80 Organizing Committee. 1977. *On Preparations for Olympiad-80 in Moscow: (information).* Moscow: Organizing Committee.

Olympic Museum Homepage. September, 2012. http://www.olympic.org/museum.

Organizing Committee for the Olympic Games-80. 1980a. "Opening Ceremonies of the 1980 Moscow Summer Olympics." Lausanne: International Olympic Committee, July 19.

———. 1980b. "Closing Ceremonies of the 1980 Moscow Summer Olympics." New York: NBC News, August 3.

———. 1981. *Games of the XXII Olympiad Moscow 1980, Official Report of the Organizing Committee of the XXII Olympiad, Moscow, 1980.* Volumes 1–3.

Organizing Committee of the XIVth Olympic Winter Games. 1984a. "Opening Ceremonies of the 1984 Sarajevo Winter Olympics." New York: ABC News, February 7.

Organizing Committee of the XIVth Olympic Winter Games. 1984b. "Closing Ceremonies of the 1984 Sarajevo Winter Olympics," New York: ABC News, February 19.

———. 1984c. *Final Report.* Sarajevo: Organizing Committee.

Organski, A. F. K., and Jacek Kugler. 1981. *The War Ledger.* Chicago: University of Chicago Press.

Pamphlet from the Information Department, Embassy of the USSR. 1988. *Soviet Sport: The Way to Medals.* Moscow: Novosti Press Agency.

Peppard, Victor, and James Riordan. 1993. *Playing Politics: Soviet Sport Diplomacy to 1992.* Greenwich, CT: JAI Press.

Perelman, Richard B. 1985b. *Olympic Retrospective: The Games of Los Angeles.* Los Angeles: Los Angeles Olympic Organizing Committee.

Promyslov, Vladimir. 1984. Letter to Dr. A. Hammer, May 16. Special Collections, Sports Library, Amateur Athletics Foundation of Los Angeles.

Pro Sport München. *Die Spiele: The Official Report of the Organizing Committee for the Games of the XXth Olympiad Munich 1972.* Volumes 1–3.

Pound, Richard W. 1994. *Five Rings over Korea.* Boston: Little Brown Company.

Reich, Kenneth. 1986. *Making It Happen: Peter Ueberroth and the 1984 Olympics.* Santa Barbara, CA: Capra Press.

Renson, Roland. 2004. "The Cool Games: The Winter Olympics 1924–2002." In Gerlach, Larry R., ed. *The Winter Olympics: From Charmonix to Salt Lake City.* Salt Lake City: University of Utah Press. 41–86.

Rice, Tim, Benny Andersson, and Bjorn Ulvaerus. 1984. *Chess.* A&M Records. CD.

Richardson, James. 1984. "Questions Emerge about Financial Conditions of Games." *San Diego Union-Tribune,* June 16. A3.

Riordan, James. 1977. *Sport in Soviet Society.* New York: Cambridge University Press.

———. 1979. *Sport in the USSR and the 1980 Olympic Games.* London: Collet's Edition.

———, ed. 1981a. *Sports under Communism: The USSR, Czechoslovakia, the G.D.R., China, Cuba.* London: C. Hurst.

———. 1991. *Sport, Politics, and Communism.* Manchester: Manchester University Press.

"Romanian Olympic Official Praises Preparation for Games." 1984. *Associated Press* June 22.

Romanov, A. O. 1963. *Sovremennye Problemy Mezhdunarodnogo Olimpiiskogo Dvizbeniia*. Moscow: Physical Culture and Sport.

Romanov, Nikolai N. 1987 *Trudnye Dorogi K Olympu*. Moscow: Fizkul'tura I Sport.

Safire, William. 2008. *Safire's Political Dictionary*. Oxford: Oxford University Press.

Samaranch, Juan Antonio. 1984. "Press Release of the International Olympic Committee, 24 April 1984." Lausanne: Comite Interntional Olympique.

Sarantakes, Nicholas Evan. 2010. *Dropping the Torch: Jimmy Carter, the Olympic Boycott, and the Cold War*. Cambridge: Cambridge University Press.

Schelling, Thomas. 2002. *The Strategy of Conflict*. Cambridge, MA: Harvard University Press.

Schmemann, Serge. 1984a. "Moscow and Friends Will Sit This One Out." *New York Times*, May 13. Section 4, Page 1.

———. 1984b. "Olympics Decision Is Final, Soviet Says." *New York Times*, May 15. 1.

Segrave, Jeffrey, ed. 1981. *Olympism*. Champaign: Human Kinetics Books.

———, ed. 1988. *Olympic Games in Transition*. Champaign: Human Kinetics Books.

Senn, Alfred. 1999. *Power Politics and the Olympic Games*. Champaign, IL: Human Kinetics.

Shaap, Dick. 1984. *1984 Olympic Games: Sarajevo/Los Angeles*. New York: Random House.

Shaikin, Bill. 1988. *Sports and Politics: The Olympics and the Los Angeles Games*. New York: Praeger.

Shneidman, Norman N. 1978. *The Soviet Road to Olympus: Theory and Practice of Soviet Physical Culture and Sport*. Toronto: Ontario Institute for Studies in Education.

Simon, David. 1984. "IOC/LAOOC/USSR NOC Meeting in Lausanne on April 24, 1984." Los Angeles: Los Angeles Olympic Organizing Committee.

Simon, William E. 1984. "Olympics for the Olympians." *New York Times*, July 29. 4.

Sobolev, S. 1951. "Letter to IOC, Moscow, April 1951." Avery Brundage Collection, No. 149, USOA NOC, 1947–69.

"Soviet Text Cites 'Rude Violations." 1984. *The Washington Post*, May 8. A28.

Spier, Fred. 1996. *The Structure of Big History: From the Big Band until Today*. Amsterdam: Amsterdam University Press.

Sydney Organizing Committee for the Games. 2000a. "Opening Ceremonies of the 2000 Sydney Summer Olympics." New York: NBC News, September 15.

———. 2000b. "Closing Ceremonies of the 2000 Sydney Summer Olympics." New York: NBC News, October 1.

———. 2001c. *Official Report of the XXVII Olympiad*. Volumes 1–2.

Toomey, Bill, and Barry King. 1984. *Olympic Challenge*. Reston, VA: Reston Publishing.

Tsebelis, George. 1992. *Nested Games*. Berkeley: University of California Press.

UCLA Special Collections Finding Aid. Accessed October 10, 2012. http://www.oac.cdlib.org.

Ueberroth, Peter. 1985. *Made in America: His Own Story*. New York: William Morrow.

United States Olympic Committee Homepage. Accessed July 10, 2001. http://www.usoc.org.

US Congress House Committee on Energy and Commerce. 1983. *1984 Summer Olympics*. 98th cong., 1st sess., September 27.

US Congress House Committee on Foreign Affairs. 1980. *U.S. Participation in the 1980 Summer Olympic Games*. 96th cong., 2nd sess., January 23, February 4.

US Congress House Committee on International Relations. 1977. *1984 Summer Olympic Games*. 95th cong., 1st sess., September 23, 29.

———. 1978. *Foreign Relations Authorization for FY79*. 95th cong., 2nd sess., January 31.

US Congress House Committee on Interstate and Foreign Commerce. 1980. *Alternatives to the Moscow Olympics*. 96th cong., 2nd sess., January 30.

US Congress Senate Committee on Foreign Relations. 1980. *1980 Summer Olympics Boycott*. 96th cong., 2nd sess., January 28.

US Department of State, Action Memorandum. 1984. *Proposed Letter from the President to President Ceuausescu of Romania*. May 16.

US Department of State, Briefing of the US Embassy in Berlin. 1984a. *GDR Treatment of Olympic Decision*. May 15.

———. 1984b. *Demarche on Olympics*. May 22.

US Department of State, Briefing of the US Embassy in Brazzaville. 1984. *Congolese Resist Soviet Pressures to Boycott Olympics*. May.

US Department of State, Briefing of the US Embassy in Bucharest. 1984a. *Romanian Participation in Los Angeles Olympics*. May 14.

———. 1984b. *Romanian Participation in the Olympics*. May.

US Department of State, Briefing of the US Embassy in Budapest. 1984a. *Deputy PM on Hungarian Olympic Participation*. May.

———. 1984b. *More Hungarian Information on the Olympic Boycott*. May.

———. 1984c. *Olympic Boycott—Hungary is Playing for Time*. May.

———. 1984d. *Soviet Boycott of Olympics—Coordination within the Warsaw Pact as Seen from Budapest*. July.

US Department of State, Briefing of the US Embassy in Ouagadougou. 1984. *Supreme Council on Sport in Africa, Executive Bureau Meetings, June 16–17*. June.

US Department of State, Briefing of the US Embassy in Prague. 1984a. *Views of the Olympic Boycott*. May.

———. 1984b. *Romanian Decision to Attend the Olympic Games*. June.

US Department of State, Memorandum for Mr. Robert McFarlane, White House. 1984. *Proposed Letter from President Reagan to Romanian President on Olympic Participation.* May 18.

Usher, Harry. "Press Conference on the TASS Story on Soviet Participation, 8 May 1984." Marina Center, Headquarters of the Los Angeles Olympic Organizing Committee, Los Angeles.

Vecsey, George. 1984. "Sports of the Times: Great Red Hopes in the Olympics." *New York Times,* June 28. B9.

Vinokur, Martin. 1988. *More Than a Game: Sports and Politics.* New York: Greenwood Press.

Waltz, Kenneth Neal. 2001. *Man, the State, and War: A Theoretical Analysis.* New York: Columbia University Press.

Wedemeyer, Bernd. 1999. "Sports and Terrorism." In Krüger, Arnd, and Riordan, James. 1999. *The International Politics of Sport in the 20th Century.* London: E & FN Spon.

Wilson, Harold Edwin. 1993. "The Golden Opportunity: A Study of the Romanian Manipulation of the Olympic Movement during the Boycott of the 1984 Los Angeles Olympic Games." PhD Dissertation, Ohio State University.

Zagara, Frank. 1984. *Game Theory: Concepts and Applications.* London: Sage Publications.

———. 1987. *Dynamics of Deterrence.* Chicago: University of Chicago Press.

INDEX

CPSIA information can be obtained at www.ICGtesting.com
Printed in the USA
LVOW10*2045250414

383286LV00011B/317/P